THE ART
OF WATCHING
FILMS

a guide to film analysis

JOSEPH M. BOGGS

Western Kentucky University

The Benjamin/Cummings Publishing Company, Inc.

Menlo Park, California / Reading, Massachusetts
London / Amsterdam / Don Mills, Ontario / Sydney

Photographs, with the exception of studio photos, by Keith Jackson.

The Benjamin/Cummings Publishing Company, Inc.
2727 Sand Hill Road
Menlo Park, California 94025

To my teachers—those who made a difference:

Thelma Howard
T. J. Kallsen
Ruel Foster
Don Bond
Leon Golden
Nancy deGrummond
Don Ungurait
Hans Braendlin

PREFACE

This book is designed as a handbook or guide to the analytical study of film. It is therefore not a textbook in the ordinary sense, but an educational tool—an attempt to set up a systematic critical and analytical approach that can be applied to a large variety of films. It does not, however, profess to provide a rigid, foolproof set of criteria for film evaluation or a mechanical checklist for transforming ordinary filmgoers into expert movie critics.

Specific and detailed examples from current and classical films are held to a minimum for two reasons. First, most current films will be unknown to students in two or three years. Second, examples from film classics may hamper the instructor's use of such films by providing answers which he or she may want the students to discover for themselves. Therefore, wherever possible, common techniques or practices will be explained without detailed examples from films. In this way students are encouraged to seek their own examples in films under study. In general, this book will try to tell students what to look for and how to look for it. It will not tell them what others have seen and recorded. There is little benefit in telling students exactly what is in a given film and then asking them to find what they have been told is there. I prefer to challenge students to look for elements that might be in any film, so that they may have the joy of discovering their own examples and describing them from their own observations.

The underlying principle and purpose of this book, then, is to provide students with enough guidance so that they may discover some new insights into films themselves and, in the process, to stimulate, challenge, and sharpen their powers of observation.

It is my goal to provide that guidance through the analytical questions provided at the end of each section and the comprehensive list of questions at the end of the book. At the discretion of the instructor, these questions should be selectively applied to the film under study by the class—as the instructor deems them relevant to his or her purposes. The real "text" of any film course is the films themselves. This book is designed as a useful tool to aid in studying that "text."

J. M. Boggs

CONTENTS

5 SOUND EFFECTS AND DIALOGUE, 122

6 THE MUSICAL SCORE, 132

chapter 1

INTRODUCTION

THE STRUGGLE
FOR SERIOUS RECOGNITION

Today, almost without question, we accept the value and potential of the motion picture as an art form. Such, however, has not always been the case. Although from its inception the film has enjoyed tremendous popularity as an entertainment medium, public recognition of its artistic value is a relatively recent phenomenon. As late as 1941, cultural historian P. A. Sorokin expressed what was perhaps the current intellectual assessment of the motion picture:

> Science gave us the movies, but Hollywood turned them into the most vulgar displays. Like our detective and mystery stories, the shows are all right for relaxation and momentary thrill, but nobody as yet has made of thrillers great classics, or of shows a great art.

Only a few antiquarians would agree with such a statement today. Yet if we are really to understand film, we must look briefly at some of the difficulties the medium has faced in its fight to gain respectable status as an art form. The intellectual snobbery reflected in Sorokin's statement, and indeed the general reluctance to take the motion picture art seriously, can be traced to several complex factors. Certainly one of these factors is the origin and development of the medium itself. In a sense, the film grew up on the wrong side of the tracks, for it was created by inventors and in some cases by showmen, who viewed it not as an important medium for artistic expression, but as a mere toy or novelty, the commercial possibilities of which far overshadowed any other considerations. Later, as the film's profit potential became clear, the men who were to become the giants of the motion picture industry entered the scene. The nature of the early film, the intentions of its creators, and the kind of men who were to head the giant film studios are clearly illustrated in the following excerpts from *King Cohn:* *

> In the beginning is a sneeze. Thomas Alva Edison takes a motion picture of Fred Ott's sneeze, and an industry is born. Drop in a penny, turn the crank and see the funny man sneeze. The public crowds into kinetoscope parlors to peep for a minute at pictures that move. Besides The Sneeze they see Sandow the Strong Man, Annie Oakley, trained bears, a tooth extraction, and How the Porto Rico Girls Entertain Uncle Sam's Soldiers.
>
> * * *
>
> This is not a business for the dilettante, the aesthete, the penny-ante player. They are shouldered aside by the new breed: Carl Laemmele, the German-born bookkeeper for an Oshkosh clothing store; Adolf Zukor from Hungary, once a sweeper in a fur store; Samuel Goldfish, late of Warsaw, glove salesman; William Fox, cloth sponger from Hungary; the Schenck brothers from Russia, Nick and Joe, who ran drugstores in the Bronx; Marcus Loew, a furrier born of immigrant parents in Manhattan; Lewis Selznik from Kiev, a jewelry salesman; Louis B. Mayer, junk dealer, born near Minsk. They have at least two things in common: They know what the public wants; they are tough. . . .

Their toughness and their knowledge of the public taste enabled these men to successfully exploit the film as an entertainment medium, but in the minds of many, the great popular success of the motion picture has been a serious obstacle to the development of the film as art. While such success created a very happy financial situation for the producers, it also imposed serious restrictions on filmmakers who wanted to utilize the full artistic potential of the medium. To communicate effectively with the mass audience, they were forced to reduce their ideas to the lowest common denominator. Many films of high artistic quality were produced in spite of this limitation, but the medium's popularity has worked against the serious acceptance of these films by those who consider anything popular and commercially successful vulgar, coarse, and common, and thereby unworthy of their attention.

A few purists have even been reluctant to recognize the existence of an artistic vision in the film "industry" because of the purely technical and mechanical nature of motion picture photography. While it is true that the motion picture camera is a mechanical tool, capable of recording on film a visual reproduction of almost any lighted object toward which it is directed, the mechanical process involved is not an end in itself, but simply a means to an end. The camera and its film are only the

---

*Bob Thomas's 1967 biography of Columbia Pictures' founder Harry Cohn.

tools used by the filmmaker—no more important in their own way than the artist's brush, oils, and canvas, or the sculptor's hammer, chisel, and marble slab. It is not, after all, the nature of the tools that determines whether a finished product is a work of art, but the nature of the human mind behind those tools—its sensitivity, its creative power, its artistic vision, and, even more important, its ability to communicate the essence of that vision through the skillful use of the medium's tools. If a motion picture seems nothing more than the product of a mechanical process, then, it is because the controlling force behind the film, usually the director, either lacks the essential artistic vision, or fails to capture the essence of that vision on celluloid.

Paradoxically, the motion picture's rapid technological progress, which has so greatly increased its artistic potential, has also been a real obstacle to the full realization of that potential. The silent film, for example, had reached a high level of visual sophistication when the element of sound was added in the late 1920s. However, filmmakers became so fascinated with this giant leap of progress toward realism that they lost sight of the film's most powerful and important element—the moving image on the screen—and the result was a temporary reversion to a more primitive visual technique and the production of films that were talky, static, and visually uninteresting. To a lesser degree, the motion picture's normal rate of artistic development has been slowed also by the innovations in film size, screen size, and projection techniques developed during the early 1950s, when the industry experimented with such radical changes as 3-D and Cinerama.

For the most part, film has been able to rise above these obstacles, and the increase of serious interest in the motion picture during the fifties and sixties indicates that the medium has finally won widespread acceptance as an art form. Film is still a popular and essentially commercial medium and will probably always be, but television and the movie rating code have relieved it of the burden of communicating with the mass audience. The rapidly changing medium also continues to suffer from growing pains, as it experiments with new techniques in cinematography, editing, and sound, and as it responds to the new freedoms from censorship first granted it by the rating code, and then brought into question by subsequent court decisions.

THE UNIQUE PROPERTIES AND POTENTIAL OF FILM

As an art form, the motion picture is similar to other artistic media, for it has the basic properties of these other media woven into its own rich fabric. Like painting and sculpture, film employs line, texture, color, form, volume, and mass, as well as subtle interplays of light and shadow. Many of the rules of photographic composition followed in the motion picture are similar to those applied in painting and sculpture. Like the drama, film communicates visually through dramatic action, gesture, and expression, and verbally through dialogue. Like music and poetry, film utilizes complex and subtle rhythms, and, like poetry in particular, it communicates through images, metaphors, and symbols. Like pantomime, film concentrates upon a moving image, and like the dance, that moving image has certain rhythmic qualities. Finally, like the novel, film has the ability to manipulate time and space, to expand or compress them, and to move back and forth freely within the wide borders of these two dimensions.

In spite of these similarities to other media, however, film is unique, set apart from all other media by its quality of free and constant motion. Because of this element, film goes beyond the static limitations of painting and sculpture in the complexity of its sensual appeal, communicating simultaneously by means of sight, sound, and motion. Film surpasses drama in its unique capacity for varied points of view, action, manipulation of time, and unlimited sense of space. Unlike the stage play, the film is capable of providing a continuous, unbroken flow, which blurs and minimizes transitions in time and space while still leaving them absolutely clear. Unlike the novel and the poem, the film communicates not in abstract symbols printed upon a page (and requiring translation by the brain into visual images and sounds), but directly through concrete images and sounds.

Furthermore, film is capable of treating an almost unlimited variety of subjects:

> It is impossible to conceive of anything which the eye might behold or the ear hear, in actuality or imagination, which could not be represented in the medium of film. From the poles to the equator, from the Grand Canyon to the minutest flaw in a piece of steel, from the whistling flight of a bullet to the slow growth of a flower, from the flicker of thought across an almost impassive face to the frenzied ravings of a madman, there is no point in space, no degree of magnitude or speed of movement within the apprehension of man which is not within reach of the film.*

Film is unlimited not only in its range of subject matter, but also in the scope of its approach to that material. In mood and treatment, it can range anywhere between the lyric and the epic; in point of view, it

*Ernest Lindgren, *The Art of the Film* (Hempstead, England: George Allen & Unwin Ltd.).

can cover the entire spectrum from the purely objective to the intensely subjective; in depth, it may focus on the surface realities and the purely sensual, or delve into the intellectual and philosophical. In the dimension of time, film can look backward to the remote past, or probe forward into the distant future; it can make a few seconds seem like hours, or compress a century into minutes. Finally, film is capable of evoking the entire spectrum of human sensitivity, from the most tender, delicate, fragile, and beautiful feelings to the most brutal, violent and repulsive.

Of even greater importance than the film medium's unlimited range in subject matter and treatment, however, is the overwhelming sense of reality it can convey, regardless of the nature of its subject matter. This sense of reality in film is due primarily to the medium's continuous flow of sight, sound, and motion, those basic cinematic properties that make everything on the screen seem to be cast in the present tense and cause the viewer to become totally immersed in the illusion projected on the screen. Thus, the most complete and utter fantasy assumes through film the shape and the emotional impact of the starkest reality.

The technological history of film can in fact be viewed as a vast evolutionary process toward a greater realism, toward erasing the borderline between art and nature. The motion picture has progressed step by step from drawings, to photographs, to projected images, to sound, to color, to wide screen, to 3-D. Experiments have even been conducted attempting to add the sense of smell to the film experience by releasing fragrances throughout the theater to reinforce or intensify the visual image on the screen. Aldous Huxley's *Brave New World* predicted a future where the sense of touch would be added through a complex electrical apparatus at each seat synchronized with the visual image:

> Going to the Feelies this evening, Henry? . . . I hear the new one at the Alhambra is first-rate. There's a love scene on a bearskin rug; they say it's marvellous. Every hair of the bear reproduced. The most amazing tactual effects.

Although Huxley's "Feelies" have not yet become a reality, the motion picture has succeeded through Cinerama and other wide- or curved-screen projection techniques in intensifying our experience to a remarkable degree. In fact, by creating images that are bigger than life, films have sometimes been made to seem more real than reality. A cartoon published shortly after the first Cinerama film *This Is Cinerama* appeared clearly illustrates the effectiveness of this device. The cartoon pictures a man attempting to find a seat during the famous rollercoaster sequence. As he moves across the row of seats, a seated spectator, in a state of real panic, reaches out to grab his arm and screams hysterically, "Sit down, you fool! You'll have us all killed!" Anyone who has seen this film knows the cartoon is no exaggeration.

DIFFICULTIES OF FILM ANALYSIS

The properties that make film the most powerful and realistic of all artistic media also make film analysis a very difficult process. To begin with, since film in its natural state is a continuous flowing form, it cannot be frozen in time and space for analysis. Once frozen, it is no longer a motion picture, for the unique property of the medium is gone. Therefore, we must direct most of our attention toward responding sensitively to the simultaneous and continuous interplay of image, sound, and motion on the screen. This necessity creates the most difficult part of our task: We must somehow manage to remain almost totally immersed in the "real" experience of a film while at the same time maintaining a fairly high degree of objectivity and critical detachment. Difficult though it may seem, this skill can be developed, and we must consciously cultivate it if we desire to become truly "cineliterate."

The technical nature of the medium also creates difficulties in film analysis. It would be ideal if we all could have at least some limited experience in cinematography and film editing. Since this is impossible, we should become familiar with the basic techniques of film production so that we can recognize them and evaluate their effectiveness. Since a certain amount of technical language or jargon is necessary for the analysis and intelligent discussion of any art form, we must also add a number of important technical terms to our vocabularies. Although many difficulties face us in our early attempts at film analysis, none of them will be insurmountable if we are willing to develop the proper attitudes, skills, and habits essential to perceptive analysis.

WHY ANALYZE FILMS?

Before turning to the actual process of film analysis, it may be worthwhile to look into certain fundamental questions which have been raised about the value of analysis in general. Perhaps the most vocal reactions against analysis come from those who see it as a destroyer of beauty, claiming that it kills the love we have for the object under study. According to this viewpoint, it is much better to accept all art intuitively, emotionally, and subjectively, so that our response is full, warm, and vibrant, uncluttered by the intellect. This kind of thinking is expressed in Walt Whitman's poem "When I Heard the Learn'd Astronomer":

> When I heard the learn'd astronomer;
> When the proofs, the figures, were ranged in
>   columns before me;
> When I was shown the charts and the diagrams, to add,
>   divide, and measure them,
> When I, sitting, heard the astronomer, where he lectured
>   with much applause in the lecture-room,
> How soon, unaccountable, I became tired and sick;
> Till rising and gliding out, I wander'd off by myself,
> In the mystical moist night-air, and from time to time,
> Look'd up in perfect silence at the stars.

If we were to agree with the poet's reaction, we would certainly throw analysis out the window completely as a cold, intellectual, bloodless, and unfeeling process that destroys the magical, emotional, and mystical aspects of experience. But if this is so, why should we bother to analyze films at all?

The flaw in Whitman's thinking lies in the either/or, black and white extremism of his view, in the polarization of poet and astronomer. It denies the possibility of some middle ground, a compromise or synthesis, which retains the best qualities of both approaches, embracing as equally valid both the emotional/intuitive and the intellectual/analytical approaches. This book is based on the opposite assumption—that the "soul" of the poet and the intellect of the astronomer *can* be present at the same time in all of us, and that these two seemingly conflicting aspects of human nature can actually work together simultaneously, enriching and enhancing each other without cancelling each other out. If this is true, mysteries, beauties, and emotional joys exist that can be experienced intellectually or rationally as well as intuitively and emotionally. Therefore, analysis does not need to destroy our love of the movies, or anything else for that matter. By creating new avenues of awareness and new depths of understanding, it can make our love for movies stronger, more real, and more enduring.

Whitman's astronomer need not be a cold, analytical observer; he could also be a poet. His knowledge that a great many things exist in the universe which can't be seen with the naked eye could make him even more sensitive when he looks up at the stars and the sky. He may have seen great beauty through the telescope and experienced moments of emotional ecstasy from the things he has viewed. If he has seen the rings of Saturn or the moons of Jupiter, he may have a mystical feeling for those planets that goes much deeper than an unschooled poet's.

To assume that analysis not only obscures but actually destroys the mystical and the beautiful is to assume that physicians, because they have carefully studied or analyzed the human body, its bone and muscle structure, its circulatory and nervous systems and all its many organs, have no sense of respect for the body. It is just as likely that they will be even more aware that the human body is one of God's miracles—the miracle of life in all its complexity, warm, vibrant, and pulsing with energy.

Analysis also suffers from another misconception: that we somehow kill the thing we analyze. As Wordsworth states it in "The Tables Turned":

> Sweet is the lore which Nature brings;
> Our meddling intellect
> Misshapes the beauteous forms of things
> We murder to dissect.

The reference to dissection, which conjures up an image of the medical student working on a cadaver or the physician performing an autopsy on a corpse, is another false conception. Film analysis does not kill, nor does it work with parts that are dead. Film analysis takes place only in the mind. Each part being studied still pulses with life, since analytical viewers, if they have anything of the poet in them at all, still see each part as connected to the lifeline of the whole. In a sense, each part should actually seem more alive, for the analytical approach not only enables us to see and understand each part more clearly—it also focuses on the vital function and energy which each part contributes to the pulsing, dynamic whole.

THE ANALYTICAL APPROACH

The analytical approach is by no means the only valid approach to film study. A great many other approaches are used successfully and validly. But the analytical framework set up in this guide grows out of an assumption that a great many teachers and students are seeking to find some kind of thorough, systematized, rational, and orderly framework in their study of film or in their study of art in general. To take such an approach does not deny the existence and importance of the emotional and intuitive responses to film. It is simply that the analytical approach is capable of being ordered and structured to fit the classroom situation. In other words, it is teachable. The emotional and intuitive responses to film, on the other hand, are so highly subjective and vary so greatly from one individual to another that they are difficult to share in a meaningful way in the classroom.

The following quote from Richard Dyer MacCann's introduction to *Film: A Montage of Theories* might well serve as the basic assumption of this book:

> Arnold Hauser contended, and I think rightly, that "all art is a game with and a fight against chaos." The film that simply says life is chaos is a film which has not undertaken the battle of art.

If we accept MacCann's judgment, the analytical approach is essential to the art of watching films. Since analysis means a separating or breaking up of any whole into its parts so as to find out their nature, proportion, function, and relationships, film analysis presupposes the existence of a unified and rationally structured artistic whole. Therefore, the usefullness of this guide is restricted to the structured film, which is developed with a definite underlying purpose and unified around a central theme.

Limiting our approach to the structured film does not necessarily deny the artistic value of the unstructured film. A great many of the films being produced by experimental or underground filmmakers do communicate effectively on a purely subjective, intuitive, or sensual plane, and are meaningful to some degree as "experiences." But many of these films are not structured or unified around a central purpose or theme, and therefore cannot be successfully approached through analysis.

It would be foolish to suggest that the structured film cannot be appreciated or understood at all without analysis. If the film is effective, we should possess an intuitive grasp of its overall meaning. The problem is that this intuitive grasp is generally weak and vague, and limits our critical response to hazy generalizations and half-formed opinions. The analytical approach makes it possible for us to raise this intuitive grasp to a conscious level, bring it into sharp focus, and thereby reach more valid and definite conclusions on the film's meaning and value.

But the fact that the analytical approach will help us to reach more valid and definite conclusions on the film's meaning and its value in no way implies that it can reduce the film art to rational and manageable proportions. Analysis does not claim, or even attempt, to explain everything about an art form. Film will always retain its special magic and its mystical qualities—none of which can ever be reduced to a simple matter of 2 + 2 = 4. The elusive, flowing stream of images will always escape complete analysis and complete understanding. In fact, no final answers exist about any work of art. A film, like anything else of true aesthetic value, can never be completely captured by analysis.

But the fact that there are no final answers should not prevent us from pursuing some important questions. Our hope is that, through analysis, we can reach a higher level of confusion about films, a level where we are reaching for the higher more significant aspects of the film art as opposed to the mundane, the practical, and the technical. If we can understand some things through analysis so that we learn to "see" them habitually, our minds will be free to concentrate on higher and more significant questions.

Analysis has the further advantage of helping us to lock the experience of a film in our minds so that we may savor it longer in our memory. By looking at a film analytically, we thus make a film more truly our own. Furthermore, because our critical judgments enter into the process, analysis should also make us more discriminating in our tastes and more selective in the films we really admire. A great film or a very good one will stand up under analysis; our admiration for it will increase the more deeply we look into it. But a mediocre film may impress us more than it should on first impression, and we may like it less after analyzing it.

Therefore, analysis can be seen to have several clear benefits. It allows us to reach more valid and definite conclusions on the film's meaning and value, it helps us to "lock" the experience of a film into our minds, and it sharpens our critical judgments. But the ultimate purpose of analysis, and its greatest benefit, is that it opens up new avenues of awareness and new depths of understanding. It seems logical to assume that the more understanding we have, the more completely we appreciate art. If the love we have for an art form is built on rational understanding, it will be more solid, more enduring, and of greater value than love based solely on irrational and totally subjective reactions. This is not to claim that analysis will create a love of films where none exists. The love of film does not come from a book or from any special critical approach. It comes only from that secret, personal union, the intimate meeting of film and viewer in a darkened room. If that love does not already exist for the viewer, this book and its analytical approach can do little to create it.

If we truly love films, however, we will find that analysis is worth the trouble, for it will bring understanding that will deepen our appreciation. Instead of cancelling out the emotional experience of watching the film, analysis will enhance and enrich that experience, for as we become more perceptive and look more deeply into the film, new levels of emotional experience will emerge.

chapter 2

THEME AND PURPOSE

DOUBLE VIEWING

The most difficult part of our task has already been stated: We must somehow manage to become almost totally immersed in the "real" experience of a film and *at the same time* maintain a fairly high degree of objectivity and critical detachment. The complex nature of the medium also makes it difficult to consider all the elements of a film in a single viewing; too many things happen too quickly on too many levels to allow for a complete analysis. Therefore, if we wish to develop the proper habits of analytical viewing, we should see a film twice whenever possible. In the first viewing we can watch the film in the usual manner, concerning ourselves primarily with plot elements, the total emotional effect, and the central idea or theme. Then in a second viewing, since we are no longer caught up in the suspense of "what happens," we can focus our full attention on the hows and whys of the filmmaker's art. Constant practice of the double-viewing technique should make it possible for us to gradually combine the functions of both viewings into one.

We must also remember that film analysis does not end the minute the film is over. In a sense, it really begins then, for most of the questions posed in this guide will require the reader to reflect on the film after leaving the theater, and a mental replay of some parts of the film will be necessary for any complete analysis.

DETERMINING THE THEME

As the sum total of all elements, the theme serves as the basic unifying factor in the film. Therefore, each element within the film must contribute in some manner and to some degree to the development of the theme, and must be analyzed in terms of this relationship. It is essential, then, that the viewer make some attempt to determine, as accurately as possible, the nature of that theme.

Unfortunately, determining theme is often a very difficult process. We cannot expect the theme to be revealed in a blinding flash of light midway through the film. Although we may easily acquire a vague, intuitive grasp of the film's basic meaning from simply watching it, accurately determining and stating the theme is quite another matter. Often we will not accomplish this until we leave the theater and begin thinking about or discussing the film in abstract terms.

Determining the theme can, in fact, be considered both the beginning and end of the analytical approach. After seeing the film, we should make a tentative identification of its theme to provide ourselves with a clear sense of the direction our close analysis will take. The analysis itself is a process that should lead to a clarified vision of the film and all its elements functioning together as a unique whole. On the other hand, if our analysis of the individual film elements does not support our original concept of the film's theme, we should be prepared to replace that concept with a more valid one.

BASIC TYPES OF FILM THEMES

The traditional use of the word *theme* as it applies to fiction, drama, and poetry, always clearly connotes an *idea,* variously referred to as the central idea, the point, the message, or the statement of the work as a whole. This concept of theme, however, is much too narrow for practical application to the film, where it must cover a wide spectrum of approaches, from Walt Disney's to Ingmar Bergman's or from Charlie Chaplin's to Sir Laurence Olivier's. To assume that all films within this spectrum are structured around some kind of central idea can only be misleading. Therefore, for our purposes, it is necessary to expand the concept of theme to mean the central concern or focus around which a film is structured (and which gives it unity). In films, these general areas of central concern or focus can be broken down into four more or less distinct categories: plot, emotion, character, and idea.

PLOT AS THEME

In many types of films, such as the adventure story or the detective story, the primary emphasis is on the chain of events itself, on what happens. Since these films are generally aimed at providing us with a temporary escape from the boredom and the drabness of our everyday lives, the action must be exciting and fast-paced. The characters, the ideas, and the emotional effects in these films are subordinate to the plot, and the final outcome is all important. However, the events and the final outcome are important only to the specific story being told, and little if any real significance in a general or abstract sense can be attached to those events. The essence or theme of such a film can best be captured, therefore, in a concise summary of the central action.

EMOTIONAL EFFECT OR MOOD AS THEME

A highly specialized mood or emotional effect serves as a focus or structural basis for a relatively large number of films. In such films, it is possible to identify a single primary mood or emotion which prevails throughout the film, or to view each segment of the film as a stairstep leading up to a single powerful emotional effect. Although plot may play a very important role in such movies, the chain of events itself is subordinate to the emotional response caused by those events. Most horror films, the Alfred Hitchcock suspense thrillers, and romantic tone poems such as *A Man and a Woman* can all be interpreted as having a mood or emotional effect as their primary focus and unifying element. The theme of such films can best be stated by simply naming the primary mood or emotional effect created.

CHARACTER AS THEME

Some films focus on the clear delineation through action and dialogue of a single unique character. Although plot is important in such films, what happens is important primarily in that it helps us to understand the character being developed. The major appeal of such characters lies in their uniqueness, in those qualities which set them apart from ordinary people. The theme of such films can best be expressed in a brief description of the central character, with emphasis on the unusual aspects of the individual's personality.

IDEA AS THEME

In most serious films,* the action and characters have a significance beyond the context of the film itself, a significance which helps us to gain

*The term *serious* as used here refers to seriousness of purpose, not of treatment.

a clearer understanding of some aspect of life, experience, or the human condition. An idea theme can, of course, be stated directly through some particular incident or through some particular character; most often, however, the theme is arrived at indirectly, and we are challenged to search our own minds in arriving at an interpretation which we feel best fits the film as a whole. This less direct approach increases the possibilities of varying interpretations, but varying interpretations by different viewers are not necessarily contradictory. They may, in fact, be equally valid, complementary statements, saying essentially the same thing in different terms, or approaching the same theme from different angles.

Perhaps the first step in determining an idea theme is accurately identifying the abstract subject of the film in a single word or phrase— for example, jealousy, hypocrisy, prejudice. If this is as specific as we can get in determining the theme, we should not despair; some themes can be stated explicitly and others cannot. At any rate, the identification of the *true subject* of the film is a valuable first step in film analysis.

If possible, however, we should attempt to carry the determination of theme beyond the mere identification of subject, and see if we can formulate a statement which accurately summarizes the subject dramatized in the film and conveyed by all its elements. If such a specific statement of theme is possible, it is likely to fall into one of the following categories:

1. *Theme as a moral statement.* Films of this nature are intended primarily to convince us of the wisdom or practicality of a certain moral principle and thereby persuade us to apply that principle to our own behavior. Such themes often take the form of a maxim or proverbial formula, such as, "The love of money is the root of all evil." Although many modern films have important moral implications, very few are structured around a single moral statement, and we must be careful not to mistake a moral implication for a moral statement as theme.

2. *Theme as a statement about life.* Films of this type focus on pointing out a "truth of life," and in doing so they may provide a sharpened awareness of reality, make a comment on the nature of human experience, or give an assessment of the human condition. As a general rule, such films attempt to add to our understanding of life without making a specific moral statement; we are left to deduce any rules of behavior for ourselves from that increased understanding.

3. *Theme as a statement about human nature.* Quite different from those films which focus on unique characters are those which fo-

cus on universal or representative characters. Such films move beyond the mere character study into the realm of "idea as theme," for such characters take on significance beyond themselves and the context of the particular film in which they appear. Since those characters are representative of mankind in general, they serve as cinematic vehicles to illustrate some truth about human nature which is widely or universally acceptable.

4. *Theme as a social comment.* Modern filmmakers are very concerned with social problems, and show their concern in films that focus on exposing the vices and follies of man as a social being or criticizing the social institutions he has established. Although the underlying purpose of such films is social reform, they rarely spell out specific methods of reform; usually they concentrate instead on clarifying the problem and emphasizing its importance, thus convincing us of the necessity for reform. A social-problem film may make its point in a variety of ways: It may treat its subject in a light, satirical, or comic manner, or attack it in a savage, harsh, and brutal manner.

Although the two types of themes have much in common, the social-comment theme differs from the human-nature theme primarily in the fact it does not concern itself with criticism of the human race in general or the universal aspects of human nature, but only with the special functions of human beings as social animals and with the social institutions and traditions they have created.

5. *Theme as a moral or philosophical riddle.* In some cases a filmmaker may purposely strive to evoke a variety of subjective interpretations by developing a film around a riddling or puzzling quality, attempting to suggest or mystify instead of communicating clearly, and attempting to pose moral or philosophical questions rather than provide answers. The typical reaction to such films is, "What's it all about?" Since this type of film communicates primarily through symbols and images, a thorough analysis of these elements will be required for interpretation, and a degree of uncertainty will remain after even the most perceptive analysis. Such films are, of course, wide open to subjective interpretation. The fact that subjective interpretation is required, however, does not mean that the analysis of all film elements can be ignored: The theme should still be the sum total of all these elements, and individual interpretation should be supported by an examination of these elements.

The thematic categories described above are intended to give the student some help in pinpointing the themes of *most* films. Certainly many exceptions will arise—films that do not seem to fit clearly into any one category as well as those that seem equally suited to more than one category. In our efforts to determine theme, we must also be aware that certain films may possess, in addition to the single unifying central concern defined as theme, other less important areas of emphasis called *subthemes* or *motifs.* These are images, patterns, or ideas that repeat themselves throughout the film, and are variations or aspects of the major theme. Above all, we should remember that the statement of theme does not equal the full impact of the film itself; it merely clarifies our vision of it as a unified work and leads us to a greater appreciation of its elements as they function together in a unique artistic whole.

EVALUATING THE THEME

Once the theme has been determined, it is important to make some kind of evaluation of it, especially in the serious film that attempts to do more than simply entertain. Theme evaluation is, for the most part, a subjective process, and any attempt to provide systematic guidelines for this kind of value judgment would be prejudicial in itself. A few generalizations, however, are permissible.

One standard commonly applied in theme evaluation is universality. A universal theme is one of lasting interest, and one that is meaningful not just to people here and now, but to all human beings in all ages. Therefore, a theme with universal appeal may be considered superior to one with an appeal strictly limited in time and place.

This does not mean that we place no value on themes that lack universality. Even if a theme's appeal is strictly limited to a specific time and place, it should have some relevance to our own experience. We will naturally consider a theme that says something significant *to us* superior to one that doesn't, regardless of its universality or lack of it.

We also have the right to expect that an idea theme be intellectually or philosophically interesting. In other words, if a film attempts to make some kind of a significant statement, that statement should be neither boring nor self-evident, but should interest or even challenge our minds.

QUESTIONS
ON THEME AND PURPOSE

1   What is the film's primary concern or focus: plot, character, emotion, or idea? On the basis of your decision, answer one of the questions below.

    a.   If the film's primary concern is plot, summarize the action abstractly in a single sentence or a short paragraph.

    b.   If the film centers around a single unique character, describe the unusual aspects of his or her personality.

    c.   If the film is structured around a mood or emotional effect, what is the mood or feeling it attempts to convey?

    d.   If the film's primary focus is an idea, answer the following questions.

        (1) What is the true subject of the film? What is it really about in abstract terms? Identify the abstract subject in a single word or phrase.

        (2) What comment or statement does the film make about the subject? If possible, formulate a sentence that accurately summarizes the idea dramatized by the film.

2   Although a director may attempt to do several things with a film, one goal usually stands out as more important than the others. Decide which of the following was the director's *primary* aim and give reasons for your choice.

    a.   Providing pure entertainment, that is, temporary escape from the real world.

    b.   Developing a pervasive mood or creating a single, specialized emotional effect.

    c.   Providing a character sketch of a unique, fascinating personality.

    d.   Pointing out a "truth of life" by making the kind of statement that sharpens the viewer's awareness of reality and helps him to accept that "life is like that."

    e.   Criticizing mankind and human institutions, and increasing the viewer's awareness of a social problem and the necessity for reforms.

    f.   Providing insight into human nature (demonstrating that human beings *in general* are like that).

    g. Creating a moral or philosophical riddle for the viewer to ponder.

    h. Making a moral statement to influence the viewer's values and/or behavior.

3 Which of the above seem important enough to qualify as secondary aims?

4 Is the film's basic appeal to the intellect, to the funnybone, to the moral sense, or to the aesthetic sense? Is it aimed primarily at the groin (the erotic sense), the viscera (blood and guts), the heart, the yellow streak down the back, or simply the eyeballs? Support your choice with specific examples from the film.

5 How well does your statement of the film's theme and purpose stand up after you have thoroughly analyzed all the film elements?

6 To what degree is the film's theme universal? Is the theme relevant to your own experience? How?

7 If you think the film makes a significant statement, why is it significant?

8 Decide whether the film's theme is intellectually or philosophically interesting, or self-evident and boring, and defend your decision.

chapter 3

STANDARD FICTIONAL
AND DRAMATIC ELEMENTS

FILM AND LITERARY ANALYSIS

Although film is a unique medium, with properties and characteristics which set it apart from other art forms such as painting, sculpture, fiction and drama, it is also, in its most popular and powerful form, a storytelling medium that shares many elements with the short story and the novel. And since film presents its stories completely in dramatic form, it has even more in common with the stage play: Both forms act out or dramatize their stories and their meanings, showing rather than telling what happens.

The greatest distinction between film and the novel, short story, or play is that film is not as handy to study; it cannot be effectively frozen on the printed page. Because their medium is print, both novel and short story are relatively easy to study. They are written to be read. The stage play is slightly more difficult to study because it is written to be performed, not read. But plays are printed, and because they rely heavily on the spoken word, imaginative and creative readers can conjure up at least a pale imitation of the experience they might have watching it performed. This cannot be said of the screenplay, however, for a film depends so greatly on visual and other nonverbal elements that cannot easily be expressed in written form. The screenplay requires so much "filling in" by our imaginations that we cannot really approximate the experience of the film by simply reading it, and only if we have already seen the film will reading the screenplay be worthwhile. Thus, most screenplays are not really published to be read, but rather to be remembered.

Still, the fact that film is less handy to study does not mean it should be ignored. And the fact that we do not generally "read" films does not mean we should ignore the principles of literary or dramatic analysis when we see a film. Literature and films *do* have many elements in common, and though they are different mediums, they communicate many things in similar ways. Perceptive film analysis is built on the same elements used in literary analysis, and if we apply what we have learned in the study of literature to our analysis of films, we are far ahead of those who do not. Therefore, before we turn to the unique elements of film, we need to look into those elements that film shares with fiction and drama.

Dividing film into its various elements for analysis is a somewhat artificial process, for the elements of any art form never exist in isolation from each other. It is impossible, for example, to isolate the concepts of plot and character: Events influence people, and people influence events; the two are always closely interwoven in any fictional, dramatic, or cinematic work. Though it is somewhat artificial to isolate these elements and consider them separately, the analytical method uses this technique for its own ease and convenience. But it does so with the assumption that we can study these elements in isolation without losing sight of their interdependence or their relationship to the whole.

THE ELEMENTS OF A GOOD STORY

What makes a good story? Any answer to this question is bound to be a subjective one; however, some general observations might be made that will apply to a large variety of film stories.

A GOOD STORY IS UNIFIED IN PLOT OR STORY LINE

As mentioned before, the structured film is one that has some broad underlying purpose or is unified around a central theme. Regardless of the nature of its theme, whether its focus is on plot, emotional effect, character, or idea, the fictional film generally has a plot, or "story line" that contributes to the development of that theme. Therefore the plot, or the story, and the events, conflicts, and characters, that constitute it, must be carefully selected and arranged in terms of their relationship to the theme.

A unified plot or story line focuses on a single thread of continuous action, where one event leads to another naturally and logically. Usually a strong cause and effect relationship exists between these events, and the outcome is made to seem, if not inevitable, at least probable. In a tightly unified plot, nothing can be transposed or removed without significantly affecting or altering the whole.

Thus, every event grows naturally out of the plot itself, and the conflict must be resolved by elements or agents present in and prepared for in the plot itself. The unified plot does not introduce out of thin air some kind of chance, coincidental, or miraculous happening, or some powerful superhuman force that swoops down out of nowhere to save the day. Consider, for example, this hypothetical scene from a western: A wagon train is attacked by Indians numbering in the thousands. Doom seems certain when suddenly, out of nowhere, appears a battalion of U.S. Cavalry troops (who just happen to be passing that way on maneuvers, one hundred miles from the fort). Although such accidental, chance occurrences happen in real life, we reject them in fiction. The arrival of the Cavalry to save the settlers would be acceptable, however, if a reason for it were established earlier in the plot (if, for example, a rider were sent for them).

Although plot unity as described above is a general requirement, exceptions do exist. In the film whose focus is the clear delineation of a single unique character, unity of action and cause-and-effect relationships between events are not so important. In fact, such plots may even be episodic, for the unity in such films comes from the contribution of each event to our understanding of the character being developed, rather than from the relation of the events of the film to each other.

A GOOD STORY IS BELIEVABLE

To really become involved in a story, we must be convinced that it is true. But "truth" is a relative term, and the filmmaker can create truth in a variety of ways.

1. *Externally observable truths.* The most obvious and common kind of truth in a film story is the approximation of life as we have experienced or observed it as conveyed in realistic or naturalistic treatments. To borrow Aristotle's phrase, these are such stories as "might occur and have the capability of occurring in accordance with the laws of probability or necessity."

2. *Internal truths of human nature.* Some of the greatest film classics, however, do not even pretend to represent the actualities of real life; instead they specialize in fairy tale or "happily ever after" endings. Here the good guy always wins, and the bad guy always loses; Cinderella

wins the love of the handsome prince, and true love conquers all. But in a very special way, these stories are also "believable," or at least can be made to seem so, because they contain what might be called "internal truths." The human mind possesses dreams, fears, and childish or naive beliefs in things which are not logical, rational, or really observable "truths," but which seem "true" to us because we want (or need) them to be true and pretend that they are. Indeed, the concept of poetic justice (the idea that virtue will be rewarded and evil will be punished) serves as an example of such an "internal truth"; simply because it is human to *want* it to be true, we seldom question the application of poetic justice in a story. Thus many film stories are convincing because they conform to some kind of inner truth, even though it has little if any resemblance to externally observable truths.

3. *Artistic semblance of "truth."* Another factor at work in making the incredible seem plausible is the filmmaker's ability to lead the viewer out of the real world and into the imaginary world of his story. When dealing with material of an implausible nature, with supernatural characters and happenings, the filmmaker must structure the film as Samuel Taylor Coleridge instructed: to create "a semblance of truth sufficient to procure for these shadows of imagination that willing suspension of disbelief for the moment, which constitutes poetic faith."

Thus we make an aggreement of sorts, an unconscious and implicit agreement at that, to "willingly suspend our disbelief," to leave our skepticism and our rational faculties outside the door as we enter the film's imaginary world. It may be more accurate to say that we leave them in the foyer, for this agreement takes place only when we are caught up in the overall spirit, mood, and atmosphere of the film. The early and thoroughly convincing establishment of a strange or fantastic environment, sense of another time, or unusual characters is extremely important in films where an extraordinary reality prevails. If the fictional reality is successfully established, we may think to ourselves, "Yes, in such a situation almost anything could happen." By communicating this pervasive and "real" sense of an unusual situation or environment, the filmmaker in effect creates a new set of ground rules by which we judge reality, and for the brief period of an hour or two we can believe thoroughly in the "truth" of *Rosemary's Baby, The Day the Earth Stood Still, King Kong, Mary Poppins,* or *The Wizard of Oz.*

Thus the plausibility of a story depends on at least three separate factors: the objective, external, and observable laws of probability and necessity; the subjective, irrational, and emotional "inner truths" of human nature; and the "semblance of truth" created by the filmmaker's convincing art.

1. *Willing suspension of disbelief—unusual characters*: When excellent acting succeeds in making some nonhuman characters seem very human, a skillful director like Mervyn Leroy can take us out of reality and make us believe in the fantasy world of a film like *The Wizard of Oz.* From the MGM release *The Wizard of Oz* © 1939 Loew's Incorporated. Copyright renewed 1966 by Metro-Goldwyn-Mayer Inc.

A GOOD STORY IS INTERESTING

An extremely important requirement of a good story is that it capture and retain our interest. Of course, a story can be interesting in many ways, and few stories (if any) will have equal appeal to all filmgoers, for whether a story is interesting or boring is, to a great extent, a subjective matter dependent on the "eye of the beholder." Some of us may be interested only in a fast-paced action-adventure film, others may be bored by anything that does not have some romantic love interest at its core, and still others may be indifferent to any story that lacks deep philosophical significance. But regardless of what we expect from a motion picture, whether it be the relaxation gained from simply being entertained or some clue to understanding the universe, we never go to the movies to be bored. Our tolerance for boredom seems very limited: A film may shock us, frustrate us, puzzle us, or even offend us, but it

2. The effective visual creation of an extraordinary setting puts us into a proper frame of mind for supernatural happenings in the horror film by leading us to believe that in a setting such as the one pictured here, almost anything can happen. *The Terror.*

must never bore us. Thus we fully expect the filmmaker to structure his or her "reality" toward a heightened intensity by doing away with irrelevant and distracting details so that we do not have to pay to watch anything dull, monotonous, or routine—those dead spots of human existence that life excels in providing us free of charge.

Even the directors in the movement known as Italian Neorealism, who stress everyday reality in their films and deny the validity of "invented" stories, argue that their particular brand of everyday reality is not boring because of its complex and significant echoes and implications. As Cesare Zavattini puts it, "Give us whatever 'fact' you like, and we will disembowel it, make it something worth watching." To most of us, the terms "worth watching" and "interesting" are synonymous.

SUSPENSE

To capture and maintain our interest, the filmmaker employs a multitude of devices and techniques, most of which are in some way related to what we call suspense. These elements create a state of heightened interest by exciting our curiosity, usually by foreshadowing or hinting about the outcome without revealing it. By withholding bits of information that would answer the dramatic questions raised by the story, and by floating some unanswered question just beyond our reach like the carrot dangling on the pole before the donkey, the filmmaker provides a motive force to keep us constantly moving with the story's flow.

ACTION

If a story is to be interesting at all, it must contain some elements of action. Stories are never static; some sort of change, movement, or action is essential if the story is to be worth telling. Action, however, is not limited to physical activities such as fights, chases, duels, or great battles. It may also be internal, psychological, or emotional. Thus in such films as *The Guns of Navarrone, The Great Escape,* or *Goldfinger,* the action is external and physical, while in *Marty,* for instance, the action occurs within the mind, the heart, and the emotions of the characters. Both sorts of films have movement and change; neither is static. The interest created by the exciting action in *The Guns of Navaronne* is obvious, and needs no explanation, but action within the mind and sensitivity of a human being is not so obvious. Nothing very extraordinary happens externally in *Marty,* but what takes place internally is extremely interesting and exciting in its own way.

Internal action stories naturally require more concentration from the viewer, and they are more difficult to treat cinematically. But they are worthwhile subjects for film and can be as interesting and exciting in their own way as those films which stress external and physical action.

A GOOD STORY IS BOTH SIMPLE AND COMPLEX

A good film story must be simple enough that it can be tightly unified and expressed cinematically within the limits of the medium. Poe's idea that a short story should be capable of being read in a single sitting also applies to the film. Experiencing a film by seeing and hearing is less tiring than reading a book, however, so our single sitting required for the film story may be a maximum of, say, two hours. Beyond that limit only the greatest films can prevent us from becoming restless or inattentive. Thus the story's action or theme must be effectively compressed into a unified dramatic structure that requires about two hours to unfold. In most cases, a limited, simple theme, such as that in *Marty,* which focuses on one person in one time period, is better suited for the cinema than a worldwide, ageless, generalized theme such as D. W. Griffith attempted to treat in *Intolerance.* Thus a story should be simple enough to be told in the time period allotted for its telling.

However, within these limits, a good story must also have some complexity, at least enough to hold our interest throughout the film. Some complexity of plot is necessary to make a story truly worth telling. Also, although a good story may contain a hint as to its eventual outcome, it must also provide some surprises, or at least be subtle enough to prevent the viewer from predicting its outcome at the midway point. Thus, a good story usually withholds something about its conclusion or significance until the very end.

However, if new elements are introduced into the plot at the very end, the "surprise" ending may be illegitimate, especially if such elements bring about an almost miraculous conclusion to the story or make too much use of coincidence or chance. On the other hand, a surprise ending can be powerful and legitimate when it is prepared for by the plot, even though the plot elements and the chain of cause and effect leading up to it may escape our conscious attention. The important thing is that the viewer never feel hoodwinked, fooled, or cheated by a surprise ending; instead the viewer should gain insight by means of the ending. The latter occurs only when the surprise ending carries out tendencies established earlier in the story. A good plot is complex enough to keep us in doubt as to its outcome, but simple enough so that all the seeds of that outcome can be planted in the plot.

The filmmaker's communication techniques must also be a proper blend of simplicity and complexity. Filmmakers must communicate some things simply, clearly, and directly, so that they are clear to all viewers. But to challenge the minds and eyes of the most perceptive viewers, they must also communicate through implication and suggestion, leaving some things open to multiple interpretations. Some viewers, of course, will be bored by films that are too complex, and make too much use of implication or suggestion; others, who like an intellectual challenge, will not be interested in films that are too direct and simple. Thus the filmmaker must seek to please both those who don't appreciate films they cannot easily understand and those who reject films they understand too easily.

Filmgoers' views of life will also greatly influence their attitudes toward a film's complexity or simplicity. If they see real life as complex rather than simple, and demand the kind of "truth" that follows the laws of necessity and probability, they will be interested only in stories that capture the complexity and ambiguity they see reflected in the world around them. Thus, a viewer may reject the escapist entertainment film because it falsifies the nature of existence by oversimplifying it, by making it seem too easy, too neat, too pat. Another viewer may reject the more complex view of life in the realistic or naturalisitic film for the opposite reason—because it is too full of ambiguities, too complex, or because it does not conform to the inner subjective "truth" of life as he or she wants it to be.

A GOOD STORY USES RESTRAINT IN THE HANDLING OF EMOTIONAL MATERIAL

A good story is honest and sincere in its handling of emotional material. A strong emotional element or effect is present in almost any story, and film is capable of manipulating our emotions in many ways. But this manipulation of emotion must be honest and appropriate to the story on the screen. We describe as "sentimental" films that overuse emotional materials in a story, and we make this negative judgment when we become aware that our emotions are being manipulated insincerely or unfairly. Usually we respond by rejecting such a film as a whole. Therefore great restraint and care must be used by the director to achieve emotional effects in as powerful and dramatic a way as possible, but without overdoing it. Overdone emotional material becomes ludicrous, and we may end up laughing at material intended to make us cry. Reactions to emotional material, of course, depend greatly on the individual viewer. For example, one viewer may consider the film *Love Story* to be a beautifully touching and poignant experience, while another may scoff and call it "sentimental trash." The difference lies in the viewers themselves. The first viewer would probably have responded fully to the film, allowing himself to be manipulated by its emotional effects without considering the filmmaker to be dishonest in his handling of emotional material. The second viewer, however, might have felt that his emotions were being manipulated unfairly and dishonestly, and rebelled against this treatment by rejecting the film.

When the emotional material in a film is understated, however, there is little danger of offending. In understatement the filmmaker makes a conscious attempt to play down the emotional material by giving it less emphasis than the situation would seem to call for. For example, in *To Kill a Mockingbird,* Atticus Finch (Gregory Peck), thanks the boogeyman, Arthur "Boo" Radley (Robert Duvall), for saving the lives of his children with the simple phrase, "Thank you Arthur . . . for my children." The effect of understatement is demonstrated here in the tremendous emotional weight carried by the simple phrase "thank you," which we often use for the most trivial favors. The normally insignificant phrase takes on great significance, and we are powerfully moved by what is *not* said. The same type of understatement is built into a line from the voice-over narration in the same film:

> Neighbors bring food with death and flowers with sickness and little things in between. Boo was our neighbor. He gave us two soap dolls, a broken watch and chain, a pair of good luck pennies, and our lives.

A wide variety of film elements and techniques influence our overall emotional response to a film. Both understatement and the overuse of emotional material are reflected in the way the plot is structured, in the dialogue and the acting, and in the visual effects employed. The filmmaker's approach to emotional material is perhaps most evident, however, in the musical score, which can communicate on a purely emotional level and thus reflects accurately the peaks and valleys of emotional emphasis and understatement.

QUESTIONS
ON STORY ELEMENTS

How does the film stack up against the five characteristics of a good story?

1 How well is it unified in plot or story line?
2 What makes the story believable? Pick out specific scenes to illustrate what kind of "truth" is stressed by the film: (a) objective "truth" which follows the observable laws of probability and necessity, (b) subjective, irrational, and emotional "inner truth" of human nature, or (c) the "semblance of truth" created by the filmmaker?
3 What makes the film interesting? Where are its high points of suspense and action, and where are its dead spots? If you are bored by the film as a whole or by certain parts, what causes you to have this reaction?
4 Is the film a proper blend of simplicity and complexity?
    a. How well is the story suited in length to the limits of the medium?

    b. Is the film a simple "formula" treatment, allowing you to predict the outcome at the halfway point, or does it effectively maintain suspense until the very end? If the ending is shocking or surprising, how does it carry out the tendencies of the earlier parts of the story?

    c. Where in the film are implication and suggestion effectively employed? Where is it simple and direct?

    d. Is the view of life reflected by the story simple or complex? What factors influenced your answer?

5 How honest and sincere is the film in its handling of emotional material? Where are the emotional effects overdone? Where is understatement used?

DRAMATIC STRUCTURE

The art of storytelling, whether it be practiced in the short story, novel, drama, or film, has always depended on a strong dramatic structure— that is, the arrangement of parts esthetically and logically in order to achieve the maximum emotional, intellectual, or dramatic impact. Two common structural patterns are followed by so many fictional films that they deserve brief treatment here. Both patterns contain the same elements: *exposition, complication, climax,* and *resolution* or *denouement.* These two types of dramatic structure differ only in the arrangement of those elements, and are identified by the way they begin.

    1. *Expository or chronological beginning:* The first part of the story, which is called the *exposition,* introduces the characters, shows some of their interrelationships, and places them within a believable time and place. The next section, in which a conflict begins and grows in clarity, intensity, and importance, is called the *complication.* Since dramatic tension and suspense are created and maintained during the complication, this stage is usually of greater length than other parts of the dramatic structure. When the complication has reached its point of maximum tension, the two forces in opposition confront each other at a high point of physical or emotional action called the *climax.* At the climax, the resolution of the conflict occurs and there follows a brief period of calm called a *denouement* in which a state of relative equilibrium returns.

    2. *In medias res beginning. In medias res* is a Latin phrase meaning "in the midst of the action," and refers to a method of beginning a story

which has had great popularity since the time of Homer. (Both his *Iliad* and his *Odyssey* begin in this fashion.) Since capturing the audience's interest is always critical, it is extremely important that this occur at an early stage and be maintained throughout the story. For this reason, many films are structured to begin *in medias res,* opening with an exciting incident after the complication has already started to develop and the action is underway. Thus a state of dramatic tension exists and interest is assured from the beginning. The necessary expository information is filled in later as the situation permits, through such means as dialogue (characters talking about the situation or events that led to the complication) or flashbacks (actual filmed sequences that go back in time to provide expository material). In this manner exposition can be built up gradually and spread throughout the film instead of being carefully and completely established at the beginning, before dramatic interest starts to build.

The following two passages from John Steinbeck's short story "Flight"* are used to illustrate the difference between the expository or chronological beginning and the *in medias res* beginning when visualized in cinematic form.

First, consider how an expository or chronological beginning might be developed from this passage:

About fifteen miles below Monterey, on the wild coast, the Torres family had their farm, a few sloping acres above a cliff that dropped to the brown reefs and to the hissing white waters of the ocean. Behind the farm the stone mountains stood up against the sky. The farm buildings huddled like little clinging aphids on the mountain skirts, crouched low to the ground as though the wind might blow them into the sea. The little shack, the rattling, rotting barn were gray-bitten with sea salt, beaten by the damp wind until they had taken on the color of the granite hills. Two horses, a red cow and a red calf, half a dozen pigs and a flock of lean, multi-colored chickens stocked the place. A little corn was raised on the sterile slope, and it grew short and thick under the wind, and all the cobs formed on the landward sides of the stalks.

Mama Torres, a lean, dry woman with ancient eyes, had ruled the farm for ten years, ever since her husband tripped over a stone in the field one day and fell full length on a rattlesnake. When one is bitten on the chest there is not much that can be done.

Mama Torres had three children, two undersized black ones of twelve and fourteen, Emilio and Rosy, whom Mama kept fishing on the rocks be-

---

*"Flight" from *The Long Valley* by John Steinbeck. Copyright 1938, © 1966 by John Steinbeck. Reprinted by permission of The Viking Press.

low the farm when the sea was kind and when the truant officer was in some distant part of Monterey County. And there was Pepé, the tall smiling son of nineteen, a gentle, affectionate boy, but very lazy. Pepé had a tall head, pointed at the top, and from its peak, coarse black hair grew down like a thatch all around. Over his smiling little eyes Mama cut a straight bang so he could see. Pepé had sharp Indian cheek bones and an eagle nose, but his mouth was as sweet and shapely as a girl's mouth, and his chin was fragile and chiseled. He was loose and gangling, all legs and feet and wrists, and he was very lazy. Mama thought him fine and brave, but she never told him so. She said, "Some lazy cow must have got into thy father's family, else how could I have a son like thee." And she said, "When I carried thee, a sneaking lazy coyote came out of the brush and looked at me one day. That must have made thee so."

In the film version of this expository or chronological beginning, the camera would first show the Torres family farm from a distance, then move gradually closer to show us the children playing near the house, with Mama Torres perhaps standing in the doorway, talking to herself as she looks out toward Pepé and the other children. A beginning of this sort would have no dramatic tension but would effectively establish the setting, introduce the major characters, and show something of their interrelationships.

In the *in medias res* beginning, the director might choose the scene described in the following paragraph, in which the dramatic tension is already clearly established and the major action of the plot is already under way.

Pepé started up, listening. His horse had whinnied. The moon was just slipping behind the western ridge, leaving the valley in darkness behind it. Pepé sat tensely gripping his rifle. From far up the trail he heard an answering whinny and the crash of shod hooves on the broken rock. He jumped to his feet, ran to his horse and led it under the trees. He threw on the saddle and cinched it tight for the steep trail, caught the unwilling head and forced the bit into the mouth. He felt the saddle to make sure the water bag and the sack of jerky were there. Then he mounted and turned up the hill.

If the film started in this way, the relationship between Pepé and his mother would have to be established later through a flashback. But providing exposition is not the only function of flashback. Few stories are structured in a pure, straight chronological sequence, and divergence from strict chronological order is very common in film, where the visual flashback gives it great structural flexibility. Through use of the flashback, the director can bring in information as he or she desires, when it is most dramatically appropriate and powerful, or when it will most effectively illuminate the theme. (*Flash-forwards*, where the visual scene jumps from the present into a future time has even been tried in such films as *Easy Rider* and *They Shoot Horses, Don't They?*, although it is doubtful whether this device will ever gain widespread acceptance.) As long as coherence is maintained so that a clear sense of the relationships between one scene and another is established, the director can violate strict chronological order at will.

Sometimes, however, a director may purposely try to confuse the time sequences. For example, in the haunting and mystifying *Last Year at Marienbad,* Resnais seems determined to keep us wondering whether the scene we are watching is taking place in time-present (this year), time-past (last year) or, in fact, whether it really took place at all.

QUESTIONS
ON DRAMATIC STRUCTURE

1   Does the film use the expository (chronological) or the *in medias res* beginning? If it begins with expository material, does it capture your interest quickly enough, or would a beginning "in the midst of the action" be better? At what point in the story could an *in medias res* beginning start?
2   If flashbacks are used, what is their purpose and how effective are they?

SYMBOLISM

In most general terms, whether it be in a work of art or in everyday communications of the most ordinary sort, a symbol is something that stands for something else and communicates that "something else" by triggering, stimulating, or arousing previously associated ideas in the mind of the person perceiving the symbol.* All forms of human communication involve the use of symbols, and we clearly understand their meaning if we already possess the ideas or concepts associated with or built into the symbol. For example, a traffic light communicates its

---

*To avoid complex distinctions between terms, the words *symbol* and *simile* are sometimes used in this book when the term *metaphor* may be more technically correct.

message to us symbolically. When the light turns green or red, we do more than observe with interest the change from one color to another; we respond to the symbolic message it gives us. To a caveman who had never seen a traffic light, however, the change in color would have no symbolic meaning, for he would lack the built-in associations with those colors that our experience in modern society has provided us. It would, therefore, be very dangerous for the caveman to walk around in the heart of a busy city without some awareness of the symbolic importance of traffic signals. It is equally dangerous for a student to approach a work of art without some understanding of the nature, function, and importance of its symbols. The things which take on symbolic meaning in a film are almost unlimited in range. In many stories, the setting takes on strong symbolic overtones. Characters are often used symbolically, and once characters become symbolic, the conflicts in which they take part become symbolic also. Therefore, it is essential that we become consciously aware of the special nature of symbolic communication in film.

In any story form, a symbol is something concrete (a particular object, image, person, sound, event, or place) that stands for, suggests, or triggers a complex of ideas, attitudes, or feelings and thus acquires significance beyond itself. A symbol therefore is a special kind of energized communication unit, which functions somewhat like a storage battery. Once a symbol is "charged" with a set of associations (ideas, attitudes, or feelings), it is capable of storing those associations and communicating them any time it is used.

UNIVERSAL AND NATURAL SYMBOLS

Universal symbols are "precharged" or "ready-made" symbols that are already charged with values and associations understood by most of the people in a given culture. By using such objects, images, or persons, which automatically evoke many complex associations, filmmakers save themselves the job of creating each of the associated attitudes and feelings within the context of their films. They need only to use these symbols appropriately to make full use of their communication potential. Thus such symbols as the American flag (triggering the complex set of feelings and values that we associate with America), or the cross (evoking a variety of values and feelings associated with Christianity), can be used effectively as symbols for a broad audience. Reactions would vary according to the viewer's attitudes toward the ideas represented, but all people from the same culture would get the general symbolic message.

Many universal symbols are charged with their meanings externally, through past associations with people, events, places, or ideas, rather than through their own inherent characteristics. For example, there is nothing inherent in the shape of a cross to suggest Christianity; rather, the religious values and ideas attached to the crucifixion of Christ over the ages have given the cross its symbolic meaning. On the other hand, some objects have natural or inherent qualities that make them particularly well-fitted as symbols. A buzzard, for example, may be used as a symbol of death, without the need to establish its symbolic value. This, of course, is partly due to its appearance. Buzzards are black, a color associated with death, but the habits of the buzzard are also important. A buzzard is a scavenger, a creature that feeds only on dead flesh, and does not even approach living creatures. Probably of even greater significance is a buzzard's *visibility* as a symbol: By soaring in long, lazy circles over an area where something is dead or dying, the buzzard actually signals the presence of death. Thus, buzzards communicate the idea of death indirectly but clearly, so an observer need not see the dead object itself to know that death is present. The habits or lifestyles of hawks and doves are equally significant in determining their symbolic meanings.

The filmmaker will use such universal and natural symbols whenever they suit his purposes, not only because they communicate ideas effectively, but also because they save the trouble of creating the associations, attitudes, and feelings that they evoke.

CREATING SYMBOLIC MEANINGS

In many cases, however, filmmakers cannot depend on precharged or ready-made symbols, but must create symbols by charging them within the context of the film itself. This is done by first loading a concrete object or image with an electrical charge of associations, feelings, and attitudes, and then employing the now "charged" symbol to evoke these associations whenever necessary. Consider, for example, how John Steinbeck develops the symbolic value of a knife in his short story "Flight":

> Pepé smiled sheepishly and stabbed at the ground with his knife to keep the blade sharp and free from rust. It was his inheritance, that knife, his father's knife. The long heavy blade folded back into the block handle. There was a button on the handle. When Pepé pressed the button, the blade leaped out ready for use. The knife was with Pepé always, for it had been his father's knife.

In charging an object with symbolic value, the storyteller actually has a dual purpose. First, he wants to expand the meaning of the symbolic object in order to communicate his meanings, feelings, and ideas, and second, he wants to make it clear that the object is being treated symbolically. Thus many of the methods used to charge an object symbolically also serve as clues that the object is taking on symbolic value. There are four primary methods of charging symbols to which we must pay special attention:

1. *Through repetition.* Perhaps the most obvious means of charging an object is by repeatedly drawing attention to it more often than a simple surface object might seem to deserve. Through such repetition, the object gains in significance and symbolic power with each appearance.

3. *Repeated images of symbolic separation:* Jean Arthur, as the farmer's wife Marion, stands inside the house while Alan Ladd, as Shane, the exgunfighter who is now the farmer's hired hand, stands outside looking in the window. This symbolic separation is repeated visually throughout the film—Shane is always an outsider, present with, but not part of, the warm family circle or the close-knit group of farmers. On several occasions, Shane is framed through an open doorway, looking in on a warm family scene inside, or sitting off to the side by himself in a meeting of the farmers. The scene shown here has additional levels of meaning: Shane and Marion have a strong but unspoken mutual attraction, and keep a "wall" up between themselves out of basic human decency and their mutual respect and love for the farmer (Van Heflin). *Shane.*

2. *Through value placed on an object by a character.* An object is also charged symbolically when a particular character places value and importance on it. By showing extraordinary concern for an object (as in Pepé's treatment of the knife, or in the Captain's treatment of his palm tree in *Mister Roberts*), or by repeatedly mentioning it in the dialogue, the character indicates that an object or idea has more than ordinary significance. Symbols charged in this way may be of relatively minor importance, functioning only to give us symbolic insight into the character in question, or they may have major significance to the overall dramatic structure, as illustrated by the famous Rosebud symbol in *Citizen Kane.*

3. *Through context in which the object or image appears.* Sometimes an object or image takes on symbolic power simply through its placement in the film, and its symbolic charge is built up through associations created (1) by its relationship to other visual objects in the same frame, (2) by a relationship established by the editorial juxtaposition of one shot with another, or (3) when it occupies an important place in the film's structure.

One particular symbolic image in the film version of Tennessee Williams's play *Suddenly Last Summer*—the Venus flytrap—illustrates all three methods of charging an image by context. The Venus flytrap is a large, white flowered plant whose leaves have two hinged blades. When an insect enters the space between them, the blades close like a mouth on it, trapping it inside. The plant then "feeds" on the insect. Once the nature of the plant and its feeding habits are made clear, the Venus flytrap is used to suggest or represent a major idea in the play—the concept of carnivorousness or cannibalism. The plant's nature is explained by Mrs. Venable (played by Katharine Hepburn), and it is seen to occupy a position near her chair so they share the same visual frame. As Mrs. Venable talks about her dead son Sebastian, we begin to see the relationship between the woman and the plant, for her conversation reveals her to be a "cannibal," savagely feeding on and deriving her nourishment from the memory of her dead son.

The same effect could be achieved through editorial juxtaposition, by cutting immediately from a close-up of Mrs. Venable's mouth as she drones on about her son to a close-up of the "jaws" of the Venus flytrap snapping shut on an unsuspecting insect.

Even if it were not further charged within the context of the film, this image could still function effectively as a symbol if its symbolic function were made clear by the importance of its position within the film's overall structure. Consider, for example, how the image might be used only at the beginning and the end of a film: As the film begins,

4. *"Charging" the symbol:* Mrs. Venable (Katharine Hepburn) explains
    the nature of the Venus Flytrap to the young psychiatrist (Mont-
    gomery Clift) in a scene from *Suddenly Last Summer.* In so doing,
    she "charges" the plant with symbolic meaning and starts a pattern or
    progression of symbolic images that continues throughout the film.

a close-up of the Venus flytrap serves as a background to the titles.
Then, as the titles draw to a close, an insect lands on the flower and is
trapped as the jaws close suddenly around it. The object is not seen
again until the film's closing shot, where it appears again, seducing another insect into its folds. In this case we would be forced, by the sheer
weight of its structural position, to consider the plant's symbolic function and its meaning to the film as a whole.

   4. *Through special visual, aural, or musical emphasis.* Film has its
own unique ways of charging and underscoring symbols and providing
clues to the audience that an object is to be seen symbolically. For example, visual emphasis may be achieved through lingering close-ups, unusual camera angles, changes from sharp to soft focus, freeze frames, or
lighting effects. Similar emphasis can be achieved through sound effects
or use of the musical score. Individual natural sounds or musical refrains
can become symbols in their own right if complex associations are built
into them by any of the three methods above.

SYMBOLIC PATTERNS AND PROGRESSIONS

Although symbols may function singly without a clear relationship to other symbols, they often interact with other symbols in what might be called symbolic patterns. In such a case, the filmmaker will express the same idea through several symbols instead of relying on only one. The resulting symbolic pattern may even have a certain progression to it, so that the symbols grow in value or power as the film progresses.

An excellent example is the complex pattern of symbols that gradually builds up to the climax of *Suddenly Last Summer.** The idea of a savage universe, inhabited by creatures who devour each other, is established by the symbol already described, the Venus flytrap, and its association with Mrs. Venable. From this point on, other symbolic images are used with the same meaning in a pattern of ever-increasing dramatic power. The next symbolic image in the pattern appears in Mrs. Venable's description of a sight she and Sebastian witnessed on the Encantadas:

> Over the narrow black beach of the Encantadas as the just-hatched sea-turtles scrambled out of the sandpits and started their race to the sea. . . . To escape the flesh-eating birds that made the sky almost as black as the beach! . . . And the sand was all alive, all alive, as the hatched sea-turtles made their dash for the sea, while the birds hovered and swooped to attack and hovered and—swooped to attack! They were diving down on the hatched sea-turtles, turning them over to expose their soft undersides, tearing the undersides open and rending and eating their flesh. . . .

Having set up three symbols of the same idea (the flytrap, Mrs. Venable, and the birds) the playwright gives us a suggestion of their significance as Mrs. Venable continues her story:

> He spent the whole blazing equatorial day in the crow's nest of the schooner watching this thing on the beach until it was too dark to see it, and when he came down from the rigging he said "Well, now I've seen Him," and he meant God. . .He meant that God shows a savage face to people and shouts some fierce things at them, it's all we see or hear of Him . . .

The next image in the pattern occurs in Catherine's (Elizabeth Taylor) description of Sebastian himself, which adds strong overtones of homosexuality to the already shocking image:

*Tennessee Williams, *Suddenly Last Summer*. Copyright © 1958 by Tennessee Williams. All rights reserved. Reprinted by permission of New Directions Publishing Corporation.

> We were *going* to blonds, blonds were next on the menu. . . . Cousin Sebastian said he was famished for blonds, he was fed up with the dark ones and was famished for blonds . . . that's how he talked about people, as if they were—items on a menu.—"That one's delicious-looking, that one is appetizing," or "that one is not appetizing"—I think because he was nearly half-starved from living on pills and salads. . . .

As the next image in the pattern begins to develop, there is an effort to link the children which constitute this image with the earlier image of the carnivorous birds.

> There were naked children along the beach, a band of frightfully thin and dark naked children that looked like a flock of plucked birds, and they would come darting up to the barbed wire fence as if blown there by the wind, the hot white wind from the sea, all crying out, "Pan, pan, pan!". . . The word for bread, and they made gobbling voices with their little black mouths, stuffing their little black fists to their mouths and making those gobbling noises with frightful grins!

At the film's climax, the image of the carnivorous birds is repeated, but this time on a completely human level, which makes it even more shocking:

> . . . Sebastian started to run and they all screamed at once and seemed to fly in the air, they outran him so quickly. I screamed. I heard Sebastian scream, he screamed just once before this flock of black plucked little birds that pursued him and overtook him halfway up the white hill.
> I ran down . . . screaming out "Help" all the way, till—. . . Waiters, police, and others—ran out of the buildings and rushed back up the hill with me. When we got back to where my Cousin Sebastian had disappeared in the flock of featherless little black sparrows, he—he was lying naked as they had been naked against a white wall, and this you won't believe, nobody has believed it, nobody would believe it, nobody, nobody on earth could possibly believe it, and I don't *blame* them!—They had *devoured* parts of him.
> Torn or cut parts of him away with their hands or knives or maybe those jagged tin cans they made music with, they had torn bits of him away and stuffed them into those gobbling fierce little empty mouths of theirs. . . .

This incident takes place in a village whose name is also symbolic: Cabeza De Lobo, which means "Head of the Wolf," another savage and carnivorous image.

Thus by means of a complex pattern of symbols, the film makes a statement about the human condition. The idea of the earth as a savage jungle where creatures devour each other is made clear by a series of symbols: the Venus flytrap, the turtle-devouring birds, Sebastian's own "hungers," and the little human "cannibals" of Cabeza De Lobo. And Williams has arranged these symbols in order so that they become increasingly vivid, powerful, and shocking as the story unfolds.

ALLEGORY

When an entire story is structured around its symbolic meanings, so that every object, event, and person on the surface level has a corresponding meaning on a symbolic level, the story is known as an allegory. In allegory, each symbolic meaning and abstraction is part of an interdependent system that tells a separate and complete story on a purely allegorical or figurative level.

A major problem with allegory is the difficulty of making both levels of meaning equally interesting. Often, so much importance is placed on the abstract symbolic level, that we lose interest in the surface level. The difficulty arises primarily from the fact that allegorical characters are almost by necessity flat or undeveloped characters. To be effective as symbols, they cannot have many unique and particular characteristics, for the more unique and particular the characters are, the less representative they can be. But these difficulties do not necessarily prevent allegory from being effective in cinematic form, as is evidenced by such excellent films as *Woman in the Dunes, Sweptaway, Lord of the Flies,* and *The Seventh Seal.*

5. *Allegory:* Peter Brook's *Lord of the Flies,* based on William Golding's novel, is an allegory on the savage nature of man. (Culver Pictures)

COMPLEX OR AMBIGUOUS SYMBOLS

Although filmmakers want to express their ideas clearly, they may not always want to express them simply or too clearly. Thus, although some symbols may be very simple and clear, others may be complex and ambiguous. Such symbols can seldom be interpreted with one clear and certain meaning; there may be no one "right answer" to what a given symbol means, but several equally valid but different interpretations. This is not to say that a filmmaker using ambiguous symbols is deliberately trying to confuse us. The intention is usually to enrich or enhance the work through complexities.

SIMILES

Closely related to symbolism is the filmmaker's use of what might be called visual similes. Whereas a symbol stands for or represents something else, a film simile is a brief comparison that helps us understand or perceive one image better because of its similarity to another image. This is usually achieved through the editorial juxtaposition of two images in two successive shots. If, for example, the filmmaker wants to show us his reaction to a group of old ladies in the midst of a gossip session, he or she may do so by cutting from a shot of the gossips talking together to a close-up of the heads of several frantically clucking chickens. Thus, in purely visual terms, the director has told us that the old ladies gossiping are like a bunch of old hens. On a more serious plane is an example of a simile taken from Eisenstein's *Strike,* where shots of workers being pursued and killed are alternated with simile shots of a butcher slaughtering a bull. In both examples, the secondary images are extrinsic, meaning that they have no place within the context of the scene itself but are imposed artificially into the scene by the director. In the realistic or naturalistic film, such extrinsic similes may seem forced, heavy-handed, or even ludicrous, destroying a sense of reality which may be very important to the film. On the other hand, comedy or fantasy films can use such images freely, and serious films that stress an interior or subjective viewpoint may also use them very effectively.

Intrinsic similes, which are taken directly from the context of the scene itself, are more natural and usually more subtle. In his short story "Flight," John Steinbeck employs a subtle use of simile which can be easily visualized in cinematic terms. The story's central character, the young man Pepé, has killed a man with his knife in Monterey, and is attempting to escape the pursuing posse alone. The following scene takes place near Pepé's home on the morning after the event, and focuses on Pepé's little brother and sister:

> Emilio and Rosy stood wondering in the dawn. They heard Mama whimpering in the house. They went out to sit on the cliff above the ocean. They touched shoulders. "When did Pepé come to be a man?" Emilio asked.
>
> "Last night," said Rosy. "Last night in Monterey." The ocean clouds turned red with the sun that was behind the mountains.
>
> "We will have no breakfast," said Emilio. "Mama will not want to cook." Rosy did not answer him. "Where is Pepé gone?" he asked.
>
> Rosy looked around at him. She drew her knowledge from the quiet air. "He has gone on a journey. He will never come back."
>
> "Is he dead? Do you think he is dead?"
>
> Rosy looked back at the ocean again. A little steamer, drawing a line of smoke, sat on the edge of the horizon. "He is not dead," Rosy explained. "Not yet."

The similes here depend primarily on the juxtaposition of dialogue and visual image. When the ocean clouds turn red, we see the similarity to "last night in Monterey," a night of bloodshed. The image of the little steamer, all alone in the vast ocean and about to disappear over the edge of the horizon, becomes an effective simile which helps us to understand Pepé's predicament and his chances. Yet because they are intrinsic similes, drawn naturally from the scene's environment, they have a quiet subtlety and an understated power which would be impossible to achieve with an extrinsic image.

The dramatic power and the communicative effectiveness of any symbol or simile are dependent also on its originality and freshness. A tired and worn out symbol can no longer carry "heavy" meanings, and a simile which has become a cliché becomes a hindrance rather than a help. This fact causes many problems in watching older films, for many of the similes and symbols used seem to be clichés today, although they may have actually been fresh and original when the film was made.

QUESTIONS
ON SYMBOLISM

1   What symbols appear in the film and what do they represent?
2   What universal or natural symbols are employed? How effective are they?

3 Which symbols derive their meaning solely from their context in the film? How are they charged with symbolic value? (In other words, how do you know they are symbols, and how do you arrive at their meaning?)

4 How are the special capabilities of film (the visual image, the sound track, and the musical score) employed to charge symbols with their meaning?

5 Which symbols fit into a larger pattern or progression with other symbols in the film?

6 How are the major symbols related to the theme?

7 Is the story structured around its symbolic meanings to the extent that it can be called an allegory?

8 Which of the symbols' meanings are clear and simple? Which symbols are complex and ambiguous? What gives them this quality?

9 Are visual similies employed effectively? Are they primarily extrinsic (imposed artificially into the scene by editing) or intrinsic (a natural part of the setting)?

10 How fresh and original are the film's symbols and similies? If they seem clichéd or time-worn, where have you encountered them before?

CHARACTERIZATION

If we are not interested in a film's most human elements, its characters, there is little chance that we will be interested in the film as a whole. To be interesting, characters must seem real, understandable, and worth caring about. For the most part, the characters in a story are believable in the same way that the story is believable; in other words, they either conform to the laws of probability and necessity (by reflecting externally observable truths about human nature), conform to some inner truth (man as we want him to be), or they are made to seem real by the convincing art of the actor.

And if the characters are truly believable, it is almost impossible to remain completely neutral toward them. We must respond toward them in some way: We may admire them for their heroic deeds and their nobility, or pity them for their failures. We may love them or identify with them for their ordinary human qualitites. And we may laugh at them for their ignorance, or laugh *with them* because theirs is a human ignorance which we all share. Or, if our reaction to them is negative, we may detest them for their greed, their cruelty, their selfishness, and their underhanded methods. Or we may scorn them for their cowardice.

CHARACTERIZATION BY APPEARANCE

Because most film actors project certain qualities of character the minute they appear on the screen, characterization in film has a great deal to do with the casting selection made. Although some actors may be versatile enough to project completely different qualities in different roles, with most actors this is not the case. Thus the minute we see actors on the screen we make certain assumptions about them based on their facial features, dress, physical build, mannerisms, and the way they move. A major aspect of film characterization is therefore revealed visually and instantaneously by our first visual impression of each character. This first impression may be proven erroneous as the story progresses, but it is certainly an important means of establishing character. Consider, for example, the immediate reactions we have to Michael Pollard and Robert Redford when they appear for the first time in *Little Fauss and Big Halsey,* or to Jack Palance as the gunfighter Wilson in *Shane.*

CHARACTERIZATION THROUGH DIALOGUE

Characters in a fictional film naturally reveal a great deal about themselves by what they say. But there is also a great deal revealed by *how* they say it. Their true thoughts, attitudes, and emotions may be revealed in subtle ways through their choice of words and through the stress, pitch, and pause patterns built into their speech. Actors' use of grammar, sentence structure, vocabulary, and particular dialects (if any) all reveal a great deal about their characters' social and economic level, educational background, and mental processes. Therefore, we must develop a keen ear, attuned to the faintest and most subtle nuances of meaning revealed through the human voice—not only by listening carefully to what is said, but also to how it is said.

CHARACTERIZATION THROUGH EXTERNAL ACTION

Although a character's appearance is an important measure of his or her personality, it may often be misleading. Perhaps the best reflection of character can be found in a person's actions. It must be assumed, of course, that real characters are more than mere instruments of the plot, and they do what they do for a purpose, out of motives that are consistent with their overall personality. Thus there should be a clear relationship between a character and his or her actions so that the actions grow naturally out of the character's personality. If the motivation for a character's action is clearly established, the character and the plot become so closely interwoven that they are impossible to separate, and every action that a person takes in some way reflects the quality of the particular personality. As Henry James stated in *The Art of Fiction,* "What is character but the determination of incident? What is incident but the reflection of character?"

Of course, some actions are more important in revealing character than others, as Aristotle implied when he said the "character is manifested in those things which an individual chooses or rejects." Even the most ordinary kind of choice can be revealing, for some kind of choice is involved in almost everything we do. Sometimes the most effective characterization is achieved not by the large actions in the film, but by the small, seemingly insignificant actions or choices. For example, a fireman may demonstrate his courage by saving a child from a burning building, yet such an act may be only a performance of duty rather than any choice on his part. His essential character might be more clearly defined by risking his life to "save" a little girl's doll, since such an action would not be imposed upon him by duty, but by his own value judgment on the importance a doll might have to a little girl.

CHARACTERIZATION THROUGH INTERNAL ACTION

There is also an inner world of "action" that normally remains unseen and unheard by even the most careful observer or listener. Yet the dimension of human nature that this world embraces is often essential to a real understanding of a character. Inner action occurs within characters' minds and emotions, and consists of secret, unspoken thoughts, daydreams, aspirations, memories, fears, and fantasies. People's hopes, dreams, and aspirations can be as important to an understanding of their character as any real achievement, and their fears and insecurities may be more terrible to them than any real catastrophic failure. Thus, although Walter Mitty is a dull, drab, insignificant creature scarcely worth caring about when judged purely by his external behavior, he becomes an exciting and interesting personality when we "read" his mind and see his daydreams.

6. *Characterization through internal action:* In *The Secret Life of Wal-*
7. *ter Mitty,* Walter Mitty (Danny Kaye) is in reality a timid, frightened creature who is henpecked by his wife (Virginia Mayo). In his daydreams, however, he sees himself in a variety of heroic roles like the western hero, defending the weak and clinging Ms. Mayo. (Culver Pictures)

The most obvious way in which the filmmaker shows us this inner reality is by taking us visually or aurally into the mind so that we see or hear the things that the character imagines, remembers, or thinks about. This may be achieved through a sustained interior view, or through fleeting glimpses revealed by means of similes. Consider, for example, how the self-consciousness of T. S. Eliot's J. Alfred Prufrock might be characterized by a simile:*

> And I have known the eyes already, known them all—
> The eyes that fix you in a formulated phrase,
> And when I am formulated, sprawling on a pin,
> When I am pinned and wriggling on the wall. . .

In this image, Prufrock compares himself to an insect, "pinned and wriggling on the wall," as he is classified and dissected by the eyes of people watching him at a social gathering. The filmmaker might handle this inner characterization in one of two ways. He may simply cut from a subjective viewpoint (Prufrock's view of the people watching him) to a shot showing the same people examining and classifying a real insect "pinned and wriggling" on the wall. Or he may choose to interpret the image

*T.S. Eliot, "The Love Song of J. Alfred Prufrock," *Collected Poems 1909-1962* (New York: Harcourt Brace Jovanovich).

more literally, by cutting to a shot picturing Prufrock himself, reduced to insect size and with a huge pin through his middle, wriggling on a wall, helpless as he is analyzed by the same people.

Another scene taken from Eliot's poem illustrates other methods of conveying the inner story:

> And indeed there will be time
> To wonder, "Do I dare?" and "Do I dare?"
> Time to turn back and descend the stair,
> With a bald spot in the middle of my hair—
> (They will say: "How his hair is growing thin!")
> My morning coat, my collar mounting firmly to the chin,
> My necktie rich and modest, but asserted by a simple pin—
> (They will say: "But how his arms and legs are thin!")

This scene might be translated into film as follows:

> Tight close-up of Prufrock's head and shoulders from behind, as he's starting slowly upstairs toward social gathering. Stops after a few steps. Close-up of hand nervously gripping railing. Close-up of feet on stairs, poised to step up but not stepping. Close-up of top of Prufrock's head, with long thin fingers trying to brush hair over bald spot. Imaginary voice on sound track, over real buzz of conversation from top of stairs: "How his hair is growing thin." Close-up of front torso of Prufrock, now moving upstairs. Hands straightening lapels of coat, smoothing necktie, checking tie-pin. Imaginary voice on sound track, rising again over blur of conversation: "But how his arms and legs are thin."

In this visualization, an important aspect of Prufrock's inner character is captured through a combination of carefully chosen close-ups and a few brief aural "glimpses" of the voices in his mind's "ear." In addition to providing glimpses into the inner action by revealing the sounds and sights the character imagines he see and hears, the filmmaker may employ tight close-ups on an unusually sensitive and expressive face (reaction shots), or may utilize the musical score for essentially the same purpose.

CHARACTERIZATION BY REACTIONS OF OTHER CHARACTERS

The way other characters view a person often serves as an excellent means of characterization. Sometimes, a great deal of information about a character will already be provided through such means before he or she first appears on the screen, as is the case in the opening scene from *Hud.* In this sequence Lonnie (Brandon DeWilde) is walking along the main street of the little Texas town at around 6:30 in the morning, looking for his uncle Hud (Paul Newman). As he passes a beer joint along the way, the owner is out front, sweeping up the pieces of glass which used to be his large front window. Lonnie notices the broken window and observes, "You must have had quite a brawl in here last night." The owner replies, "I had *Hud* in here last night, that's what I had." The man's emphasis on the name Hud and his tone of voice in saying it clearly express that "Hud" is a synonym for "trouble." An effective bit of reactive characterization is also seen in *Shane,* as the gunfighter Wilson (Jack Palance), a personification of pure evil, walks into a saloon, empty except for a mangy dog curled up under a table. As Wilson enters, the dog puts his ears back and his tail between his legs and slinks fearfully out of the room.

CHARACTERIZATION BY CONTRAST: DRAMATIC FOILS

One of the most effective techniques of characterization is the use of contrasting characters whose behavior, attitudes, opinions, lifestyles, physical appearances, and so on are opposite to those of the main character, and thus serve to clearly define and emphasize his personality. The effect is similar to that achieved by putting black and white together—the black appears blacker, and the white appears whiter. The tallest giant and the tiniest midget might be placed side by side at the carnival side show, and the filmmaker sometimes uses characters in much the same way. Consider, for example, the effective contrasts in the characters played by Andy Griffith and Don Knotts on the old *Andy Griffith Show.* Griffith, as Sheriff Taylor, was tall, a little heavy, and projected a calm, self-confident, easy-going personality. Knotts, as Deputy Fife, was the exact opposite: short, skinny, insecure, and a perpetual bundle of nerves.

CHARACTERIZATION BY EXAGGERATION OR REPETITION: CARICATURE AND LEITMOTIF

In order to etch a character quickly and deeply on our minds and memories, actors often exaggerate or distort one or more dominant features

8. *Dramatic foils:* In the film version of Herman Melville's allegory of good and evil, *Billy Budd,* Terence Stamp as the sweet, naive, and innocent Billy contrasts sharply with the grim, satanic Master of Arms Claggart (played by Robert Ryan). The striking opposites in their characters are emphasized by their features, facial expressions, clothing, and voice qualities. Stamp is baby-faced, his features soft and smooth, his expressions sweet, almost effeminate, his eyes light blue, wide open, innocent. Ryan's face is mature, lined, the jaw and mouth strong and hard set; his facial expressions are sour and cynical, his eyes are dark, narrow, piercing, and malevolent. The fair complexion and blond (almost white) hair and white shirt worn by Stamp also contrast visually with Ryan's dark hair and clothing. Stamp's voice is soft, sometimes melodious; Ryan's is deep, unctuous, and cold.

or personality traits, a device which is called *caricature* from the technique in cartooning. The perpetual nervousness of Barney Fife mentioned above, or Gomer Pyle's eternal naiveté, provide excellent examples from television. A physical feature, such as the way a person moves, may also be caricatured—for example, Chester's exaggerated stiff-legged limp on the old *Gunsmoke* series, or Walter Brennan's hopping and skipping limp on *The Real McCoys.* Voice qualities and accents may also function in this way, as illustrated by the back-woods nasal employed by Ken Curtis as Festus Haigan on *Gunsmoke,* and the New England aristocratic speech of Jim Backus as Mr. Howell on *Gilligan's Island.*

A similar means of characterization, called *leitmotif,* is the repetition of a single phrase or idea by a character until it becomes almost a trademark or theme song for that character. Because it essentially exaggerates and emphasizes (through repetition), such a device acts very much like caricature. Examples of *leitmotif* might be seen in the *Beverly Hillbillies'* Jethroe Clampett and his obsession for "vittles" and his cousin Ellie May's preoccupation with her "critters." Perhaps Charles Dickens rates as the all-time master of both techniques. Recall Uriah Heep from *David Copperfield*, for example, who continually wrings his hands (caricature) and says, "I'm so 'umble" (*leitmotif*). Modern films such as *Catch 22* still employ such techniques effectively.

CHARACTERIZATION THROUGH CHOICE OF NAME: NAME-TYPING

An important method of characterization often overlooked in film is the use of names possessing appropriate qualities of sound, meaning, or connotation to help describe the character, a technique known as name-typing. Since a great deal of thought goes into the choice of names, they should not be taken for granted, but should be carefully examined for the connotations they communicate. Some names, such as Dick Tracy, are rather obvious and clear connotations can be seen: Dick is a slang word for detective; Tracy derives from the fact that detectives "trace" criminals. Others may have only generalized connotations. Gomer Pyle, for example, has a small-town or country-hick ring to it, while Cornelius Witherspoon III has an opposite kind of sound. Certain sounds in names have generally unpleasant connotations. The "sn" sound, for example, evokes primarily unpleasant associations, since a large majority of the words beginning with that sound are unpleasant—for example, snide, sneer, sneak, snake, snail, sneeze, snatch, snout, snort. Thus a name like Snerd or Snavely has an unpleasant ring automatically. Sometimes a name will draw its effect both from its meaning and its sound, such as Flem (read "phlegm") Snopes. In this vein, because of the connotative power of names, film actors' names are often changed to fit the image they project. (John Wayne's real name, for example, was Marion Morrison, and Cary Grant's real name was Archibald Leach.)

STOCK CHARACTERS AND STEREOTYPES

It is not essential, or even desirable, that every character in a film have a unique or memorable personality. Stock characters are minor characters whose actions are completely predictable. Typical of their job or profession (such as a bartender in a Western), they are in the film simply because the situation demands their presence. Thus they serve more as a natural part of the setting than anything else, much as stage properties like a lamp or a chair might function in a play.

Stereotypes, on the other hand, are characters of somewhat greater importance to the film who fit into preconceived patterns of behavior common to or representative of a large number of people, at least a large number of "fictional" people. Examples of stereotypes are the rich playboy, the Western hero's "sidekick," the pompous banker, and the old maid aunt. Our preconceived notions of such characters allow the director to economize greatly in treating them.

STATIC AND DEVELOPING CHARACTERS

It is often useful to determine whether or not the most important characters in a film are static or developing characters. Developing characters are those who are deeply affected by the action of the plot (internal, external, or both) and who undergo some important change in personality, attitude, or outlook on life as a result of the action of the story. The change they undergo is an important, permanent one, not just a whimsical shift in attitude that will change back again tomorrow. The character will somehow never be the same person he or she was when the action of the film began. This change may be of any type, but it is significant to the total make-up of the individual undergoing the change. Developing characters may become sadder and wiser, or happier and more self-confident. They may gain some new awareness of life, or become more mature, more responsible, or more moral or less so. They may become simply more aware and knowing, and less innocent or naive.

Static characters, however, as the term implies, remain essentially the same throughout the action of the film, either because the action does not have as important an effect on their lives (as might generally be the case with the hero of an action-adventure film), or simply because they are insensitive to the meaning of the action, and thus are not really capable of growth or change, as is the case with the title character in *Hud*.

FLAT AND ROUND CHARACTERS

Another important distinction is made between *flat* and *round* characters. Flat characters are two-dimensional, predictable characters who lack the complexity and unique qualities associated with what we call psychological depth. They often tend to be representative character types rather than real flesh and blood human beings. Unique individualistic characters who have some degree of complexity and ambiguity and who cannot easily be categorized are called *round* or *three-dimensional* characters.

There is nothing inherently superior about round or developing characters over flat or static characters. The terms imply different functions rather than value judgments. What is important is that the characters function effectively within the framework of the story's theme or purpose. Static characters can be complex and vitally interesting without undergoing any character change. Flat characters may function better than round characters when attention needs to be directed *away* from personalities and *toward* the meaning of the action, for example in an allegory such as *Lord of the Flies* or *Woman in the Dunes.*

QUESTIONS
ON CHARACTERIZATION

1   Identify the central (most important) character or characters. Which characters are static and which ones are developing? Which characters are flat and which ones are round?
2   What methods of characterization are employed, and how effective are they?
3   Which of the characters are realistic, and which ones are exaggerated for effect?
4   Is each character's motivation sound? Which actions grow naturally out of the characters themselves, and where does the filmmaker seem to be manipulating them to fit his purposes?
5   What facets of the central character's personality are revealed by what he chooses or rejects?
6   Which minor characters function to bring out personality traits of the major characters, and what do they help reveal?
7   Pick out bits of dialogue, visual images, or scenes which you consider

especially effective in revealing character, and tell why they are effective.

8 Which characters function as stock characters and stereotypes, and how can the presence of each be justified in the film?

CONFLICT

In his essay "Why Do We Read Fiction?" Robert Penn Warren observes, "A story is not merely an image of life, but of life in motion . . . individual characters moving through their particular experiences to some end that we may accept as meaningful. And the experience that is characteristically presented in a story is that of facing a problem, a conflict. To put it bluntly: No conflict, no story." Conflict is the mainspring of every story, whether it be told on the printed page, on the stage, or on the screen. It is this element, then, that really captures our interest, that heightens the intensity of our experience, and that quickens our pulses and challenges our minds.

Although there may be several conflicts within a story, some kind of *major conflict* lies at its core or focal point that ultimately has the greatest importance to the story as a whole. This major conflict usually has some of the following characteristics, which may be helpful in identifying it.

To begin with, the major conflict is obviously of greater importance to the characters involved, and there is some worthwhile and perhaps lasting goal to be gained by the resolution of the conflict. Because it is highly significant to the characters, and because significant conflicts have important effects on people and events, the major conflict and its resolution almost always bring about some kind of important *change,* either in the people involved or in their overall situation.

The major conflict also has a reasonably high degree of complexity; it is not the sort of problem that can be quickly and easily resolved by some kind of obvious or simple solution. Thus its outcome remains in doubt throughout the greater part of the film. The complexity of the struggle is also influenced by the fact that the forces which constitute the major conflict are nearly equal in strength, a fact which adds greatly to the dramatic tension and power of the work.

In some films, the major conflict and its resolution may also contribute greatly to the viewer's experience, for it is this conflict, and its resolution (or sometimes its lack of resolution), that does the most to clarify or illuminate the nature of human experience.

TYPES OF MAJOR CONFLICTS

Various types of major conflicts exist. Some, for example, may be primarily physical in nature, such as a fistfight or a shoot-out on a western street. Others may be almost completely psychological, as is often the case in the films of Fellini or Bergman. In a large majority of films, however, the conflict has both physical and psychological implications, and it is often difficult to tell where one stops and the other begins. It is perhaps simpler and more meaningful to classify major conflicts under the broad headings of external and internal.

1. *External conflict.* In its simplest form, an external conflict may consist of a personal and individual struggle between the central character and another character. On this level the conflict is nothing more than a contest of human wills seeking opposing or similar goals, as might be illustrated by a prizefight, a duel, or even by two suitors seeking to win the affections of the same girl. Yet these basic and simple human conflicts have a tendency to be more complex than they first appear. Conflicts can seldom be isolated completely from other individuals, society as a whole, or the value systems of the individuals involved. Thus they often grow into representative struggles between groups of people, different segments of society or social institutions, or different value systems.

Another type of external conflict is one that pits the central character or characters against some nonhuman force or agency, such as fate, the gods, the forces of nature, or the social system. Here the forces the characters face, though they may be man-made, are essentially nonhuman and impersonal. They present an entirely different kind of problem or obstacle than do human opponents. A clear example of this type of conflict might be seen in the legendary John Henry's pile-driving race with the steam hammer, where a human being struggles to prove his worth against the dehumanizing forces of technology.

2. *Internal conflicts.* An internal conflict is one that centers on an internal, psychological conflict within the central character, so that the forces in opposition are simply different aspects of the same personality. For example, in Walter Mitty we have a conflict between what a man actually is (a small, timid, incompetent creature, henpecked viciously by an overbearing wife) and what he wants to be (a brave and competent hero). By escaping constantly into the world of his daydreams, Mitty reveals himself to be living in a permanent state of conflict between his heroic dreams and the drab reality of his existence. In all such internal

conflicts, we see a character caught in a squeeze between two sides of his or her own personality, torn between equally strong but conflicting desires, goals, or value systems. In some cases, this inner conflict is resolved, and the character grows or develops as a result, but in many cases, like that of Walter Mitty, there is no resolution.

SYMBOLIC OR ABSTRACT VALUES IN CONFLICTS

Although some conflicts in films are clearly self-contained and have no meaning beyond themselves, most conflicts tend to take on abstract or symbolic qualities so that the individuals or the forces involved represent something beyond themselves. It seems natural for the forces in opposition to align themselves with different generalized concepts or value systems, and even the most ordinary whodunit and typical western at least vaguely imply a conflict between law and order and lawlessness and chaos, or even simply between good and evil. Other abstract ideas that might be represented by a film's conflict are civilization versus barbarism, sensual values versus spiritual ones, change versus tradition, realism versus idealism, practical views versus aesthetic views, and the individual versus society. Thus almost any conflict can be stated in abstract or generalized terms. Because a comprehension of such abstract interpretations is often essential to determining and understanding a film's theme, the major conflict should be analyzed as carefully as possible on both the concrete and abstract planes.

QUESTIONS
ON CONFLICT

1 Identify the major conflict.
2 Is the conflict internal (man against himself), external, or a combination of both? Is it primarily a physical or psychological conflict?
3 Express the major conflict in general or abstract terms (for example, brains versus brawn, man against nature.)
4 How is the major conflict related to the theme?

SETTING

Simply stated, the setting is the time and place in which the story of a film takes place. Although it may often seem unobtrusive or be taken for granted, setting is one of the essential ingredients in any story form and thus makes an extremely important contribution to the film's theme or its total effect. Because of its complex interrelationships with other story elements, such as plot, character, theme, conflict, and symbolism, setting should be analyzed carefully in terms of its effect on the story being told. And because of its important function on a purely visual plane, it must also be considered as a powerful cinematic element in its own right.

In examining the setting as it relates to the story, it is necessary to consider four factors in terms of the effect each has on the story as a whole:

1. *Temporal factors.* The time period in which the story takes place.

2. *Geographical factors.* The physical location and its characteristics, including such things as the type of terrain, climate, population density, its visual and psychological impact, and any other physical factors of the locale which may have an effect on the story's characters and their actions.

3. *Prevailing social structures and economic factors.*

4. *Customs, moral attitudes, and codes of behavior.*

All of these factors have an important effect on the problems, conflicts, and character of human beings. Therefore they must be considered as integral parts of any story's plot or theme.

SETTING AS A MOLDER OR DETERMINER OF CHARACTER

The four aspects of setting listed above are especially important to understanding what might be called the naturalistic interpretation of the role of setting. This interpretation is based on the belief that man's character, his destiny, or his fate, are all determined for him by forces outside himself, that he may be nothing more than a product of his own heredity and environment, and that his cherished and precious freedom of choice is only an illusion. Thus, by considering the environment as a significant shaping force or even a dominant controlling one, this interpretation forces us to consider carefully how a character's environment has made him what he is—in other words, how his complete and total nature has been dictated by such factors as his time in history, the particular place on earth he inhabits, his place in the social and economic structure, and the customs, moral attitudes, and codes of behavior imposed upon him by his society. These environmental factors may be so pervasive that they serve as something much more important than a backdrop for the film's plot.

In some cases the environment may even function as an antagonist in the plot, as when the protagonist or central character struggles against the environmental forces exerted upon him, seeking to express some freedom of choice, or to escape from an oppressive trap. Thus the serious consideration of the cruel, indifferent, or at least powerful forces of the environment is often a key to understanding the character of modern man and his dilemma.

SETTING AS A REFLECTION OF CHARACTER

The environment in which a person lives may also provide the viewer with clues to understanding his or her character. This is especially true in regard to the effect man has on those aspects of his environment over which he has some control. Houses, for example, may serve as excellent indications of character. Their usefulness is illustrated by the following examples of exterior views as they might appear in a film's opening establishing shot.

Picture a small, neat, white, green-shuttered cottage with red roses around the doorstep and bright and cheerful curtains at the windows. It is surrounded by a newly whitewashed picket fence. Such a setting has been traditionally used in films to suggest the happy honeymoon couple, full of youth, vigor, and optimism for a bright future.

On the other extreme, consider the visual image evoked by Poe's description of the Usher house in his classic short story "The Fall of the House of Usher": bleak, gray walls, vacant eye-like windows, crumbling stones, rotten woodwork, and a barely perceptible zigzag crack in the masonry from roof to foundation. This opening picture, a reflection of the Usher family's decadent state, becomes even more significant as the story progresses, for Roderick Usher and the house in which he lives are so closely interwoven symbolically and metaphorically that they become one: The house's vacant eye-like windows portray the eyes of Roderick

Usher, and the zigzag crack in the masonry is equated with the crack in Usher's mind.

Thus, the filmgoer must be aware of any type of interaction between environment and character, whether setting is serving as a molder of character or merely as its reflection.

SETTING FOR VERISIMILITUDE

One of the most obvious and natural functions of the setting is to create a "semblance of reality" that gives the viewer a sense of a real time, a real place, and a feeling of being there. Because they recognize the great importance that an authentic setting plays in making a film believable, filmmakers may often search for months to find a proper setting, and then move crew, actors, and equipment thousands of miles in order to capture an appropriate backdrop for the story they are attempting to film.

To be thoroughly convincing, the setting chosen should be authentic in even the most minute detail, and even the slightest anachronism may be detrimental. Thus a filmmaker shooting a story set in the Civil War period must be careful that the skies do not show jet vapor trails or the landscapes do not include high tension power lines.

Some films are so effective in capturing the unique qualities of the time and place in which they are set that these factors become the most important elements of the film, being more powerful and memorable than the characters or the story line. *McCabe and Mrs. Miller, Ryan's Daughter,* and *The Last Picture Show* are good examples.

SETTING FOR SHEER VISUAL IMPACT

When it is permissible within the limits of a film's theme and purpose, filmmakers will use setting with a high degree of visual impact. For example, the plot and structure of such westerns as *Shane* or *True Grit* do not demand great scenery, but the directors of these films realized that the sheer beauty of the wide western landscape, with its snowcapped mountains and rainbow-colored rock formations, is usually effective for its own sake, so long as it does not violate the overall tone or atmosphere of the film. David Lean is especially successful in choosing settings with a powerful visual impact, as demonstrated in *Dr. Zhivago, Ryan's Daughter,* and *Lawrence of Arabia.*

SETTING TO CREATE EMOTIONAL ATMOSPHERE

In certain specialized films, setting is extremely important in creating the pervasive mood or emotional atmosphere which permeates the film. This is especially true in the horror film, and to some extent in the science fiction or fantasy film, where the unusually charged emotional atmosphere created and maintained by the setting becomes an important factor in achieving the willing suspension of disbelief on the part of the viewer. Setting may also create a mood of tension and suspense in keeping with the overall tone of the film, in addition to adding credibility to plot and character elements.

9. *The Psycho house—a setting for emotional atmosphere, characterization, and visual impact:* In contrast to the drab, ordinary, run-down Bates Motel in Alfred Hitchcock's *Psycho* is the Bates home, located on a hill behind the motel. Its strange, foreboding, haunted quality contributes both to the emotional atmosphere of the film and to the characterization of Norman Bates (Tony Perkins), not only as a reflection of his character but as a determining factor in his character as well. The starkness of the house, silhouetted against the sky, also contributes a strong visual impact to the film.

SETTING AS SYMBOL

The setting of a film story may also take on strong symbolic overtones when it is used to stand for or represent not just a location but some idea associated with the location. An example of such a symbolic environment may be seen in the garden setting for *Suddenly Last Summer.* * The garden becomes a symbol for the world view reflected by the other symbols: that men are carnivorous creatures living in what is essentially a savage jungle, where they devour each other in a constant struggle of fang and claw, obeying only the jungle law of the survival of the fittest. That this world view is reflected in the setting is illustrated by Tennessee Williams's own description of the set:

> The interior is blended with a fantastic garden which is more like a tropical jungle, or forest, in the prehistoric age of giant fern-forests when living creatures had flippers turning to limbs and scales to skin. The colors of this jungle-garden are violent, especially since it is steaming with heat after rain. There are massive tree-flowers that suggest organs of a body, torn out, still glistening with undried blood; there are harsh cries and sibilant hissings and thrashing sounds in the garden as if it were inhabited by beasts, serpents and birds, all of a savage nature. . . .

SETTING AS MICROCOSM

A specialized type of symbolic setting is the type known as a *microcosm,* meaning "the world in little," in which the human activity in a·small and limited setting is actually representative of human behavior or the human condition in the world as a whole. In such a setting special care is taken to isolate the characters from all external influences, so that the "little world" of the setting seems self-contained. The limited group of people, which contains representative human "types" from various walks of life or levels of society, might be isolated on a desert island, an airplane, a stagecoach, or in a western town. The implication of the microcosm often comes very close to being allegorical: The viewer should see strong similarities to what happens in the microcosm in the world at large, and the film's theme should have universal implications. Such films as *Lord of the Flies, Ship of Fools,* and *High Noon* can all be seen as microcosms; television's *Gilligan's Island,* however, lacks the universal implications of a microcosm, though it possesses many microcosmic qualities.

---

*Tennessee Williams, *Suddenly Last Summer.* Copyright © 1958 by Tennessee Williams. All Rights Reserved. Reprinted by permission of New Directions Publishing Corporation.

10. *Microcosm:* Characters isolated from external influences become a self-contained "little world," as does this group in Alfred Hitchcock's *Lifeboat.* (Copyright © 1944 Twentieth Century-Fox Film Company Ltd. All Rights Reserved)

QUESTIONS
ON SETTING

1 Which of the four environmental factors (temporal, geographical, social and economic levels, and customs, moral attitudes, and codes of behavior) play significant roles in the film? Could the same story take place in any environment?

2 Which environmental factors are most important, and what effect do these factors have on the plot or the characters?

3 Why did the director choose this particular location for filming this story?

4 How does the film's setting contribute to the overall emotional atmosphere?

5 What kind of important interrelationships exist between setting and the characters, or between setting and plot?

6 Is the setting symbolic in any way? Does it function as a microcosm?

THE SIGNIFICANCE OF TITLE

In most films, the full significance of the title can be determined only after seeing the film. In many cases, the title will have one meaning to a viewer before seeing the film, and a completely different, richer and deeper meaning afterwards. Titles are often ironic, expressing an idea exactly the opposite of the meaning intended, and many titles are allusions to biblical passages, mythology, or other literary sources. For example, the title *All the King's Men* is taken from "Humpty Dumpty," and serves to remind the reader of the whole nursery rhyme, which is actually a summary of the novel in a nutshell. *All the King's Men* concerns a southern dictator (king), who rises to a high position of power (sat on a wall), but is assassinated (had a great fall). As in the case of the egg, even "all the King's men" are unable to put him together again. On another level, the title literally tells us what the novel is about. Although Willie Stark, the politician, is the primary energy force in the novel, Jack Burden, his press secretary and right-hand man, is actually the focal character, and the novel is very much concerned with the lives of others who work for Stark in one capacity or another. Thus, the story is in a sense about "all the King's men."* On yet another plane, the title serves to link the character of Willie Stark to Huey Long, on whose career the novel is loosely based. Long's favorite nickname for himself was "The Kingfisher," from a character on the old Amos and Andy radio show, and Long once wrote a song around his campaign slogan, "Every man a king, but no one wears a crown."

Some titles may call our attention to a key scene in the film that becomes worthy of especially careful study when we realize that the title has been taken from it. Although the title seldom names the theme, it is usually an extremely important clue in determining it. Thus, thinking carefully about the possible meanings of the title after seeing any film is essential.

QUESTIONS
ON SIGNIFICANCE OF TITLE

1   Why is the title appropriate? What does it mean in terms of the whole film?
2   How many different levels of meaning can you find in the title? How does each level apply to the film as a whole?

*Since this title is more appropriate to the novel than the film, the discussion here focuses on the novel.

3 If the title is ironic, what opposite meanings or contrasts does it suggest?

4 If you recognize the title as being an allusion, why is the work or passage alluded to an appropriate one?

5 If the title calls your attention to a key scene, why is that scene important?

6 How is the title related to the theme?

IRONY

Irony, in the most general sense, is a literary, dramatic, and cinematic technique involving the juxtaposition or linking together of opposites. By emphasizing the sharp and startling contrasts, reversals, and paradoxes of human experience, irony is capable of adding an intellectual dimension and achieving both comic and tragic effects at the same time. To be clearly understood, irony must be broken down into its various types and explained in terms of the contexts in which it appears.

DRAMATIC IRONY

Dramatic irony derives its effect primarily through a contrast between ignorance and knowledge. When a character speaks or acts in ignorance of the true state of affairs but the audience possesses knowledge that he or she does not have, dramatic irony may be employed effectively to create two separate meanings to each line of dialogue: (1) The meaning of the line as it is understood by the unenlightened character (a literal or face-value meaning), and (2) the additional meaning the line may have to the enlightened audience (an ironic meaning, opposite to the literal meaning).

By knowing something which the character does not know, we gain pleasure from being "in" on the joke or secret. In *Oedipus Rex,* for example, Oedipus does not realize that he has already killed his father and married his mother when he refers to himself as "the child of Good Luck" and "the most fortunate of men." Since we are aware of the truth, however, we hear the line as a painful joke. On a less serious plane is an example from *Superman.* We know that Clark Kent is really Superman, but Lois Lane does not. Therefore, every time Lois accuses Clark of cowardice because he disappears whenever trouble starts, we have a pleasurable reaction because of our inside knowledge.

Dramatic irony may also function in a purely visual way, either for comic effect or to build suspense, when the camera shows us something which the character on the screen can't see. For example, a character trying to elude a pursuer in a comic chase may be crawling toward the same corner as his pursuer, but only *we* will see and anticipate the coming shock of sudden confrontation. Horror films employ similar scenes to both intensify and prolong suspense. Because of its great effectiveness in enriching both the emotional and intellectual impact of a story, dramatic irony has been a popular technique in literary and dramatic art since Homer employed it in *The Odyssey;* it remains popular and effective to this day, and some television situation comedies (such as *The Lucy Show*) are literally built around it.

IRONY OF SITUATION

Irony of situation is essentially an irony of plot. It involves a sudden reversal or backfiring of events, so that the end result of a character's actions is exactly the opposite of his or her intentions. Almost the entire plot structure of *Oedipus Rex* involves irony of situation: Every move that Oedipus and Jocasta make to avoid the prophesies actually helps to bring them about. This particular type of irony is most often associated with O. Henry. An excellent example is his story "The Ransom of Red Chief," where two hoodlums kidnap a child who is such a demon that they end up having to pay his parents to get them to take the boy back.

IRONY OF CHARACTER

Irony of character occurs when a character possesses strong opposites or contradictions within himself, or when his actions involve sharp reversals in expected patterns of behavior. Oedipus, for example, is probably the most ironic character ever created, for the opposites built into his character constitute an almost endless list: He is both the detective and the murderer he is seeking; he sees, yet he is blind (in direct contrast to his foil, the blind "seer" Tiresias); he is the great riddle-solver, but doesn't know his own identity; he is his mother's husband, and his children's brother; and in the end, when he finally "sees," he blinds himself. Superman, in his alter ego as mild-mannered reporter Clark Kent, is another example of an ironic character, an irony which is intensified by Lois Lane's thinking him not only mild-mannered, but cowardly.

Irony of character may also be present when a character violates our stereotyped view of him, as illustrated by this imaginary scene: Two soldiers, played by Woody Allen and John Wayne, are pinned down in a foxhole by an enemy machine gun. When mortar shells begin falling around the foxhole, the John Wayne character panics, buries his head under his arms and begins sobbing uncontrollably, while the Woody Allen character puts his bayonet between his teeth, grabs two grenades in each hand, and charges the machine-gun nest alone.

IRONY OF SETTING

Irony of setting occurs when an event takes place in a setting which is exactly the opposite of the expected, normal, or usual setting for such an event—for example, an orgy in a church, a birth in a graveyard, or a free-for-all in a Quaker meeting hall.

IRONY OF TONE

Because it communicates simultaneously on several different layers, film is especially suited for many types of irony, but irony of tone can be especially effective. In essence, irony of tone involves the juxtaposition of opposites in attitudes or feelings, as exemplified in literature by Erasmus's *The Praise of Folly,* in which the reader must read between the lines to discover that the work is actually a condemnation of Folly. Swift's classic essay, "A Modest Proposal," is another example. Here the author's proposal, put forth in rational, calm, and modest style, is actually an outrageous proposal—that the Irish people sell their year-old children to be eaten like suckling pigs by the wealthy English landlords. In film, such irony may be effectively provided through contrasting emotional attitudes communicated simultaneously by the sound track and the visual image. Consider, for example, the juxtaposition of an optimistic Pollyanna-type song such as "Everything Is Beautiful" with visual images of the mutilated victims of war atrocities or the inmates of a leper colony.

Many different kinds of irony are possible in film because of film's ability to communicate on more than one level at a time. In fact, the multilayered nature can reach a point of complexity where its effect is difficult to describe. This is the case, for example, in the final scene of *Dr. Strangelove,* which combines three separate contrasting elements: (1) the visual picture, composed of multiple shots of atomic mushroom clouds filmed in slow motion; (2) the sound track, which is Vera Lynn's voice, sticky and sweet, singing "We'll Meet Again Some Sunny Day"; and (3) the significance of the action, which is the end of all life as we know it.   The ironic effect is provided by the ingenious touch of the Vera Lynn song, which adds a sweet, haunting quality to the pictorial element, so that we become aware of the almost breathtaking beauty of the mushroom clouds. This ironic combination of beauty and horror creates an unbelievably powerful effect.   Such effects are rare in film, but the filmgoer must be constantly aware of the potential for ironic expression in the musical score, juxtaposition of sight and sound, and in transitions of almost any kind.

PHILOSOPHICAL IMPLICATIONS
—COSMIC IRONY

Although irony is basically a means of expression, the continuous use of ironic techniques might indicate that the director holds a certain philosophical attitude, constituting what might be called an ironic world view.   Because irony pictures every situation as possessing two equal sides, or truths, which end up cancelling each other out or at least working against each other, the overall effect of ironic expression is to show the ridiculous complexity and uncertainty of human experience. Life is seen as a continuous series of paradoxes and contradictions, characterized by ambiguities and discrepancies, and no truth is ever absolute.   Somehow, such irony reminds us that life is a game in which the players never win, and in which the players are aware of the impossibility of winning and the absurdity of the game, even while they continue to play.   On the positive side, however, irony's ability to make life seem both tragic and comic at the same moment keeps us from taking things too seriously or too literally.

Looked at on a cosmic scale, an ironic world view implies the existence of some kind of supreme being or creator. Whether he be called God, Fate, or Destiny makes little difference. The implication is that the supreme being manipulates events in such a way as to deliberately frustrate and mock mankind, and entertains himself with what is essentially a perpetual cruel joke on man.

And although irony usually has a humorous effect, the humor of cosmic irony bites a little deeper. It may bring a laugh, but not of the usual kind. It will not be a belly laugh, but a sudden outward gasp of air, almost a cough, that catches in the throat between the heart and mind. And we laugh perhaps because it hurts too much to cry.

QUESTIONS
ON IRONY

1   What examples of irony can be found in the film?

2   Is irony employed to such a significant degree that the whole film takes on an ironic tone? Is an ironic world view implied?

3   Do any particular examples of irony achieve comic and tragic effects at the same time?

4   Where in the film is suspense or humor achieved through dramatic irony?

5   How do the ironies contribute to the theme?

chapter 4

VISUAL ELEMENTS

THE IMPORTANCE OF THE VISUAL IMAGE

Because the visual element is the film's basic means of communication, it is the most important factor in distinguishing between the fictional film and the so-called "literary" forms of fiction and drama. The very term *literature* refers to the written word, and it is defined as including "all writings in verse or prose, especially those of an imaginative or critical nature." Even in colloquial use, literature means printed matter of any kind. Therefore, although it shares many of the techniques common to the literary form, film in itself is not "literary." Its emphasis is on the moving visual image, which generally communicates what is most significant or interesting.

In the strictest sense of the word, drama is not literature either. Aside from the fact that a play is written before the actors can memorize their lines, for the spectator drama has no reality as "literature." But a play's significance and its techniques can be understood through an intelligent and imaginative reading of the script, since drama relies primarily on the medium of words. Thus, although drama is intended to be performed rather than read, it can be studied from the printed page as literature. For the most part, however, the same is not true of film. So much is missing from the average screenplay, since the moving visual elements themselves are not there, that we almost need to have seen a film to make the reading of a screenplay worthwhile. Usually, only about half the running time of a film is taken up with dialogue, the rest of the story being communicated by strictly nonverbal means, through images, music, and natural sounds. Thus Artaud's statement that "our theatre must speak a concrete physical language intended for the senses rather than the mind, independent of the dictatorship of speech" has a greater application to the film than it does to the average play.

The "concrete physical language of the senses" in film is its flowing and sparkling stream of images, its compelling pace and natural rhythms, and its pictorial style, all of which are nonverbal means of communication. It follows naturally that the aesthetic quality and dramatic power of the image itself are extremely important to the overall quality of a film. Although the nature and quality of the story, and the editing, musical score, sound effects, dialogue, and acting can do much to enhance the power of a film, even these important elements cannot save a film where the visual image is shoddy or mediocre.

As important as the quality of the visual image may be, however, it must not be considered so important that the purpose of the film as an artistic, unified whole is ignored. A film's photographic effects should not be created for their own sake as independent, beautiful, or powerful images. They must, in the final analysis, be justified psychologically and dramatically as well as aesthetically in terms of the film as a whole, as important means to an end, not as ends in themselves. The creation of beautiful images for the sake of beautiful images violates a film's aesthetic unity and therefore may actually work against the film.

The same principle applies to overly clever or self-conscious technique. Technique must not become an end in itself; any special technique must have some kind of underlying purpose related to the purpose of the film as a whole. Thus, every time a director or cinematographer employs an unusual camera angle or uses a new photographic technique, he or she should do so for the purpose of communicating (either sensually or intellectually) in the most effective way possible, not simply because he wants to show off or try out a new trick he has learned. A sense of naturalness, a feeling that it had to be done that way, is more praiseworthy than a showy, neat, and clever camera trick.

Although the visual element is the motion picture's primary and most powerful level of communication, the cinematography can often completely dominate a film, taking it over by sheer force. When this occurs, the artistic structure of the film is weakened, its dramatic power fades, and watching the film becomes simply an orgy of the eyeballs.

THE CINEMATIC FILM

In the simplest terms, a cinematic film is a film that takes advantage of all the special properties and qualities that make the film medium unique. The first and most essential of these is the quality of continuous motion. The cinematic film is truly a "motion picture"—a flowing, ever-changing stream of images and sounds sparkling with a freshness and vitality all its own, a fluid blend of image, sound, and motion possessed by a restless compulsion to be vibrantly alive, to avoid the quiet, the still, and the static.

The second quality of the cinematic film evolves naturally out of the first. The continuous and simultaneous interplay of image, sound, and motion on the screen sets up varied, complex, and subtle rhythms. Clear, crisp visual and aural rhythms are created by the physical movements or sound of objects on the screen, by the pace of the dialogue, by the natural rhythms of human speech, by the frequency of editorial cuts, by the varying duration of shots between cuts, and by the musical score. The pace of the plot itself also has distinct rhythms. All of these serve to intensify the film's unique sense of pulsing life.

The cinematic film also makes maximum use of the great flexibility and freedom of the medium: its freedom from the spoken word, and its ability to communicate directly, physically, and concretely through images and sounds; its freedom to spirit us about on a kind of magic carpet ride, to show us significant action from any vantage point, and to vary our point of view at will; its capability to manipulate concepts of time and space, expanding or compressing them at will; and its freedom to make quick and clear transitions in time and space.

Although film is essentially a two-dimensional medium, the cinematic film overcomes this limitation by creating an illusion of depth. It creates the impression that the screen is not a flat surface, but a window through which we observe a three-dimensional world.

All of these qualities are present in the truly cinematic film; if they are not present in the subject matter, it is up to the director or the cinematographer to build them in. Otherwise, he or she will not be able to communicate the film's dramatic scenes in all the fullness of the medium's potential.

THE ELEMENTS OF CINEMATIC COMPOSITION

Because the cinematic film is a unique medium, the problems in composition it poses for the director and cinematographer are also unique. First, they must be aware every single shot (a single uninterrupted running of the camera) is only a segment, a brief element in a continuous flow of visual images, and that its character must really be created with reference to its contribution to that total visual flow. The most difficult aspect of creating a shot is that the image itself will move, will in fact be in a constant state of flux. They cannot, therefore, make every single frame in a shot conform to the aesthetic principles of composition used in still photography. Therefore, the cinematographer's choices in each shot are dictated by the nature of film medium, and every shot must be designed with the goals of cinematic composition in mind. These goals are (1) directing our attention to the object of greatest interest, (2) keeping the image in constant motion, and (3) creating an illusion of depth.

DIRECTING OUR ATTENTION TO THE OBJECT OF GREATEST INTEREST

Above all, the shot must be so composed that it draws our attention into the scene and toward the object of greatest dramatic significance and interest. Only when this is achieved can the film's dramatic ideas be effectively conveyed. Several methods of directing our attention are open to the filmmaker.

1. *Size and closeness of object.* Normally, the eye is directed toward larger, closer objects rather than smaller, more distant objects. Therefore, the image of an actor's face appearing in the foreground (closer to the camera, and therefore larger) would be more likely to serve as a focal point for our attention than a face in the background, appearing smaller and more distant. In a normal situation then, the size and relative distance of the object are important factors in determining the greatest area of interest. (*See photo 11.*)

11

12

2. *Sharpness of focus.* On the other hand, the eye is also drawn almost automatically to that which it can see best. Therefore, if an actor in the foreground, even in an image taking up half the screen, is in soft focus (slightly blurred) and a face in the background, though smaller and more distant, is in sharp, clear focus, our eyes are attracted to the background figure, since that is the one which can be seen best. An object in sharp focus is capable of diverting our attention away from a closer, larger object in soft focus. (*See photo 12 above.*)

3. *Movement.* The eye is also drawn to an object in motion, and a moving object is capable of diverting our attention away from a static object. Thus, a single moving object in an otherwise static scene will draw our attention to itself. On the other hand, if movement and flow have been established in a general way as part of the background, it may become generalized background movement and be ignored in favor of static, but more dramatically important objects.

4. *Extreme close-up.* Perhaps the most dictatorial control the cinematographer has on our attention is achieved by use of the tight or extreme close-up. By bringing us so close to the object of interest (an actor's face, for example) that we cannot look elsewhere, the face so fills the screen that there is nothing else to see.

5. *Arrangement of people and/or objects.* The director also focuses our attention by his or her arrangement of people (and/or objects) in relation to each other. Since each arrangement is determined largely by the nature of the dramatic moment being enacted and the complex in-

terrelationships involved, the director must depend more on his or her
intuitive sense of rightness than any visual formulas for his positioning.

6. *Foreground framing.* The director may even go so far as to
frame the object of greatest significance with objects or people in the
near foreground. In *The Graduate,* for example, Mike Nichols frames
the bride, groom, and clergyman in the front of the church between the
head and raised arm of Dustin Hoffman as he bangs against the glass
window in the balcony. (*See photo 13 above.*)

7. *Lighting and color.* Special uses of light and color also help to
draw the eye to the object of greatest significance. High contrast areas
of light and dark create natural centers of focal interest, as do bright
colors present in a subdued or drab background.

In composing each shot, the filmmaker continually employs these
techniques, either separately or in conjunction with each other, to keep
our attention on the object of greatest dramatic significance and interest, thereby gently guiding our thoughts and emotions where he or she
wants them to go. Such guiding of the viewer's attention is the most
fundamental concern in cinematic composition, but not the only one.

14.   In this picture, the director uses lighting to make the star, Barbra Streisand, stand out from the others seated around the table. *Funny Girl.* (Culver Pictures)

15.   Dark or shaded areas can also become the focus of attention, as in this picture.   The shadows over the face of the caped figure create a sense of mystery and draw our attention toward him. *Jack the Ripper.*

16.   Lighting and focus both work together in this picture. Although
Brandon De Wilde is closer to the camera, differences in sharpness of
focus and lighting direct our attention to Paul Newman. *Hud.*

KEEPING THE IMAGE IN CONSTANT MOTION

Since the most essential property of the cinematic film is its quality of
continuous motion—its flowing, ever-changing stream of images—the director or cameraman must also build this quality of movement and flux
into every single shot.   To create the flowing stream of constantly
changing images, the cinematographer employs several techniques.

1. *Fixed-frame movement.* The fixed camera frame approximates
the effect of looking through a window.   The camera remains in the
same position, pointing at exactly the same spot, as we might look at
something with a frozen stare.   Movement and variety are then worked
into the shot through movement of the subject.   The movement introduced can be rapid, frantic movement of real physical "action," or
a calmer, subtle movement of actors speaking and gesturing normally,
or even just changing facial expressions.   Several different types of
movement are possible within the set frame established by the fixed

camera. This movement can be *lateral* (from the left to right of the frame), movement in *depth* (toward or away from the camera) or *diagonal movement* (a combination of lateral and in-depth movement). Since purely lateral movement creates the impression of movement on a flat two-dimensional surface (which the screen is) it calls attention to the two dimensional limitations of film. To avoid this and to create the illusion of a three-dimensional "reality," the cinematographer will use more in-depth movement (toward or away from the camera), or diagonal movement, than purely lateral movement.

2. *Panning and tilting movement.* Usually when the camera remains in a fixed physical location, however, it takes an added capability of capturing movement by approximating the head and eye movements of a human spectator. Thus, most of the movements of the camera are made to incorporate what is essentially a human field of view. With the body stationary, if we turn the head and neck from left to right and add a corresponding sideward glance of the eyes within the head, our field of view takes in an arc of something better than 180 degrees. If we simply move the head and eyes up and down in a vertical plane, our eyes span an arc of at least 90 degrees. Most movements of the camera—either horizontal (called *panning*) or vertical (called *tilting*)—fall within these natural human limitations. A closer look at these camera movements may make these limitations clear.

Panning. The most common use of the camera pan is to follow the lateral movement of the subject. In a western film, for example, the panning camera may function as follows:

> The wagon train has been attacked by Indians and moved into a defensive circle. The camera for this shot is set up in a fixed location looking over the shoulder of one of the settlers as he attempts to pick off circling Indians with a rifle. The movement of the circling Indians is from right to left. The camera (and the rifle) move to the right and pick up subject (target Indian). Then, both camera and rifle swing laterally to left as subject Indian rides by; when he reaches a center position, the rifle fires and we watch him fall off the horse and roll to the left of center as he bites the dust. Then the camera either pans back to the right to pick up a new target, or an editorial cut starts the next shot with the camera picking up a new target Indian (far right) and the pattern is repeated.

Another type of pan is used to change from one subject to another. This might be illustrated by a sterotyped duel or shoot-out scene in the middle of the street of a western town. The camera occupies a fixed position on the side of the street, halfway between the dueling gunfighters.   After establishing the tense, poised image of the gunman on the right, the camera leaves him and slowly pans left until it focuses on the other man, also tense and poised.

Since normally the eye jumps instantaneously from one object of interest to another, a pan must have a dramatic purpose or it will seem unnatural and conspicuous.   There are several possible reasons for using a pan.   In the gunfight scene, for instance, the slow fluid movement of the camera from one man to the other may help expand time, intensifying the suspense and the viewer's anticipation of the first draw.   Also, it may reflect the tension in the environment as a whole by registering the fear and suspense on the faces of the onlookers across the street, who become secondary subjects, as we see their facial expressions in passing or catch glimpses of them frantically diving for cover.   Finally, the pan may simply help to clearly establish the relative distance between the two men.   Although this type of pan can be effective, it must be used with restraint, particularly if there is a great deal of dead screen (screen with no objects of real interest) between the two subjects.

On rare occasions, a complete 360–degree pan may be dramatically effective, especially when the situation calls for a sweeping panoramic view of the entire landscape.   Such might be the case in a western where the fort is completely surrounded by Indians at the rim of the surrounding hills.   A full 360–degree pan would clearly indicate the impossibility of escape and the helplessness of the situation.   Also, a character waking up in unfamiliar and unexpected surroundings, such as a jail cell, might call for a 360–degree pan shot, since a person coming to in this situation would turn his or her body enough to completely survey the surroundings.

Tilting. The human quality of the camera is also illustrated by the camera movement known as *tilting*, which approximates the vertical movement of our head and eyes.   The following hypothetical sequence illustrates how the tilt is used.   The camera occupies a fixed position at the end of an airport runway, focused on a jet airliner taxiing toward the camera.   As the plane lifts off, the camera tilts upward to follow its flight until it passes directly overhead.   At this point, although it would be technically possible to create an axis to follow the plane in one continuous shot, the shot stops, and a new shot begins with the camera facing in the opposite direction.   The second shot picks up the plane still overhead and tilts downward to follow its flight away from the camera, approximating visually the way we would normally observe the incident if we were standing in the camera's position.   As the plane turns right and begins to climb for altitude, the camera follows it in a diagonal movement which combines the elements of both panning and tilting. Thus, though the camera is in a fixed location, it is flexible enough to follow the movement of the plane as represented by the following arrows: take-off to directly overhead ↑, cross-over to turn ↓, turn and climb ↗. In most panning and tilting shots, then, the movement of the camera approximates our normal *human* way of looking at things. Many shots in every film will be photographed in this manner, showing the story unfold as a person watching the scene might view it.

In the techniques described so far the camera has, in every case, remained in a fixed position. But the fixed-location camera, even though it can pan and tilt, does not provide enough variety and fluid movement to create a cinematic film. The cinematic film depends, to a large degree, on a camera freed of its human limitations, a living camera with superhuman creative abilities. Thus the truly cinematic camera, in many cases, functions as a superhuman eye.

3. The zoom lens. One way in which the camera can be freed from its purely human limitations is through the use of the zoom lens. Consisting of a complex series of lenses which keep the image constantly in focus, the zoom lens gives the camera the apparent power to vary its distance from any subject. It creates the effect of smooth and fluid movement toward or away from the subject without actually requiring any movement of the camera. Zoom lenses also have the ability to magnify the subject ten or more times, so that in effect we seem to move ten times closer than the actual distance from camera to subject.

For example, if the camera occupies a fixed position in a baseball stadium above and behind home plate, and is aimed out toward the center fielder, standing some four hundred feet away, the figure will be extremely small, the same size that he would appear to the naked eye. By zooming in on the center fielder, however, the lens elements move in proper relationship to each other so that the fielder stays in focus constantly, while we in effect glide fluidly and smoothly towards him until his standing figure almost fills the screen, as if we were seeing him from a distance of forty feet or closer. Though the camera is actually simply magnifying the image, it gives the effect of moving toward the subject. By reversing the process, the effect is that of moving away from the subject. Thus, through the use of the zoom lens, the camera not only allows us to see things more clearly than might be otherwise possible, but also gives us a sense of fluid motion in and out of the frame itself, increasing our sensual interest and involvement. Furthermore, all of the above variations are possible without changing the physical location of the camera.

4. *The mobile camera.* When the camera itself becomes mobile, the possibilities of movement increase tremendously. By freeing the camera from a fixed position, the cinematographer can create a constantly shifting viewpoint, giving us a moving image of a static subject. For example, by mounting the camera on a boom or crane device which itself is mounted on a truck or dolly, the cinematographer can move it fluidly and smoothly alongside, above, in front of, behind, or even under a running horse. With the mobile camera, almost any demand for movement created by a story situation may be met.

5. *Editing and movement.* The editing process also contributes greatly to the cinematic film's ever-changing stream of images. The editing, in fact, often creates the most vibrant visual rhythms in a film, as the editorial cuts and transitions propel us instantaneously from a long shot to a close-up, from one camera angle to another, and from one setting to another.

Thus the cinematographer employs a wide variety of techniques that he or she uses either separately or in various combinations to keep the visual image in constant motion:

a. The movement of the subject within the fixed frame.

b. Apparent movement of the viewer in or out of the frame (zoom lens).

c. Vertical or horizontal movement of the camera (tilting and panning).

d. Completely free movement of the camera and constantly changing viewpoint (mobile camera and editorial cuts).

Subject movement will also most likely be present in varying degrees in all of the above.

6. *"Dead" screen and "live" screen.* The director must also be concerned with keeping the image alive in another sense. In almost every shot, he or she will attempt to communicate a significant amount of information in each frame. To achieve this, each shot must be composed so that the visual frame is loaded with cinematic information and large blank areas of "dead" screen are avoided (unless, as in some cases, there is a dramatic purpose for dead screen. (*See photos 17–19 on pp. 80–81.*)

17. *The "packed screen":* The most obvious way to keep the screen alive is to pack almost every square inch of its surface with visual information, as in the case with this scene from *For Whom the Bell Tolls.* The visual frame contains nine highly expressive faces, all conveying different kinds of information in what is obviously a very tense moment.

18. *Background in motion:* Sometimes the background helps to keep the screen alive by providing motion. This type of background motion is a very subordinate type, which does not take our attention away from the primary subject. Such is the case in the picture here, where the slowly turning mill machinery keeps the otherwise static shot "alive" and provides a three-dimensional background which is both visually interesting and aesthetically pleasing. *Mill of the Stone Women.*

19. *Strong visual impact in a static background:* If the three characters
in the scene shown here were filmed against a solid white wall, our
eyes would be so overwhelmed with dead screen that we would lose
interest in the action taking place. With the stairs there, the background still dominates the frame, but fills what could be dead screen
with a strong and pleasing visual tension and contributes a powerful
three-dimensional effect as well. *The Wicked City.*

CREATING THE ILLUSION OF DEPTH

Cinematic composition must also concern itself with creating an illusion
of depth or three-dimensionality on what is essentially a two-dimensional screen. To achieve this, the cinematographer employs several different techniques.

1. *Movement of subject.* When using the fixed frame, the director
sets up the movements of the subject to create an illusion of depth—by
filming the subject moving toward or away from the camera, either head
on or at a diagonal. Purely lateral movement, perpendicular to the direction in which the camera is aimed, creates a purely two-dimensional
effect, and is kept within reasonable limits to avoid a "flat" image.

2. *Movement of camera.* The mobile camera, mounted on a truck
or dolly, may also create the illusion of depth by moving toward or
away from a relatively static subject. As it passes by or goes around ob-

jects on its way, we become aware of the extent of the depth of the image. Since the camera "eye" is actually moving, the objects on both sides of its path are constantly changing their position in relation to each other. They change according to the changing angles from which they are viewed by the moving camera.

3. *Apparent camera movement (zoom lens).* The zoom lens, which by magnifying the image gives us the sensation of moving closer to or further away from the camera, is also employed to create the illusion of depth, as well as that of movement. Because camera position does not change during zooming, there is no real change in perspective, meaning that the objects to the sides do not change their position in relation to each other as they do in true camera movement. For this reason, the zoom lens does not create the illusion of depth quite as effectively as the mobile camera.

4. *Change of focal planes.* Most cameras, including still cameras, are designed to focus on objects at different distances from the lens. Be-

20.   *Change of focal planes:* Foreground face in focus.
21.   *Change of focal planes:* Second face in focus.

22.   *Change of focal planes:* Third and fourth faces in focus.

cause the eye is ordinarily drawn to the object it can see best, that which is in sharpest focus, the cinematographer may sometimes create a kind of three-dimensionality through simply adjusting the camera lens to focus on objects in different depth planes. If, for example, the visual frame includes four faces, all at varying distances from the camera, the cinematographer may create the illusion of depth by first focusing on the nearest face, and then, while the shot is being taken, moving the plane in focus back to the second face, and then on to the third and fourth faces, thus, in effect, carrying us into a three-dimensional visual frame.

5. *Deep-depth focus or deep focus.* In direct contrast to the change in focal planes is the use of special lenses that allow the camera to focus simultaneously on objects anywhere from two feet to several hundred feet away with equal clarity. This depth of focus approximates most clearly the ability of the human eye to see a deep range of objects in clear focus.

6. *Three-dimensional arrangement of people and objects.* Perhaps most important in creating a three-dimensional image is the placement of the people and objects to be filmed in a three-dimensional arrangement, so that the cinematographer has a truly three-dimensional scene to photograph. Without this arrangement, there is no real purpose for the various effects and techniques described above.

23. *Deep focus:* All four faces in focus.

7. *Foreground framing.* A three-dimensional effect is also achieved when the shot is set up so that the subject is framed by an object or objects in the near foreground. With the object forming the frame in clear focus, a strong sense of three-dimensionality is achieved. When the foreground frame is thrown out of focus or seen in very soft focus, the three-dimensional effect is weakened somewhat but not lost, and the entire mood or atmosphere of the scene takes on a different character.

24.   Foreground framing, with frame in focus.

25.   Foreground framing, with frame out of focus.

8. *Special lighting effects.* By carefully controlling the angle, direction, intensity, and quality of the lighting employed the director may further add to the illusion of depth, as is illustrated by the difference in the two pictures below.

26.   A flat lighting effect creates essentially a two-dimensional picture.

27.   By changing the angle, direction, intensity, and quality of the lighting, the same grouping takes on a three-dimensional quality.

On some occasions, the director may even control the source and direction of the lighting for the purpose of expanding the limits of the visual frame. By positioning the light source out of camera range to either side or behind the camera, he or she can cause the shadows of objects outside the visual frame to fall inside the frame, thus suggesting the presence of those objects within the frame. When these shadows come from objects behind the camera, they can add greatly to the three-dimensionality of the shot.

The effects described in this section, of course, have nothing to do with specialized three-dimensional projection systems such as 3-D and Cinerama, but most of these techniques provide a fairly effective illusion of depth.

28. *Three-dimensional shadows:* In this scene from Charles Laughton's *The Night of the Hunter,* the orphaned boy, John, stands guard over his sleeping sister Pearl and looks out the window at the villainous "preacher" Harry Powers (Robert Mitchum). Mitchum sits on a bench in the yard, a gas lamp behind him casting his shadow through the window and onto the room's back wall. If the scene were evenly lit, with no shadows, it would have only two important planes of depth: Pearl, sleeping in the foreground, and John, standing in the background. Although the shadows add only one *real* plane of depth (the wall), our mind's eye is aware of objects or shapes in five different planes: Mitchum seated in the yard; the window frame; Pearl sleeping on the bed; John; and the back wall. Even more important to the scene's dramatic power is the very real sense of Mitchum's presence in the room as his shadow looms over and threatens the shadow of John on the wall.

QUESTIONS
ON CINEMATIC QUALITIES

1 To what degree is the film "cinematic"? Cite specific examples from the film to prove that the director succeeds or fails in (a) keeping the image constantly alive and in motion, (b) setting up clear, crisp visual and aural rhythms, (c) creating the illusion of depth, and (d) using the other flexibilities and special properties of the medium.

2 Does the cinematography strive for clear, powerful, and effective communication of the dramatic scenes in a natural way, or does it self-consciously show off the skills and techniques of the cinematographer?

3 Which methods does the director use to draw our attention to the object of greatest interest or significance?

4 Does the director succeed in keeping the screen alive by avoiding large areas of dead screen?

5 What are the primary or most memorable techniques used to create the illusion of a three-dimensional image?

EDITING

Also extremely important is the contribution made by the editor, whose function is to assemble the complete film, as if it were a gigantic and complex jigsaw puzzle, from its various component parts and sound tracks. The great Russian director V. I. Pudovkin, believing that editing is "the foundation of the film art," observed that "the expression that the film is 'shot' is entirely false, and should disappear from the language. The film is not *shot*, but built, built up from separate strips of celluloid that are its raw material . . . ." Alfred Hitchcock reinforces this viewpoint: "The screen ought to speak its own language, freshly coined, and it can't do that unless it treats an acted scene as a piece of raw material which must be broken up, taken to bits, before it can be woven into an expressive visual pattern."

Because of the tremendous importance of the editing process, the editor's role can be almost equal to that of the director. Regardless of the quality of the raw material provided by the director, it may be worthless unless careful judgment is exercised in deciding when each segment will appear and how long it will remain on the screen. And this "assembly of parts" must be done with artistic sensitivity, perception, and aesthetic judgment as well as a true involvement in the subject and a clear understanding of the director's intentions. Therefore, for the most part, the director and the editor must be considered almost equal partners in the construction of a film. In some cases, the editor may be the true structuring genius, the master builder or architect of the film. In fact, if the editor has the clearest vision of the film's unity, he or she may even make up for a lack of a clear vision on the part of the director.

THE RESPONSIBILITIES OF THE EDITOR

To fully appreciate the important role which editing plays in film, we must look carefully at the basic responsibility of the editor: to assemble a complete film which is a unified whole, in which each separate shot or sound contributes significantly to the development of the film's theme and total effect. To fully understand the editor's function, it is also important that we comprehend the nature of the jigsaw puzzle. The basic unit with which the editor works is the *shot*, a strip of film produced by a single continuous run of the camera. By joining or splicing a series of shots together so that they communicate a unified action taking place at one time and place, the editor assembles what is known as a *scene.* He or she then links a series of scenes together to form what is called a *sequence,* which constitutes a significant part of the film's dramatic structure much in the way that an act functions in a play. In assembling these parts effectively, the editor must successfully perform each of the following functions.

1. *Selectivity.* Although we can not possibly see or appreciate the editor's selectivity at work because we do not see the film which ends up on the cutting room floor, the most basic editing function is selecting the best shots from several takes—choosing those segments which provide the most powerful, effective, or significant visual and sound effects—and eliminating inferior, irrelevant, or insignificant material.

2. *Coherence and Continuity.* The film editor is also responsible for putting the pieces together into a coherent whole. To achieve this, he or she must guide our thoughts, associations, and emotional responses effectively from one image to another, or from one sound to another, so that the interrelationships between separate images and sounds are

absolutely clear and so that smooth transitions between scenes and sequences can be achieved. To achieve this goal, the editor must carefully consider the aesthetic, dramatic, and psychological effect of the juxtaposition of image to image, sound to sound, or image to sound, and carefully place each piece of film and sound track together accordingly.

3. *Transitions.* In the past, filmmakers made widespread use of several special optical effects to create smooth and clear bridges between the film's more important divisions, such as transitions between two sequences which take place at a different time or place. Such formula transitions include the following:

a. *Wipe.* A new image is separated from the previous one by a clear horizontal, vertical, or diagonal line that moves across the screen to "push" the old image off the screen.

b. *Flip-frame.* The entire visual frame appears to flip over to reveal a new scene, creating a visual effect very similar to turning a page.

c. *Dissolve.* The gradual merging of the end of one shot into the beginning of the next, produced by super-imposing a fade-out onto a fade-in of equal length, or imposing of one scene over another.

d. *Fade-out–Fade-in.* The last image of the first sequence fades momentarily to black and the first image of the next sequence is gradually illuminated.

Each of these transitional devices has its own effect on the pace of the film and the nature of the transition taking place. Generally speaking, dissolves are relatively slow transitions, and are used to make the viewer aware of major scene changes or elapsed time. Flips and wipes are faster, and are employed when the logic of time-lapse or place change is more apparent to the viewer. For the most part, modern filmmakers have given up the extensive use of these traditional formulas, and often rely on a simple cut from one sequence to another without any clear transitional signal. The sound track has also taken on some of the transitional functions formerly handled through purely optical means.

Regardless of the nature of transitions, whether they be long and obvious (as in a slow dissolve), or short and quick, (as in a simple instantaneous cut), the editor is the person who must put them together so they have continuity, creating a logical flow from one sequence to another or merely from one image to another.

When possible, the editor will often smooth out the visual flow from one shot, scene, or sequence to another through the use of the *form cut.* This type of cut is accomplished by framing objects or images of similar contour or shape in two successive shots, so that the first image smoothly flows into a similar second image at the point of the cut or dissolve. In Kubrick's *2001*, for example, a piece of bone flung into the air dissolves into a similarly shaped orbiting bomb in the following sequence; in Eisenstein's *Potemkin,* the handle of a sword or dagger in one sequence becomes the similarly shaped large cross around a priest's neck in the following shot. Similar to the *form cut* are cuts that create a smooth visual flow by using a color or a textural link between the two shots at the point where they are joined. For example, a glowing sun at the end of one shot may dissolve into a campfire at the beginning of the next. There are, of course, limitations to this type of transition, and when they are overdone they lose the sense of naturalness which makes them effective.

Within an individual sequence consisting of shots built up within the same physical setting and time frame, the editor must also assemble shots carefully for coherence within the sequence itself. For example, a great many sequences require an opening "establishing" shot to provide the viewer with a broad picture of the new setting before cutting to a detailed look at the character in action, so that we get a feel of the environment in which the scene occurs. The editor must decide if such an establishing shot is necessary for a clear understanding of the relationship of the closer and more detailed shots which follow it. The accompanying series of illustrations demonstrates the coherent structuring of shots in an editorial sequence:

29.   *Editing sequence #1:* To help us get our bearings, the editor begins with a complete view of the setting and the actors' relative positions in that setting.

30. *Editing sequence #2:* In the second shot, he takes us closer to the actors, giving the impression that the viewer himself is moving in closer to the actors so that he can see them better and hear what they are saying.

31. *Editing sequence #3:* The third shot takes us even closer, and the actors are now clearly recognizable. The volume of the sound track would also increase with each cut, taking us closer to the actors, and, by this shot, their voices in dialogue should be clearly audible.

32. *Editing sequence #4:* The fourth shot takes us into the dialogue itself, and with the camera looking over the man's shoulder, we see
the woman as she talks.

33. *Editing sequence #5:* In order to provide motion and variation in
what is essentially a very static scene, the editor now cuts to a shot
taken over the woman's shoulder, focusing on the man either reacting to her dialogue or responding verbally.

34. *Editing sequence #6:* In the sixth shot, the editor cuts to a close-up of the woman's face, giving the viewer an even more intimate viewpoint, where expressions revealed in mouth and eyes become easy to read. This kind of shot would be especially effective in a reaction shot, the camera focusing on her face while the man's voice is heard on the sound track.

35. *Editing sequence #7:* Once again, for variety and motion, the editor cuts to a close-up of the man's face, either because he is speaking or because he is reacting to what she says.

36.   *Editing sequence #8:* In order to prepare for the shot which follows (#9), the editor now cuts to the eighth shot, which backs off to a position over the man's shoulder again, and reestablishes the fact that she is preparing to pour a cup of coffee from the pot in her hand.

37.   *Editing sequence #9:* In shot #9, the editor cuts to the shot he prepared for with shot #8—a close-up of the coffee pot as the coffee is about to be poured. The entire sequence here is obviously not extremely exciting or dramatic pictorially. If there is any excitement to it, it is in the dialogue. But the editor has done his share by keeping the visual image alive and by establishing a logical continuity between the different shots by the order in which he joined them together.

4. *Rhythms, Tempo, and Time Control.* A great many factors work together and separately to create rhythms in the motion picture: the physical objects moving on the screen, the real or apparent movement of the camera, the musical score, the pace of the dialogue and the natural rhythms of human speech, as well as the pace of the plot itself: All of these factors set up unique rhythms that blend into the whole. But all these rhythms are natural, imposed on the film by the nature of its raw material. Perhaps the most dominant tempo of the film, its most compelling rhythm, is created by the frequency of editorial cuts and the varying duration of shots between cuts. The rhythms set up by these cuts are unique because, although they divide the film into a number of separate parts, they do so without interrupting the continuity and the fluid form of the medium. Thus editorial cuts set up clear rhythmic patterns which do not break the flowing stream of images and sound, but impart to it an externally controllable and unique rhythmic quality.

The rhythms established by editorial cutting are such a natural part of the film medium that we are often unaware of cuts within a given scene, yet we respond unconsciously to the tempo they create. One reason we may remain unconscious of such rhythms is that they often duplicate the manner in which we actually look at things in real life, by glancing quickly from one point of attention to another. Our emotional state is often reflected in how quickly our attention shifts from one point to another. Thus slow-cutting simulates the impressions of a tranquil observer, whereas quick-cutting creates the visual impressions of a highly excited observer. Our response to this built-in sense of visual "glancing" rhythms allows the editor to manipulate us, exciting or calming us almost at will.

Although the editor will generally alternate one tempo with another throughout the film as a whole, the cutting speed of each scene should be determined by the content of that scene, so that its rhythm corresponds to such things as the pace of the action, the speed of the dialogue, and the overall emotional tone.

5. *Expansion of time.* Skillful editing can also greatly expand our normal concepts of time, through intercutting a normal action sequence with a series of related details. Take, for example, the brief action of a man walking up a flight of stairs. By simply alternating between a full shot of the man walking up the stairs with detailed shots of his feet taking two or three steps up, the scene and sense of time of the action are expanded. If close-ups of his face and his hand gripping the rail are added, our feeling of the time which the action takes is even further expanded.

6. *Compression of time.* By using fragmented flash-cutting, short "machine-gun bursts" of images sandwiched together, the editor can compress an hour's action into a few seconds. For example, by choosing representative actions out of the daily routine of a factory worker, the editor can suggest an entire eight-hour shift in a minute or two. By overlapping each shot so that the first part of each shot is superimposed over the last part of the one preceding it, a more fluid compression of time is achieved.

Another editorial technique used to compress time is the *jump-cut,* which involves simply cutting out a strip of insignificant or unnecessary action from a continuous shot. For example, a continuous shot in a western follows the movement of the sheriff as he walks slowly across the street, from left to right, from the sheriff's office to the saloon. If the continuous following of his movement slows the pace too much, the editor may cut out the section of film which shows him crossing the street, jump-cutting from the point at which he steps into the street to his arrival at the sidewalk on the other side. Thus the jump-cut speeds up the action by removing an unnecessary section of it, a section which is still easily understood when the scene, the moving subject, and the direction of movement are the same.

One of the most effective techniques of editorial cutting is *parallel cutting,* which is the quick alternating back and forth between two actions taking place at separate locations. Parallel cutting creates the impression that the two actions are occurring simultaneously, and can be a powerful suspense-building device. A common use of parallel cutting is seen in the traditional western "Cavalry to the rescue" sequence, where the settlers in their circled wagons are under Indian attack, and the U.S. Cavalry is on the way. By cutting back and forth between the besieged settlers and the hard-riding Cavalry troops, the editor makes the eventual confrontation seem closer and closer, and effectively builds suspense between the two related scenes.

An entirely different kind of time compression is achieved by cutting to brief flashbacks or memory images, a technique which merges past and present into the same stream and often helps us to understand a character better.

7. *Creative juxtaposition.* Often the editor is called upon to communicate creatively within the film. Through unique juxtapositions of images and sounds, editors can often express an attitude or tone toward the material itself (as might be the case with an ironic transition) or they may be called upon to create, through a brief series of visual and aural images, what is commonly known as a *montage.* The term mon-

tage refers to an especially effective series of images and sounds which, without any clear logical or sequential pattern, form a kind of visual poem in miniature. The unity of a montage is derived from complex internal relationships, which we understand instantly and intuitively.

In creating a montage, the editor uses a brief series of visual and aural images as a impressionistic shorthand to create a certain mood, atmosphere, sense of time or place transition, or a physical or emotional impact. As defined by the great Russian director and film theorist Sergei Eisenstein, a montage is assembled from separate images which provide a "partial representation which in their combination and juxtaposition, shall evoke in the consciousness and feelings of the spectator. . . that same initial general image which originally hovered before the creative artist."

An example of the montage concept can be borrowed from poetic imagery: in Shakespeare's Sonnet 73, he compares his time of life (old age) to three separate images: (1) winter: "when yellow leaves, or none, or few, do hang upon those boughs which shake against the cold. . ." (2) twilight: "as after sunset fadeth in the west"; and (3) a dying fire.

> That time of year thou mayst in me behold
> When yellow leaves, or none, or few, do hang
> Upon those boughs which shake against the cold,
> Bare ruined choirs where late the sweet birds sang.
> In me thou see'st the twilight of such day
> As after sunset fadeth in the west,
> Which by and by black night doth take away,
> Death's second self, that seals up all in rest.
> In me thou see'st the glowing of such fire,
> That on the ashes of his youth doth lie
> As the deathbed whereon it must expire,
> Consumed with that which it was nourished by.
> This thou perceivest, which makes thy love more strong,
> To love that well which thou must leave ere long.

A cinematic montage might be created around these images, all of which have universal associations with death and old age, with visual and aural images edited as follows:

Shot 1: Close-up of wrinkled faces of aged couple, both in rocking chairs. Their eyes are dim, and stare into the distance as their chairs rock slowly back and forth. Sound—creaking of rocking chairs, loud ticking of old grandfather clock.

Shot 2:   Slow dissolve to close-up of withered leaves, barely clinging to bare branches, light snow falling, thin layer of snow upon the black, bare branches.   Sound of a low moaning wind.   Grandfather clock continues to tick.

Shot 3:   Slow dissolve to seacoast scene, the sun's edge just barely visible on the horizon of the water; then it slips away, leaving a red glow and gradually darkening sky, light visibly fading.   Soft, rhythmic sound of waves washing up on shore—grandfather clock continues ticking in the background.

Shot 4:   Slow dissolve from red glow in sky to a glowing bed of coals in a fireplace . . . a few feeble fingers of flame flicker, then sputter out and die.   The glowing coals, as if fanned by a slight breeze, glow brighter, then grow dimmer and dimmer.   Continued sound link of ticking grandfather clock.

Shot 5:   Return to same scene as shot #1, close-up of wrinkled faces of aged couple, rocking in their rocking chairs.   Sound of creaking chairs and the continuous tick of grandfather clock; gradual fade to black.

QUESTIONS
ON EDITING

1   How does the editing effectively guide your thoughts, associations, and emotional responses from one image to another so that smooth continuity and coherence are achieved?

2   Is the editing smooth, natural, and unobtrusive, or is it tricky and self-conscious?   How much does the editor communicate through creative juxtapositions, such as ironic transitions, montages, and the like, and how effective is this communication?

3   What is the overall effect of editorial intercutting and transitions on the pace of the film as a whole?

4   How does the cutting speed (which determines the average duration of each shot) correspond to the emotional tone of the scene involved?

5   What segments of the film seem overlong or boring?   Which parts of these segments could be cut without altering the total effect?   Where are additional shots necessary to make the film completely coherent?

CINEMATIC POINT OF VIEW

The term *point of view* must be considered in a rather specialized sense as it pertains to cinematography, for it differs significantly from the term as used in a literary sense. One primary difference is that there is no need for consistency in the cinematic viewpoint. Not only would true consistency of viewpoint be boring in a film, but it would also be too restricted for effective communication. What is important about point of view in film is that it maintain continuity and coherence. Thus, though we may be freely spirited about from one vantage point to another, we need only to respond intuitively to the different ways in which we see things, so that the changing vantage points make sense to us visually, but not necessarily logically.

In considering cinematic point of view, the filmmaker is primarily concerned with the following matters:

1. From what position and through what kind of "eyes" does the camera see the action?

2. What effect does the position of the camera and its particular ways of seeing the action have on our view of the action?

3. How is our response affected by changes in the point of view?

There are essentially four different points of view employed in the motion picture:

1. the objective point of view

2. the subjective point of view (camera as participant in the action)

3. the subjective-interpretive point of view (director's viewpoint)

4. the indirect-subjective point of view.

Generally, all four viewpoints can be used in every film to varying degrees, depending on the demands of the dramatic situation and the creative vision and the style of the director.

THE OBJECTIVE POINT OF VIEW

The objective point of view is illustrated by John Ford's "philosophy of camera." He considered the camera to be a window, with the audience outside the window viewing the people and events taking place within.

We are asked to watch the actions as if they were taking place at a distance, and we are not asked to participate in it. Thus, the objective point of view employs as static a camera as possible to produce the "window effect," and concentrates on the actors and the action without drawing attention to the camera. The objective camera suggests a relatively great emotional distance between camera and subject, as though the camera were simply recording, as straightforwardly as possible, the characters and actions of the story taking place. For the most part, the director uses the most natural, normal, straightforward types of camera positioning and camera angles to capture the action unfolding before the camera. Thus the objective camera does not comment on or interpret the action, but merely records it, letting it unfold before our eyes. We see the action from the viewpoint of an objective, impersonal observer. If the camera moves, it does so unobtrusively, calling as little attention to itself as possible.

There are distinct advantages to using the objective point of view. Continuity and clear communication of the dramatic scene in most films demand that some use be made of the objective point of view. But overuse of the objective view is dangerous, because its objective and impersonal qualities may cause us to lose interest. The objective viewpoint forces us to pinpoint subtle but perhaps very significant visual details by ourselves.

THE CAMERA AS PARTICIPANT IN THE ACTION—
SUBJECTIVE POINT OF VIEW

The subjective point of view provides us with the visual viewpoint and emotional intensity felt by a character participating in the action. Alfred Hitchcock, whose philosophy of camera is opposite to that of Ford, specializes in creating a strong sense of direct involvement on the part of the audience, and employs elaborate camera movement to create visual sequences that bring us into the suspense, literally forcing us to become the characters and experience their emotions.

An important tool in creating this kind of subjective involvement, according to Hitchcock, is skillful editing and a viewpoint close to the action, as the following passage from his essay "Direction" indicates:

> So you gradually build up the psychological situation, piece by piece, using the camera to emphasize first one detail, then another. The point is to draw the audience right inside the situation—instead of leaving them to watch it from outside, from a distance. And you can do this only by breaking the action up into details and cutting from one piece to the other,

so that each detail is forced in turn on the attention of the audience and reveals its psychological meaning. If you played the whole scene straight through, and simply made a photographic record of it with the camera always in one position, you would lose your power over the audience. They would watch the scene without becoming really involved in it, and you would have no means of concentrating their attention on those particular visual details which make them feel what the characters are feeling.*

With the more subjective point of view, our experience becomes more intense and more immediate as we become involved intimately in the action. Generally, this viewpoint is characterized by the moving camera, which forces us to see exactly what the character is seeing and in a sense to become the character.

It is almost impossible to sustain a purely subjective point of view throughout a film, as was attempted in *Lady in the Lake.* The story of this film was told entirely through the eyes of its detective hero, and the only time the hero's face was seen was in a reflection in a mirror. His hands and arms occasionally appeared, below eye level, as they might normally be seen from the hero's viewpoint. The difficulty of sustaining such a viewpoint over an entire film, however, should be obvious, for clarity of communication and continuity usually demand that the film switch back and forth between the objective and subjective points of view.

This change in point of view from objective to subjective is often accomplished in the following manner. First, an objective shot which shows a character looking at something off screen (called a *look of outward regard*) cues us to wonder what he is looking at. Then the following shot, called an *eye-line shot,* shows us subjectively what the character is seeing. Because the simple logical relationship between the two shots provides a smooth and natural movement from an objective to a subjective point of view, this pattern is typical in film. The alternation of objective and subjective viewpoints, as well as the tight link between sight and sound, is further illustrated by the following scene:

> 1. Establishing shot: objective camera view from street corner, focusing on a workman using an air hammer in center of street (apparent distance 50 to 75 feet). Sound: loud chatter of air hammer mingled with other street noises.
> 2. Cut to subjective view: close-ups of air hammer, and violently shaking lower arms and hands of workman, from workman's point of view. Sound of hammer almost deafening—no other sounds heard.

*From "Direction" by Alfred Hitchcock, in *Footnotes to the Film* edited by Charles Davy; reprinted by permission of Peter Davies Ltd., publishers.

3.   Cut back to objective camera: heavy truck turns corner beyond workman, bears down on him at top speed. Sound: loud chatter of air hammer, other street noises, rising sound of approaching truck.

4.   Cut to subjective view: close-up of air hammer and workman's hands as seen from his viewpoint . . . Sound: First only deafening sounds of air hammer, then a rising squeal of brakes mixed with hammer noise.

5.   Quick cut to a new subjective view: front of truck closing quickly on camera from ten feet away. Sound: Squeal of brakes louder, hammer stops, woman's voice screaming, cut short by sickening thud . . . darkness and momentary silence.

6.   Cut back to objective viewpoint (from street corner): unconscious figure of workman in front of stopped truck, curious crowd gathering into circle. Sound: mixed jumble of panicked voices, street noises, ambulance siren in distance.

In this way the constant alternation between the objective viewpoint and the subjective view provides both a clear understanding of the dramatic flow of events and also a strong sense of audience involvement.

DIRECTOR'S INTERPRETIVE POINT OF VIEW

In other types of shots, the filmmaker chooses not only what to show us, but also how we will see it. By photographing the scene from special angles or with special lenses, or in slow or fast motion, and so on, he or she imposes upon the visual image a certain tone, emotional attitude, or style. We are thus forced to react emotionally in a certain way to what we see, thereby experiencing the director's point of view. The director is always manipulating our viewpoint in subtle ways, but with the director's interpretive point of view we are *consciously* aware that he wants us to see the action in some *unusual way*.

INDIRECT-SUBJECTIVE POINT OF VIEW

The indirect-subjective point of view does not really provide a participant's point of view, but it does bring us close to the action so that we feel intimately involved and our visual experience becomes more intense. Consider, for example, a close-up shot that conveys the emotional reaction of a character. We recognize that we are not the character, yet we are drawn into the feeling that is being conveyed in a subjective way. A close-up of a face contorted in pain makes us feel that pain more vividly than an objective shot from a greater distance. Another example is the kind of shot that was common in the old western. With the stagecoach under attack by outlaws, the director inserts close-up shots of pounding hoofs to capture the furious rhythm and pulsing excitement of the chase, bringing us close to the action and increasing the intensity of our experience. This point of view is called indirect-subjective, because it gives us the feeling and immediacy of participating in the action without showing the action through a participant's eyes.

There are examples of all four points of view in the following typical western sequence showing a stagecoach being attacked by bandits:

1. *Objective point of view.* Stagecoach and horses as seen from the side (from a distance of 50 to 75 feet) being pursued by bandits. Shot here could either be from a panning camera in fixed position or from a mobile camera tracking alongside or parallel to the path of the stagecoach.

2. *Subjective point of view of a participant.* Camera shot from the stage driver's point of view, looking out over horses' backs, with arms and hands holding and slapping reins seen below eye level.

3. *Indirect-subjective point of view.* Close-up of stage driver's face from side, as he turns his head to look back over his shoulder (a look of outward regard). His face registers fear, determination.

4. *Subjective point of view of a participant.* Camera shot of bandits in hot pursuit of stagecoach, from the point of view of driver looking back over top of stage.

5. *Indirect subjective point of view.* Close-up of face of driver, now turned frontward again, registering strain, jaw set in determination, sweat streaming down face, screaming at horses.

6. *Director's interpretive point of view.* Slow-motion close-up of horses' heads in profile, their eyes wild with strain, mouths in agony straining at their bits, flecks of foamy sweat shaking from their necks. (By filming this shot in slow motion, the director in effect comments on the action, telling us how he wants us to see it. The slow-motion photography at this point conveys the horses' exhaustion, intensifies the tremendous effort they are putting out, and gives us a sense of the futility of the stage's chances for escape.)

TECHNIQUES FOR SPECIALIZED VISUAL EFFECTS

THE HAND-HELD CAMERA

Related to the concept of cinematic point of view is the specialized dramatic effect achieved through use of the hand-held camera. Here the jerky, uneven movement of the camera heightens the sense of reality gained from the subjective viewpoint of a participant in motion. If the viewpoint is not intended to be a subjective (participant) view, the same technique can give the sequence the feel of a documentary or newsreel. The hand-held camera, jerkiness and all, is especially effective in filming violent action scenes, where the random, chaotic camera movement fits in with the spirit of the action, as in a riot scene, or in close-ups of fight scenes.

ROLE OF CAMERA ANGLES

Cinematographers, of course, do more with the camera than simply position it for one of the four basic viewpoints. The angle from which they photograph a certain event or object is also an important factor in cinematic composition. Sometimes they may employ different camera angles simply for the sake of variety or to create a sense of visual balance between one shot and another. But camera angles are also extremely effective at communicating special kinds of dramatic information or emotional attitudes. Since the objective point of view stresses or employs a normal, straightforward view of the action, unusual camera angles are employed primarily for other points of view, such as the subjective viewpoint of a participant in the action, or for the subjective interpretive viewpoint of the director.

One type of objective camera angle is particularly worthy of mention: When an extremely high camera angle is combined with a slow fluid camera movement, as though the camera were slowly floating over the scene, the impression is given that a remote, external, detached spectator is carefully examining the dramatic situation below in an objective, almost scientific manner.

1. *Subjective Point of View—Participant.* When the camera is placed below eye level, creating a *low-angle shot,* the size and importance of the subject are exaggerated. If a child is the principal figure in a film, low angle shots of adults may be very much in evidence, as the

38.   *Extremely high camera angle:* When the mobile camera seems to
      float slowly high above the action, we become emotionally very re-
      mote and detached, as though our objectivity (like our viewpoint) is
      almost godlike. *Appointment with a Shadow.*

director attempts to show us the scene from a child's perspective. For
example, in *Night of the Hunter* two children are attempting to escape
from the clutches of Robert Mitchum, a Satanic itinerant preacher who
has already murdered their mother. As the children attempt to launch
a boat from the bank, Mitchum's figure is seen from a low angle as he
crashes through the brush lining the bank and plunges into the water.
The terror of the narrow escape is intensified by the low camera angle,
which clearly communicates the helplessness of the children and their
view of the monstrous Mitchum. A different effect is achieved in *Lord
of the Flies,* where Ralph, pursued to the point of exhaustion by the
savage boys on the beach, falls headlong in the sand at the feet of a Brit-
ish Naval officer. The low-angle shot of the officer, exaggerating his
size and solidity, conveys a sense of dominance, strength, and protec-
tiveness to Ralph. Thus, low camera angles effectively convey in an ex-

aggerated way the participants' emotional perception of the adults. The opposite effect is generally achieved by placing the camera above eye level (creating a high-angle shot), where the viewpoint seems to dwarf the subject and diminish its importance. Consider, for example, the subjective camera angle (high-angle shot) which might show Gulliver's view of the Lilliputians. The accompanying picture sequence illustrates the different effects achieved by changing the camera angles.

39.   Eye-level (or normal) angle.   41.   High camera angle.

40.   Low camera angle.   42.   Extremely low angle.

2. *Director's interpretive viewpoint.* The director may also employ certain camera angles to suggest the feeling he or she wants to convey about a character at a given moment. In *Touch of Evil,* for example, Orson Welles employs a high camera angle to look down on Janet Leigh as she enters a prison cell, a shot which emphasizes her despair, her state of mind, and her helplessness. By making us see the character as he sees her, the director interprets the emotional value or atmosphere of the scene for us.

In addition to the use of varying camera angles, directors have a great many other techniques at their command to aid in the creation of special dramatic effects. Although those discussed below are by no means the only techniques available, this list gives some idea of the tools at the filmmaker's disposal.

SPECIAL COLORED OR LIGHT-DIFFUSING FILTERS

A variety of filters are used to create a wide range of specialized effects. Directors may use special filters to darken the blue of the sky, thereby sharpening by contrast the whiteness of the clouds, or they may add a light-colored tone to the whole scene by filming it through a colored filter. A love scene, for example, in *A Man and a Woman* was filmed with a red filter, which imparted a romantic warmth to the whole sequence. On rare occasions, a special filter may be used to add a certain quality to a whole film. An example is Zeferelli's film version of *Taming of the Shrew,* where a subtle light-diffusing filter was used to soften the focus slightly and subdue the colors in a way that gave the whole film the quality of a Rembrandt painting. This technique, called the *Rembrandt effect,* was designed to give the film a mellow, aged quality, intensifying the sense that the action was taking place in another time period. A similar effect was employed in *McCabe and Mrs. Miller* and *Summer of '42,* but in the latter the quality suggested was not of an historical era but of the hazy images of the narrator's memory.

THE USE OF SPECIAL LENSES

Special lenses are often employed to provide subjective distortions of normal reality. Wide-angle and telephoto lenses, for example, distort the depth perspective of an image in opposite ways. A wide-angle lens exaggerates the perspective, so that the distance between an object in

43.   The wide-angle lens exaggerates the distance between the subjects, making them seem further apart than they actually are.

44.   The telephoto lens compresses or shortens the apparent distance between the two subjects, making them seem closer to each other than they actually are.

45.   *Fish-eye lens:* The nervous strain and tension created by men working and living in close quarters for long periods of time is expressed
as a visual claustrophobic scream through the distortions of a fish-
eye lens. *Dark Star.*

the foreground and one in the background seems much greater than it
actually is. With the telephoto lens, depth is compressed, so that the
distance between foreground and background objects seems less than it
actually is. The two photographs on page 108 demonstrate the effects
of the telephoto and wide-angle lenses. (The actors are seated in exactly
the same position in both pictures.) The effect of this distortion becomes more apparent when background to foreground movement is introduced. In *The Graduate,* for example, the hero was filmed running
toward the camera in a frantic race to interrupt the wedding ceremony,
and a telephoto distortion made him appear to gain very little headway
in spite of his effort, thus emphasizing his frustration and his desperation. Had a wide-angle lens been used in the same way, his speed would
have been greatly exaggerated. A special type of extreme wide-angle
lens, called a *fish-eye,* which bends both horizontal and vertical planes
and distorts depth relationships, is often used to create unusual subjective states such as dreams, fantasies, or drunk scenes.

VARIATIONS IN FILMING SPEED

If the action on the screen is to seem normal and realistic, the film must
move through the camera at the same rate at which it is projected, which
is generally twenty-four frames per second. If the scene is filmed at

greater than normal speed, however, and projected at normal speed, the action will be slowed. This is called *slow motion,* and is used effectively for a variety of purposes. For example, it may be used to call our attention to the poetic nature or beauty of motion itself. Or it may be used to stretch out a moment in time, to portray a character's subjective state of mind.

If a scene is filmed at less than normal speed and projected at normal speed, the result is called *fast* or *speeded motion.* Fast motion, which resembles the frantic, herky-jerky movements of the old silent comedies, is usually employed for comic effects or to compress the time of an event. An extreme form of fast motion is called *time-lapse photography,* and has the effect of greatly compressing time. In time-lapse filming, one frame is exposed at regular intervals, which may be as long as thirty minutes apart. This technique may be employed to compress something which normally takes hours or weeks into a few seconds, such as the blossoming of a flower or the construction of a house.

46.   *Freeze frame:*   In the freeze frame, some kind of normally continuous motion (such as the swinging pictured here) is first established, and then the action is suddenly frozen. Some part of the image usually appears blurred when the image is frozen, giving the desired effect of suddenly arrested motion. The freeze frame also has a rough, grainy-textured look.

THE FREEZE FRAME

Another effective device is the *freeze frame,* where motion stops completely and the image on the screen remains still, as though the projector had suddenly stopped or the living image on the screen had suddenly been frozen still. Once we have become accustomed to movement on the screen, the sudden use of a freeze frame is almost stunning in its abruptness, and it forces us to become much more attentive to the still image, because it is so shockingly still in comparison to what we have been seeing. The freeze frame has a number of applications, but its most common use is to mark the end of a powerful dramatic sequence and serve as a kind of transition to the next sequence, or to serve as the ending of the entire film.

QUESTIONS
ON CINEMATIC VIEWPOINT AND VISUAL EFFECTS

1   Although the director will probably employ all four cinematic viewpoints in making the film, one point of view may predominate to such a degree that it leaves the impression of a single point of view. With this in mind, answer the following questions:
   a.   In terms of your reaction to the film as a whole, do you feel that you were primarily an objective, impersonal observer of the action, or did you have the sense of being a participant in the action? What specific scenes can you remember that used the objective point of view? In what scenes did you feel like a participant in the action? How were you made to feel like a participant?
   b.   In what scenes were you aware that the director was employing visual techniques to comment on or interpret the action, forcing you to see the action in a special way? What were the techniques used to achieve this, and how effective were they?
2   Although a thorough analysis of each visual element is impossible, make a mental note of those pictorial effects that struck you as especially effective, ineffective, or unique, and consider them in light of the following questions:
   a.   What was the director's aim in creating these images, and what camera tools or techniques were employed in the filming of them?

b. What made these memorable visual images effective, ineffective, or unique?

c. Justify each of these impressive visual effects aesthetically in terms of its relationship to the whole film.

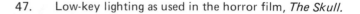

LIGHTING

Lighting is as important as the camera positioning and other special techniques. By controlling the intensity, direction, and degree of diffusion (character) of the light, the director is able to create the impression of spatial depth, delineate and mold the contours and planes of the subject, convey emotional mood and atmosphere, and create special dramatic effects.

Thus, the way a given scene is lighted is an important factor in determining its dramatic effectiveness. Variation in lighting is used in extremely subtle ways to create moods and impart to the scene a suitable dramatic atmosphere for the action which is to take place. Because lighting throughout a film should correspond to the mood of each scene,

47.   Low-key lighting as used in the horror film, *The Skull.*

48.   Low-key lighting.

49.   High-key lighting.

close observation of the nature of the lighting employed is helpful in
determining the mood or tone of the film as a whole. Two terms are
employed to designate different general intensities of lighting: *Low-key*
refers to lighting where most of the set is in shadow and just a few highlights define the subject. Since this type of lighting is effective in

heightening suspense or creating a somber mood, it is used in the mystery or horror film. *High-key* lighting, on the other hand, has more light areas than shadows, and the subjects are seen in middle grays and highlights, with far less contrast. High-key lighting is suitable for comic and light moods, such as would prevail in a musical. Generally speaking, high-contrast scenes, with a wide range of difference between light and dark areas, create more powerful and dramatic images than scenes that are evenly lighted.

The direction of the light also plays an important role in creating an effective visual image. Flat overhead lighting, for example, creates an entirely different effect from strong side lighting from floor level. Back lighting and front lighting also create strikingly different effects, as shown in the illustrations below.

50.   Overhead lighting.   51.   Strong side lighting.

52.   Back lighting.   53.   Front lighting.

54   55

Character of light: Harsh or hard lighting creates stark contrasts between light and shadow areas, emphasizing or strengthening the lines,
contours, and features of the face (left). Soft or diffused lighting has
the opposite effect. Strong shadow lines are erased and the face is defined by subtle differences in shades of gray, thus softening the features (right).

Whether light is artificial or natural (as in exterior scenes) the director has the means to control what is commonly referred to as the *character* of the light. The character of light can generally be classified as
one of three types: (1) direct, harsh, or hard, (2) medium and balanced,
or (3) soft and diffused.

The three factors of light—intensity, direction, and character—all
play a significant role in the dramatic effectiveness of the visual image.

QUESTIONS
ON LIGHTING

1   How would you characterize the lighting of the film as a whole: (a)
    direct, harsh, and hard, (b) medium and balanced, or (c) soft and
    diffused? Does high-key or low-key lighting predominate?
2   How does the lighting contribute to the overall emotional attitude
    or tone of the film?
3   In what individual scenes is the lighting especially effective, and
    what makes it effective?

OTHER IMPORTANT FACTORS

COLOR VERSUS BLACK AND WHITE

Although there is a continuing theoretical argument about the relative merits of color versus black and white film, on a practical level there is very clearly no longer a real struggle. Because a vast television audience awaits almost any decent film, the great majority of films today are made in color to better their chances for eventual sale to this medium. The apparently insatiable desire of the TV audience to see absolutely everything in color has drastically reduced the number of black and white films being produced.

The fact that black and white is simply a more powerful and effective medium for some films has been almost entirely overlooked. The director's decision to use black and white or color for a given film should be determined by the overall spirit or mood of the film. A clear demonstration of the correct use of color and black and white can be seen in comparing Sir Laurence Olivier's productions of *Henry V* and *Hamlet. Henry V,* a heroic or epic drama, much of which is set outdoors with battlefield action and much pagentry, colorful costuming, pomp and ceremony, was ideally suited for color, and was so produced by Olivier. The mood of the entire film is positive; it emphasizes the glorious heroic character of King Henry V, who emerges victorious. *Hamlet,* on the other hand, which Olivier chose to make in black and white, is a tragedy, a somber, serious play of the mind. Most of the settings are interior ones, and some are at night. The brooding, serious, intellectual quality of the hero himself has a starkness to it, a pensive gloom which could not have been captured nearly so well in color as it was in the black and white production.

The overall effect of black and white can be somewhat paradoxical, for somehow it often seems true to life, more "realistic," in spite of the fact that we see the world around us in color. For example, it is difficult to imagine that *Dr. Strangelove* in color would be quite as "real" as it was in black and white. And one wonders if *Catch 22* might not have been much more powerful in black and white for the same reason. Perhaps a sense of stark reality is provided by the black and white treatment of a basically unreal or exaggerated treatment. It is impossible also to avoid warm images in the color film, and such warmth works against the cold, bitterly ironic tone which underlies *Catch 22.*

The essentially opposite effects of color and black and white might also be explained in terms of another pair of films, *Shane* and *Hud,* both of which have western settings. Color is perfectly suited for *Shane,* a romantic western in the epic tradition set in a magnificently huge and beautiful landscape with snowcapped mountains always present in the background. *Hud,* on the other hand, is a contemporary character study of a heel, set in a drab, barren, and sterile landscape. The film emphasizes the harsh realities and glorifies nothing; this story could find adequate expression only in black and white.

Generally, films that seem to demand treatment in color are those with a romantic, idealized, or light, playful, or humorous quality, such as musicals, fantasies, historical pageants, and comedies. Also, those with exceptionally beautiful settings might be better filmed in color. The more naturalistic, serious, somber stories stressing the harsh realities of life and set in drab, dull, or sordid settings cry out for black and white. There are those, of course, that fall into a middle ground and can be treated equally well either way.

Some films have made effective use of mixtures of black and white *and* color, such as *The Wizard of Oz,* which employed black and white for the frame (reality) and changed to color for the dream sequence in *Oz,* or *A Man and a Woman,* which used a large variety of different film types and effects.

SIZE AND SHAPE OF THE PROJECTED IMAGE

Similar to the choice of black and white or color for a film is the choice among different sizes and shapes of the final projected image. Essentially, there are two basic shapes for the projected image: the *standard screen,* the width of which is 1.33 times its height, and *wide screen,* (commonly known by a variety of trade names, such as Cinemascope, Panavision, and Vistavision), the width of which varies from 1.85 to 2.85 times its height. The different dimensions and shapes of these screens cause different types of compositional problems, but generally speaking, the wide screen lends itself naturally to a panoramic view of a vast landscape or large numbers of people, as well as rapid motion such as might be characteristic in westerns, war dramas, historical pageants, or fast-paced action-adventure dramas. The standard screen is more suited for an intimate love story set in a small apartment, requiring the frequent use of tight close-ups and with very little movement of subjects in space. A wide screen can actually distort an image and detract from the visual effectiveness if it is confined to a physical set too narrow for its field of view.

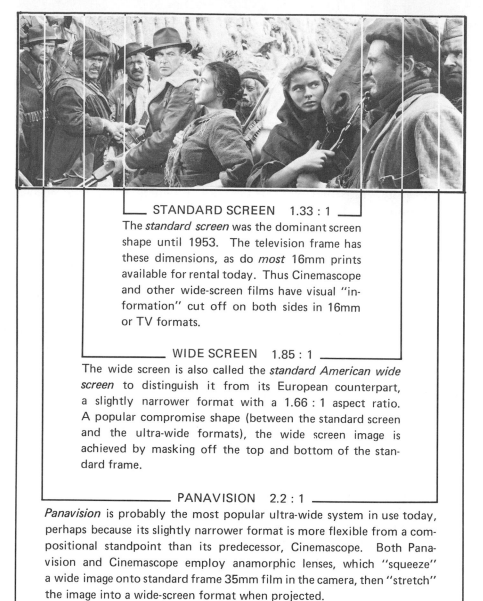

STANDARD SCREEN   1.33 : 1

The *standard screen* was the dominant screen shape until 1953. The television frame has these dimensions, as do *most* 16mm prints available for rental today. Thus Cinemascope and other wide-screen films have visual "information" cut off on both sides in 16mm or TV formats.

WIDE SCREEN   1.85 : 1

The wide screen is also called the *standard American wide screen* to distinguish it from its European counterpart, a slightly narrower format with a 1.66 : 1 aspect ratio. A popular compromise shape (between the standard screen and the ultra-wide formats), the wide screen image is achieved by masking off the top and bottom of the standard frame.

PANAVISION   2.2 : 1

Panavision is probably the most popular ultra-wide system in use today, perhaps because its slightly narrower format is more flexible from a compositional standpoint than its predecessor, Cinemascope. Both Panavision and Cinemascope employ anamorphic lenses, which "squeeze" a wide image onto standard frame 35mm film in the camera, then "stretch" the image into a wide-screen format when projected.

CINEMASCOPE   2.55 : 1

Cinemascope actually can be said to have two aspect ratios. In the fifties its dimensions were 2.55 : 1; it has since been narrowed slightly (to 2.35 : 1) to accommodate an optical sound track. When theaters began installing special screens for Cinemascope in the fifties, many of these screens were curved slightly to enhance the three-dimensional effect. Although popular with the public, the system had many critics, among them director George Stevens who claimed "the wide screen is better suited to a boa constrictor than a man." The lines drawn on the above photo from *For Whom the Bell Tolls* show the amount of side information lost when any of the wide screen films are reduced to the 16 mm or TV format.

57. Standard screen   1.33 : 1

58. Wide screen   1.85 : 1

59. Panavision   2.2 : 1

60. Cinemascope   2.55 : 1

SMOOTH- VERSUS ROUGH-GRAIN FILM

The type of film stock used may also have an important effect on the nature of the visual image. Some film stock is capable of reproducing an image which is extremely smooth or "slick." Such film also registers a wide range of subtle differences between light and dark, enabling the director to create fine tones, artistic shadows, and contrasts. Such images often have a more powerful visual effect than reality, due to their clarity and artistic perfection.

Another type of film stock, rough- or high-grain, produces an opposite effect: a rough, grainy-textured image with harsh contrasts between blacks and whites, and almost no subtle differences in contrast. Because newspaper pictures and newsreels also have this coarse, rough-grained effect, this type of film has become associated with a kind of documentary "here and now" kind of reality, as though the "reality" had to be captured quickly, with little concern for clarity and artistic perfection. The same film may employ both types of stock for different effects.

61.   Smooth-grain film stock: *Sons and Lovers.* (Copyright © Twentieth Century-Fox Film Company Ltd. All Rights Reserved)

62.   Rough-grain film stock: *Mothra.*

For example, a romantic love scene would probably be done in slow or smooth-grain film, whereas a riot or a furious battle scene may be done with rough-grain film.

QUESTIONS
ON COLOR, BLACK AND WHITE, AND SCREEN SIZE

1   Was the filmmaker's choice of black and white or color film correct for this story? What factors do you think influenced this decision? Try to imagine the film as it would appear in the other film type. What would the important differences in total effect be?
2   Is the film designed for standard or wide-screen projection? What factors do you think influenced this decision?

chapter 5

SOUND EFFECTS
AND DIALOGUE

SOUND AND THE MODERN FILM

Film is primarily a visual medium, and its areas of greatest significance and interest are generally communicated through visual means. But sound plays an increasingly important role in the modern film, because its here-and-now reality relies heavily on the three elements which make up the sound track: sound effects, dialogue, and the musical score. These elements create additional levels of meaning and provide sensual and emotional stimuli which increase the range, depth, and intensity of our experience far beyond what can be achieved through visual means alone.

Because we are more *consciously* aware of what we see than what we hear, we generally accept the sound track without much thought, responding intuitively to the information it provides while ignoring the complex techniques employed to create those responses. The intricacy of a finished sound track is illustrated by Leonard Bernstein's description of the sound mixer's contribution to a single scene from *On the Waterfront:*

> For instance, he may be told to keep the audience unconsciously aware of the traffic noises of a great city, yet they must also be aware of the sounds of wind and waves coming into a large, almost empty church over those traffic noises. And meantime, the pedaling of a child's bicycle going around the church must punctuate the dialogue of two stray characters who have wandered in. Not a word of that dialogue, of course, can be lost, and the voices, at the same time, must arouse the dim echoes they would have in so cavernous a setting. And at this particular point no one (except the composer) has even begun to think how the musical background can fit in.*

*Leonard Bernstein, *The Joy of Music* (New York: Simon and Schuster). Copyright© 1954, 1955, 1956, 1957, 1958, 1959 by Leonard Bernstein.

Five different layers of sound are at work simultaneously in the brief scene that Bernstein describes, and each one contributes significantly to the total effect. Compared to many scenes in the modern film, the sounds in this one are simple and traditional. They are not nearly as complex as the sound track for *M*A*S*H*,* for example, where sound is at least as significant as the visual element, if not more so. Thus, the modern sound track demands more and more of our conscious attention, so much so in fact, that if we want to fully appreciate a modern film we should perhaps go prepared as much to "hear" the film as to see it.

"VISIBLE" AND "INVISIBLE" SOUND

In the early days of the sound film, the emphasis was naturally placed on recorded sound which was synchronized with the visual image. As the popular term *talking pictures* indicates, the audience of that time was fascinated by the reproduction of the human voice. Although sound effects were employed, they were generally limited to those sounds which would naturally and realistically emanate from the images on the screen, that is, to *visible sounds.*

Although the dramatic power of the human voice and the sense of reality conveyed through sound effects certainly contributed new dimensions to the film art, the tight link between sound and image proved very confining, and filmmakers began to experiment with other uses of sound. They soon discovered what stage directors had known all along: that *invisible sound,* or sound emanating from sources *not* on the screen, could be used to extend the dimensions of film beyond what is seen, and to achieve more powerful dramatic effects as well. Once they realized the unique and dynamic potential of invisible sound, they were able to free sound from its restricted role of simply accompanying the visual image. Invisible sounds now function in a highly expressive or even symbolic way as independent "images," sometimes carrying as much significance as the visual image, and occasionally even more.

This creative use of invisible sound is important to the modern film for a variety of reasons. To begin with, many of the sounds around us in real life are invisible, simply because we find it unnecessary or imposible to look at their sources. Realizing this, filmmakers now employ sound as a separate storytelling element capable of providing information by itself. Sound used in this way complements the visual image instead of merely duplicating its effects. For example, if we hear the sound of a closing door, we can tell that someone has left the room even if we do not see an accompanying visual image. Thus the camera is freed from what might be considered routine chores, and can focus on the subject of the greatest significance or interest. This is especially important when the emphasis is on reaction instead of action, when the camera leaves the face of the speaker to focus on the face of the listener.

In some cases invisible sound may have a more powerful effect alone than would be possible with an accompanying visual image. The human mind is equipped with an "eye" much more powerful than that of the camera. An effective "sound image" can trigger a response in our imaginations which is much stronger than any visual image that might be projected on a screen. In the horror film, for example, invisible sounds can create a total, terror-charged atmosphere. Story elements that heighten and intensify our emotional response—the clank of chains, muffled footsteps on a creaking stair, a stifled scream, the opening of a creaking door, the howl of a wolf, or even unidentifiable sounds—are much more effective when the sources are *not* seen.

As demonstrated by the description of the scene from *On the Waterfront* above, invisible sounds (such as the sounds of city traffic, wind and waves, and the child's bicycle) are routinely used to intensify the film-goer's sense of really "being there." Thus, the sound track suggests a concrete reality beyond the limits of the visual frame by encircling the viewer with the natural sounds of the scene's immediate environment.

Sound is also effectively substituted for the visual image in comedy, usually to "depict" comic catastrophes which are set up and made completely predictable through visual means. For example, in a scene picturing a crazy inventor trying out a homemade flying machine, the picture may show the launching, while the predictable crash is left to the sound track. A dual purpose is achieved here: Our imaginations intensify the humorous effect of the crash by forming their own picture of it, while the camera focuses on the reactions registered on the faces of the on-lookers, which become the focal point of comic interest. Such use of sound also has clear practical benefits, considering the danger to the stuntman and the destruction of expensive properties which must occur if the crash is actually shown. By using sound for the crash, the would-be pilot needs only to stagger on screen, battered and dirty, draped in a few recognizable fragments of the plane.

Thus sound effects achieve their most original and effective results not through simultaneous use with the visual image, but as independent "images," enhancing and enriching the picture rather than merely duplicating it.

"POINTS OF VIEW" IN SOUND

In the objective point of view the characters and the action of a scene are perceived as if by a somewhat remote observer, who looks calmly on the scene and its events without becoming emotionally or physically involved. Camera and microphone perceive the characters externally, from the sidelines, without stepping in to assume the role of a participant. The subjective viewpoint, on the other hand, is that of a participant in the action, one who is intensely involved, either emotionally or physically, in the happenings on the screen. In the completely subjective view, therefore, camera and microphone become the eyes and ears of a character in the film, seeing exactly what he sees and hearing what he hears. As already noted, since maintaining the subjective point of view consistently is difficult if not impossible in film, most directors choose to alternate between the two, first establishing each situation clearly from an objective viewpoint, then cutting to a relatively brief subjective shot, then repeating the same pattern again. Since the camera and the microphone are, in effect, joined together in each shot to create the impression of a single viewpoint, volume and sound quality vary in direct relationship to camera positioning. The alternation between the objective and subjective viewpoints and the tight link between camera and microphone are illustrated by the following scene:

1. Establishing shot: objective camera view from street corner, focusing on a workman using an air hammer in center of street (apparent distance 50 to 75 feet). Sound: loud chatter of air hammer, mingled with other street noises.

2. Cut to subjective view: close-ups of air hammer, and violently shaking lower arms and hands of workman, from workman's point of view. Sound of hammer almost deafening—no other sounds heard.

3. Cut back to objective camera: heavy truck turns corner beyond workman, bears down on him at top speed. Sound: loud chatter of air hammer, other street noises, rising sound of approaching truck.

4. Cut to subjective view: close-up of air hammer and workman's hands as seen from his viewpoint. Sound: first only deafening sounds of air hammer, then a rising squeal of brakes mixed with hammer noise.

5. Quick cut to new subjective view: front of truck closing quickly on camera from ten feet away. Sound: squeal of brakes louder, hammer stops, woman's voice screaming, cut short by sickening thud . . . darkness and momentary silence.

6. Cut back to objective viewpoint; from street corner: unconscious figure of workman in front of stopped truck. Curious crowd gathering into circle. Sound: mixed jumble of panicked voices, street noises, ambulance siren in distance.

Sometimes the sound track is used to provide an even more intensely subjective point of view, one that communicates what goes on in a character's mind. The link between camera and microphone is slightly different here, for the camera will usually only suggest the subjective view by picturing the character's face in tight close-up, and rely on the sound track to make the subjectivity of the viewpoint clear. In most cases the sound quality will be distorted slightly to signal that the sounds being heard are not a part of the natural scene, but come from inside the character's mind. The particular type of close-up employed by the camera also serves to make this clear, for such close-ups move in even tighter than a normal close-up, and focus our attention not just on the character's face, but only on the eyes. The eyes thus become a kind of window of the mind through which the camera "reads" the character's thoughts. The soft focus with which such sequences are often filmed is another clue to their subjective nature. If they are not used simply as transitions to a visual flashback, the camera in such sequences remains in tight close-up while the character's thoughts, or the sounds and voices from his or her memory, are handled by the sound track.

63.   The eyes as a "window of the mind." Director Claude Lelouch moves the camera in for a tight close-up on the eyes of Anouk Aimee as he prepares for a memory voice-over or a visual flashback in *A Man and a Woman.*

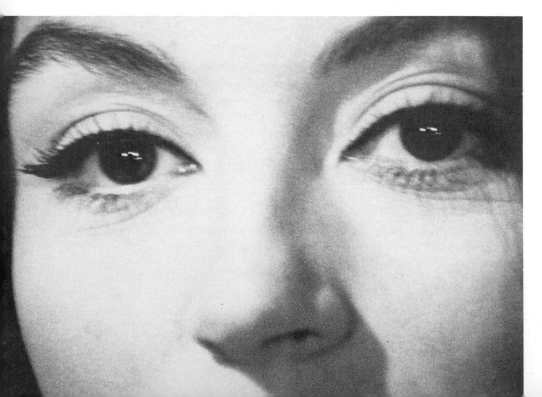

Unusual inner emotional states are also represented by the sound track, through use of variations in volume, reverberation, echoes, or other distortions in the voices or natural sounds heard by the character. Physical reactions such as extreme shock, excitement, or even illness are sometimes suggested by drum-beats, which supposedly represent internal symptoms of these reactions, such as a high pulse rate, or a pounding heart. Extreme amplification and distortion of natural sounds are also used to suggest a hysterical state of mind.

DIALOGUE

In a typical stage play dialogue is an extremely important element, and it is essential that almost every word be heard. To accomplish this end, stage actors use a certain measured rhythm, carefully speaking their lines in turn and incorporating brief pauses in the question-response pattern, so that each line of dialogue can be clearly heard by the person occupying the worst seat in the house. This limitation does not apply to film, however, where dialogue can be treated much more realistically. In *Citizen Kane,* for example, Orson Welles employed the overlapping dialogue, fragmented sentences, and interruptions which are common in everyday conversation without loss of essential information or dramatic power. This was achieved, as it now is in most films, through careful microphone positioning and recording, skillful editing and mixing of the recorded sound, and subtle variations in sound quality (volume, clarity, reverberation, and tonal qualities). Through such means, the modern filmmaker creates the impression of a highly selective ear tuned to what it wants or needs to hear. The most important sounds are singled out, emphasized, and made clear; those of less importance are blurred or muted.

The old adage that a picture is worth a thousand words is especially true in the film medium. Filmmakers must, first of all, use dialogue with great restraint to avoid repeating what has already been made clear by the visual image. Furthermore, both the dramatic power and the cinematic qualities of film are reduced if dialogue is used to communicate information that could be expressed more powerfully through visual means. In some cases, the most dramatically effective results are achieved through sparse or monosyllabic dialogue, and in a few films dialogue is dispensed with entirely. This is not to say that dialogue never dominates the screen. It does when the dramatic situation demands it. But as a general rule, dialogue in film is subordinate to the visual image, and it will seldom have the importance here that it has on the stage.

SOUND AS A TRANSITIONAL ELEMENT

Sound is also an extremely important transitional device in films, serving either to show the relationship between shots, scenes, or sequences, or to make a change in image from one shot or sequence to another seem more fluid or natural.

A fluid and graceful transition between sequences is achieved through the slight overlapping of sound from one shot into the next, where the sound from the last shot continues even after the visual image which accompanied it has faded or dissolved into an entirely new image, usually representing a passage of time, a change of setting, or both. A similar effect is created by the converse of this, where the sound track of the coming sequence slightly precedes the visual image which matches it. In many cases, there is some overlapping also of the two sound tracks, with one rising in volume while the other is still fading. This provides a smooth sound flow from one sequence to another when abrupt changes in sound are not desirable (as they sometimes are).

Also employed for transitional purposes are *sound links*, which are bridges between scenes or sequences (changes in place or time) created through the use of similar or identical sounds in both sequences. For example, a buzzing alarm clock at the end of one sequence becomes a buzzing telephone switchboard at the start of the next. Sound is thus used as a somewhat artificial link between the two sequences to create a sense of fluid continuity. Sometimes even dialogue links provide transition between two sequences: A question asked by a character at the close of one sequence may be answered by another character at the first of the following sequence, even though the two scenes may be set in a different time and place.

Sometimes dialogue transitions are ironic in nature, resulting in a sharp or startling contrast of opposites between the two scenes being joined. Consider, for example, the effect if the last line of a dialogue in the first scene has a character saying: "I don't care what happens! Nothing on the face of the earth could entice me to go to Paris!" and the next sequence opens immediately with the same character walking by the Eiffel Tower.

VOICE-OVER NARRATION

The filmmaker also employs sound that has no *direct* relationship to the natural sounds and dialogue involved in the story. A human voice offscreen, called voice-over narration, has a variety of functions. It is

64.   *The pictured narrator:* Arthur Kennedy (as Tom) serves as the time-
      present narrator as the film story of *The Glass Menagerie* unfolds in
      flashbacks. (Culver Pictures)

perhaps most commonly used as an expository device, conveying necessary background information or filling in gaps for continuity which
cannot be dramatically presented. Some films use voice-over narration
only at the beginning to give necessary background, place the action in
historical perspective, or provide a sense of authenticity. Others may
employ voice-over at the beginning, occasionally in the body of the film
for transition or continuity, and at the end. The flavor of a novelistic
first-person point of view is often provided through the use of voice-
over. This may be accomplished by setting the story in a frame: A narrator is visually introduced who then tells the story through a series of
flashbacks (as in *Little Big Man* and *The Glass Menagerie*); or the narrator may never be introduced visually, but only as the voice of a participant recalling past events. In *To Kill a Mockingbird*, for example, the
voice-over is obviously that of an adult relating childhood recollections,
but the narrator is never pictured.

     The film versions of some novels must depend on voice-over to tell
a story which cannot effectively be told through cinematic means.
Such is the case in *The Old Man and the Sea,* where the most important
part of the story takes place in the old man's mind, in his reactions to

what happens rather than in the events themselves. The voice-over becomes a noncinematic compromise, as Spencer Tracy, who plays the part of the old man Santiago, simply reads passages from the novel that communicate the character's thoughts and feelings about the action.

The voice-over technique is sometimes employed in direct contrast to the visual image for an ironic effect. For example, in *Two for the Road,* Albert Finney writes a letter to his wife while he is travelling alone. As he writes the letter, its content (which describes an ordinary hum-drum day on the road, lonely without her) serves as a voice-over narration for the visual sequence which shows what kind of a day he really had—a very exciting one where he meets a beautiful girl and enjoys a casual affair with her.

Generally voice-over narration can be very effective if used with restraint. It is not, however, a truly cinematic technique, and overusing it can be seriously detrimental to the quality of the film.

SILENCE AS A "SOUND" EFFECT

In certain situations a short *dead track,* the complete absence of sound, may be as effective as the most powerful sound effect. There is a ghostly, unnatural quality about film without sound that forces us to look more intently at the visual image. Because the natural rhythms of sound effects, dialogue, and music become as natural to the film as the rhythms of breathing, when these rhythms stop we immediately develop a feeling of almost physical tension and suspense, as though we are holding our breath and can't wait to start breathing again. This effect is used to great advantage in conjunction with the freeze frame. The sudden change from vibrant, noisy movement to silent, frozen stillness can almost stun us for a moment.

The most common use of dead track is simply to increase, by contrast, the impact and shock effect of sudden or unexpected sounds which follow these moments of silence.

RHYTHMIC QUALITIES OF DIALOGUE AND SOUND EFFECTS

Both dialogue and sound effects are also important for the rhythmic patterns or cadences they create, for these sound rhythmic elements often match the visual rhythms and reflect the mood, emotion, or pace of the action. Thus the pace of the dialogue and the rhythmic qualities of the sound effects influence the pace of the film as a whole.

QUESTIONS
ON SOUND EFFECTS AND DIALOGUE

1 Where in the film are off-screen or invisible sounds effectively employed to enlarge the boundaries of the visual frame, or to create mood and atmosphere?

2 What sound effects in particular contribute to a sense of reality and a feeling of "being there"?

3 Where is sound employed to represent subjective states of mind, and how effective is it?

4 If voice-over sound tracks are used for narration or internal monologues (thoughts of a character spoken aloud), can you justify their use, or could the same information have been conveyed through purely dramatic means?

5 Is dialogue used unnecessarily, repeating information already adequately communicated by the visual image? Where?

6 Where in the film is silence employed as a sound effect to intensify suspense, to increase the impact of sounds which follow, or to create other special dramatic effects? How effective are the results?

7 How do the pace of the dialogue and the rhythmic effects of the sound effects influence the pace of the film as a whole?

chapter 6

THE MUSICAL SCORE

THE REMARKABLE AFFINITY OF MUSIC AND FILM

Music has such a remarkable affinity to film that the addition of what we call the *musical score* was almost an inevitability. Even in the earliest films, the audience felt a very real vacuum of silence because the pulsing vitality provided by the moving image seemed unnatural, almost ghostly, without some form of sound corresponding to the action. By the time realistic sound could be provided through the addition of recorded dialogue and sound effects, music had already proven itself as a highly effective accompaniment for the emotions and rhythms built into the images on the screen. The addition of music made possible an artistic blending of sight and sound, a fusing of music and movement so effectively integrated that composer Dimitri Tiomkin was moved to remark that a good film is "really just ballet with dialogue." Muir Mathieson, in *The Technique of Film Music,* put it this way: "Music, having a form of its own, has ways of doing its appointed task in films with distinction, judged purely as music, and with subtlety, judged as a part of the whole film. It must be accepted not as a decoration or a filler of gaps in the plaster, but as a part of the architecture."

Perhaps the fact that both film and music divide time into rather clearly defined rhythmic patterns provided the most important common bond. There are certain natural rhythms inherent in the physical movements of many objects on the screen. Trees swaying in the breeze, a walking man, a galloping horse, a speeding motorcycle, or a machine capping bottles on an assembly line—all set up natural rhythms that create an almost instinctive need for corresponding rhythmic sounds. Another rhythmic pattern is provided by the pace of the plot itself, by how quickly or slowly it unfolds. Still another is created by the pace of the dialogue and the natural rhythms of human speech. A decided tempo is also established by the frequency of editorial cuts and the varying duration of shots between cuts, which gives each sequence a unique rhythmic character.

Although editing divides the film into a number of separate parts, the continuity and the fluid form of the medium remain, since the cuts create clear rhythmic patterns but do not break the flowing stream of images and sound. Because music possesses these same qualities of rhythm and fluid continuity, it can easily be adapted to the film's basic rhythms and its liquid contours or shapes. This affinity between music and film has led us to accept them almost as a unity, as part and parcel of the same package, as though music somehow exists magically alongside every film.

THE IMPORTANCE OF THE MUSICAL SCORE

Although we often accept film music without question and sometimes even without noticing it, this does not mean that its contribution to the film experience is insignificant. Music has a tremendous effect on our response, greatly enriching and enhancing our overall reaction to almost any film. It accomplishes this in several ways: by reinforcing or strengthening the emotional content of the visual image, by stimulating the imagination and the kinetic sense, and by suggesting and expressing emotions which cannot be conveyed by pictorial means alone.

Because it has a *direct* and very significant effect on our reaction to film, the term *background music,* which is so often applied to the musical score, is a misnomer. Music actually functions as an integral or complementary element. In spite of its direct effect on our response, however, there is general critical agreement on one point: The role of music in film should be a subordinate one.

Two schools of thought exist on the proper degree of this subordination. The older, traditional view is that the best film music is that which performs its various functions without making us consciously aware of its presence. In other words, if we don't notice the music, it's a good score. Therefore, the music for a "good" score shouldn't be too "good," for really good music draws attention to itself and away from the film.

The modern view allows the music, *on appropriate occasions,* not only to demand our conscious attention but even to dominate the picture, so long as it remains essentially integrated with the visual, dramatic, and rhythmic elements of the film as a whole. At such moments, we may become conscious of how intrinsically beautiful the music is, though we should not be so moved that we lose sight of its appropriateness to the image on the screen.

Both modern and traditional views are therefore in agreement on one essential point: Music that calls *too much* attention to itself at the expense of the film as a whole is not effective. Regardless of the *degree* of subordination, a good score will always be a significant structural element, performing its proper functions in a perfectly integrated whole, serving as a means to an end rather than an end itself.

GENERAL FUNCTIONS OF THE MUSICAL SCORE

The two most general and basic functions of the musical score are the creation of structural rhythms and the stimulation of emotional responses, both of which greatly enhance and reinforce the effect of the visual image.

The film score creates a sense of structural rhythm in both the film as a whole and its individual shots by developing a sense of pace and movement corresponding to the movement of the image on the screen and to the pace of the editorial cutting. In this way, the composer articulates and underscores the basic rhythms of the film.

The film score also serves to complement and enhance the narrative and dramatic structure by stimulating emotional responses which parallel each individual sequence and the film as a whole. Since even the slightest and most subtle moods or emotional atmospheres are established, intensified, maintained, and changed through the effective use of film music, the musical score becomes an accurate reflection of the emotional patterns and shapes of the film as a whole. This does not mean that a film's structured visual rhythms can be separated from its emotional patterns, for both are closely interwoven into the same fabric. Effective film music will therefore usually parallel one and complement the other.

The simplest and oldest method of adding music to film is simply the selection of a piece of familiar music (classical, pop, folk, jazz, blues, rock, and so on) that fits the rhythmic, emotional, or dramatic demands of the sequence at hand. An excellent example of the use of familiar music was the choice of the "William Tell Overture" for the old *Lone Ranger* radio show. The classical overture provided not only a perfect rhythmic counterpart to the galloping hoof beats and served as a stimulus to the visual imagination, but also gave the program a seriousness of tone which it would not have possessed otherwise. In similar manner, Stanley Kubrick employed such diverse types of music as "Thus Spake Zarathustra," Strauss waltzes, and "When Johnny Comes Marching Home" to very effective ends in *2001* and *Dr. Strangelove.*

Many directors, however, prefer to use music specially created and designed for the film at hand, composed either after the film and its accompanying sound effects track are completed, or while the film is being made so that composer and director can work together in the same creative atmosphere. Many films, of course, use a combination of familiar and original music.

Film music especially composed for the film it accompanies can be divided into two types:

1. *Mickey Mousing.*   So named because it grew out of animation techniques, *Mickey Mousing* is the exact, calculated dovetailing of music and action.   This ballet-like synchronization precisely matches the rhythm of the music with the natural rhythms of the objects moving on the screen, and requires a meticulous analysis of the filmed sequence by the composer.   Although some sense of emotional tone, mood, or atmosphere can be included in Mickey Mouse scoring, the primary emphasis is on the kinetic (the sense of movement and action) and rhythmic elements of the sequences in which it is used.

2. *Generalized* or *implicit.*   In this technique, no attempt is made at precise matching of music and movement; instead the emphasis is on capturing the *overall* emotional atmosphere or mood of a sequence and the film as a whole.   Often, this is achieved by rhythmic and emotive variations on only a few recurring main motifs or "themes."   Although basic rhythms in such scores are varied to *suggest* the rhythmic structure of individual action sequences, their primary function is to convey an emotion that parallels the story.

QUESTIONS
ON THE MUSICAL SCORE:
GENERAL FUNCTIONS

1   Where in the film is music used to match exactly the natural rhythms of the moving objects on the screen? At what points in the film does the music simply try to capture a scene's overall emotional mood?

2   Where does the film employ rhythmic and emotive variations on a single musical theme or motif?

3   Does the musical score remain inconspicuous in the background, or does it occasionally break through to assert itself?

4   If the music does demand your conscious attention, does it still perform a subordinate function in the film as a whole? How?

5   Where in the film is the main purpose of the music to match structural or visual rhythms? Where is it used to create more generalized emotional patterns?

6   How would the total effect of the film differ if the musical score were removed from the sound track?

SPECIALIZED FUNCTIONS OF FILM MUSIC

In the modern film, music is used to perform many varied and complex functions, some of which are rather specialized. Although it is impossible to list or describe all of these functions, some of the most basic ones are worthy of our attention.

COVERING WEAKNESSES OR DEFECTS IN THE FILM

A nonstorytelling function of the musical score is to disguise or cover up weaknesses in acting and dialogue. When such defects are evident, the director or composer can use heavy musical backing to make weak acting or banal dialogue appear more dramatically significant than it otherwise would. Television soap operas use organ music for this purpose with great frequency (and little sense of shame).

HEIGHTENING THE DRAMATIC EFFECT OF DIALOGUE

Music is often employed as a kind of emotional punctuation for dialogue, expressing the feeling underlying what is said. Generally, the musical accompaniment of dialogue must be extremely subtle and unobtrusive, stealing in and out so quietly that we respond to its effects without conscious awareness of its presence.

TELLING AN "INNER STORY"

Music often moves beyond a merely subordinate or complementary role and assumes a primary storytelling function, enabling the director to express things which cannot be expressed through verbal or pictorial means. This is especially true when a character's state of mind undergoes extreme and rapid changes which neither words nor action can adequately express. A good example of this occurs in *On the Beach*. An American submarine captain, played by Gregory Peck, takes an Australian girl (Ava Gardner) to a mountain resort for a final fling at trout fishing before the lethal radioactive clouds reach Australia. The American, whose family was killed in the nuclear war, has failed to adapt to the reality of the situation, and continues to think and talk of his family as though they were alive, making it impossible for him to accept the love of the Australian girl. The two are in their room in the lodge, listening to the dissonant, off-key voices of the drunken fishermen downstairs singing "Waltzing Matilda." In an underplayed dramatic scene, Peck finally realizes the futility of his ties with the past and accepts the love of the Australian girl. As they embrace, the loud and drunken voices become soft, sober, and melodious, and blend into perfect harmony, re-

65. *Music to tell an "inner story":* An important change in a character's state of mind is conveyed by music in this scene from *On the Beach.* (Culver Pictures)

flecting not any actual change in the voices downstairs, but the "inner story" of the change in Peck's state of mind. The use of massed voices of choirs to express an inner mystical or spiritual transformation is a more obvious example of the same function.

PROVIDING A SENSE OF TIME AND PLACE

Certain pieces of music or even musical styles are associated with specific time periods and locations, and composers can utilize such music to provide an emotional atmosphere which a given setting normally connotes. For example, a sense of scenic spaciousness is conveyed by standard western songs, such as "The Call of the Faraway Hills" from *Shane;* completely different qualities, such as the hustle and bustle of people having a good time, and a merry, more communal feeling, is conveyed by "town" or "saloon" music. Therefore, when the locale in a western changes from the range to the town or saloon, the visual transition is often preceded slightly by a switch to standard saloon music (player piano accompanied by shouting, laughter, general crowd noises, and an occasional gunshot or two). Thus the music not only tells us that a change of scene is coming, but also prepares us mentally for the visual scene before it appears, thereby serving a transitional function. Music associated with different countries or even different ethnic groups can be used in a similar way. Certain instruments are also associated with definite settings or groups of people: the zither, the mandolin, the sitar, the banjo, the Spanish guitar, and the Hawaiian guitar all have fairly concrete geographical connotations, and these connotations can be varied or even changed completely by the style in which the instruments are played.

The time period in which the film is set is also made realistic through the use of appropriate music and instrumentation, as illustrated by the use of the quaint, old sound of a harpsicord for a period piece set in the past, or other-worldly or futuristic electronic music for a science fiction film.

FORESHADOWING COMING EVENTS OR
BUILDING DRAMATIC TENSION

Any time a surprising change of mood or an unexpected action is about to occur on the screen, we will almost always be prepared for that change by the musical score. By preparing us emotionally for a shocking turn of events, the score does not soften the effect of the shock, but actually intensifies it by signalling its approach. In its own way, the music says, "Watch carefully now. Something shocking or unexpected is going to happen," and we respond to the musical signal by becoming more attentive. Even the fact that we know what is going to happen does not relieve the tension thus created, for suspense is as much a matter of "when" as it is of "what." Music used in this way does not coincide exactly with what is happening on the screen, but precedes it, introducing a feeling of tension while the images on the screen retain their calm.

Foreshadowing or tension-building music deliberately plays on our nerves in a variety of ways: by gradually increasing in volume or pitch, switching to a minor key, or introducing percussion instruments and dissonance. The introduction of dissonance into a musical score that has been harmonious to that point automatically creates a sense of nervousness and anxiety. Dissonance in such a situation expresses disorder, chaos, and a breakdown of the normal patterned order of harmony, causing us to become nervous and insecure, exactly the state of mind desired for effective foreshadowing or the building of dramatic tension.

ADDING LEVELS OF MEANING
TO THE VISUAL IMAGE

Sometimes music forms unique combinations with the visual image to create additional levels of meaning by making us see the visual scene in a fresh, unusual way. Take, for example, the opening scene in *Dr. Strangelove,* which is a picture of a midair refueling operation. Extremely delicate maneuvering is required to correctly place the refueling boom, trailing like a giant winged hose from the tail of the tanker plane, into the fuel-tank opening in the nose of the giant B-52 bomber, which is flying slightly behind and below the tanker. The music accompanying this sequence is the familiar love song "Try a Little Tenderness," played on romantic violins. If we are alert enough to recognize the song and think of its title, the music not only seems very appropriate to the delicate maneuvering required for the refueling operation, but also leads us to see the whole thing as a gentle love scene, a tender sexual coupling of two giant birds. Since this is the opening sequence of the film, the music also helps to establish the satiric tone that runs throughout the film as a whole.

Highly ironic levels of meaning can be achieved by using music that suggests a mood exactly opposite to the mood normally suggested by what is occurring on the screen. This technique is illustrated at the conclusion of *Dr. Strangelove,* in which the sticky-sweet voice of Vera Lynn singing "We'll Meet Again Some Sunny Day" accompanies the visual image of a nuclear holocaust as it destroys the world.

CHARACTERIZATION THROUGH MUSIC

Music also can play a role in characterization. Mickey Mouse scoring may be used, for example, to emphasize a peculiar or rhythmic pattern set up by a certain character's physical movement. The score for *Of Human Bondage,* for example, utilized a "crippled" theme, which rhythmically paralleled the main character's limp, thus reinforcing that aspect of his character. Some actors and actresses, such as John Wayne, Robert Mitchum, and Marilyn Monroe, have distinctive walks that exhibit definite rhythmic patterns and can therefore be reinforced musically.

Instrumentation can also be used to aid in characterization in an effect which might be called "Peter and the Wolfing." Here instruments and types of music represent and signal the presence of certain characters. Many films of the thirties and forties used this technique, causing the audience to associate the villain with sinister-sounding music in a minor key, the heroine with soft, ethereal violins, and the hero with strong, "honest" music. Although such heavy-handed treatment is not common today, *leitmotifs* (the repetition of a single musical theme or phrase to announce the reappearance of a certain character) are still employed to some extent.

A good composer may also use the musical score to add qualities to an actor or actress which that person does not normally have. In the filming of *Cyrano de Bergerac,* for example, Dimitri Tiomkin felt that Mala Powers did not really look French enough for the part of Roxanne. Therefore he "Frenchified" her by using French-style thematic music whenever she appeared on the screen, thus building up associations in the viewer's mind to achieve the desired effect.

TRIGGERING CONDITIONED RESPONSES

The composer also takes advantage of the fact that we have been conditioned to associate certain musical stereotypes or musical codes with certain situations, and such codes can be used with great economy and effectiveness. The sudden introduction of a steady tom-tom beat accompanied by a high wailing wind instrument ranging through a simple four- or five-tone scale effectively signals the presence of Indians even before they appear as a part of the visual image. The familiar "Cavalry to the rescue" bugle call is an equally familiar example. Such musical codes cannot be treated in a highly creative way, for to do so would cause them to lose some of their effectiveness as code devices. Composers do, however, try to make them *seem* as fresh and original as possible.

Even stereotyped musical codes can create unusual reactions when they are used ironically. In *Little Big Man,* for example, a lively fife and drum "good guys victorious" score accompanies scenes of General Custer's troops as they brutally massacre an Indian tribe. The ironic effect catches us in a tug-of-war between the music and the visual image: So compelling is the rhythm of the heroic music that we can scarcely resist tapping our toes and swelling with heroic pride, while our visual sensibilities are appalled by the unheroic action taking place on the screen.

TRAVELING MUSIC

Film music is at its best when used to characterize rapid movement. Such music, sometimes called "traveling music," is often employed almost as a formula or a shorthand code to give the impression of various means of transportation, and these formulas are varied to fit the unique quality of the movement being portrayed. Thus stagecoach music is different from horse-and-buggy music, and both differ essentially from "lone rider" music. The old steam engine even requires a different type of "railroad music" from the diesel locomotive. On rare occasions, "traveling music" performs a wide variety of functions, as is illustrated by the use of Flatt and Scruggs's "Foggy Mountain Breakdown" to accompany the famous chase scenes in *Bonnie and Clyde.* The strong, almost frantic sounds of the fast-fingered five-string banjo create a desperate yet happy rhythm that captures precisely the derring-do and spirit of the Barrow Gang, the slapstick comedy, desperation, and blind excitement of the chases themselves, and the nostalgic "good old days" flavor of the film as a whole.

ACCOMPANYING TITLES

The music that accompanies the main titles of a film usually serves at least two functions: First, it often articulates rhythmically the title information itself, making it somehow more interesting than it is. If the music consciously captures our attention anywhere in the film, it is during the showing of the titles and credits. Second, music is especially important here, for at this initial stage it usually establishes the general mood or tone of the film. It may even introduce story elements through the use of lyrics, as was done in *High Noon* and *Cat Ballou*. Since the opening or establishing scene is generally underway before the credits are completed, it can also dramatically or rhythmically match the visual image behind the credits.

MUSICAL "SOUNDS" AS A PART OF THE SCORE

Certain sound effects or noises from nature can be used in subtle ways for their own sake, to create atmosphere in the same way that music does. Crashing waves, rippling streams, bird calls, and moaning winds all possess clear musical qualities, as do many man-made sounds such as foghorns, auto horns, industrial noises of various kinds, steam whistles, clanging doors, chains, squealing auto brakes, and engine noises. Such sounds can be built up and artistically mixed into an exciting rhythmical sequence which, because of its "naturalness," may be even more effective than music in conveying a mood.

MUSIC AS INTERIOR MONOLOGUE

In the modern film, songs with lyrics that have no clear or direct relationship to the scenes they accompany are increasingly used as part of the sound track. In many cases, such songs are used to reveal the private moods, emotions, or thoughts of a central character, as was the case with the lyrics of "The Sounds of Silence" from *The Graduate* and the song "Everybody's Talkin' at Me" from *Midnight Cowboy*. Such lyrics function on a more or less independent level as a highly subjective and poetic means of communication, capable of expanding the meaning and emotional content of the scenes they accompany.

The examples just described represent only the most common and obvious uses of music in the modern film; it would be impossible to comment on them all. The important point here is that we must be aware of the various emotions and levels of meaning that music communicates.

ECONOMY IN FILM MUSIC

Generally speaking, economy is a great virtue in film music, both in duration and instrumentation. The musical score should do no more than is necessary to perform its proper functions clearly and simply. However, because of some irresistible temptation to dress up scenes with music whether they need it or not, the normal dramatic film usually ends up with too much music rather than not enough. The proper amount of music employed, of course, depends largely on the nature of the picture itself—some films require a lot of music; others are so realistic that music would only interfere with the desired effect. The fact remains that in many cases the most dramatically effective musical score is that which is used most sparingly.

So far as economy of instrumentation is concerned, the Hollywood tendency seems to be more toward large orchestras, even though smaller combinations can be more interesting and colorful, or even more powerful in their effect on the film as a whole.

QUESTIONS
ON THE MUSICAL SCORE:
SPECIALIZED FUNCTIONS

1 Which of the following functions of film music are used in the film, and where are they used?
    a. To cover weaknesses and defects in the film.
    b. To heighten the dramatic effect of dialogue.
    c. To tell an "inner story" by expressing a state of mind.
    d. To provide a sense of time or place.
    e. To foreshadow coming events or build dramatic tension.
    f. To add levels of meaning to the visual image.
    g. To aid in characterization.
    h. To trigger conditioned responses.
    i. To characterize rapid movement (traveling music).

2 Does the music accompanying the titles serve basically to underscore the rhythmic qualities of the title information, or to establish the general mood of the film? If lyrics are sung at this point, how do these lyrics relate to the film as a whole?

3 Where are sound effects or natural noises employed for a kind of rhythmic or musical effect?

4 If lyrics sung within the film provide a kind of interior monologue, what feeling or attitude do they convey?

5 How effectively does the score perform its various functions?

chapter 7

ACTING

THE IMPORTANCE OF ACTING

When we consider going to a movie, the first question we usually ask has nothing to do with the director or the cinematographer, but with the actors: "Who's in it?" Asking this question is natural on our part, because the art of the actor is the most clearly visible one. The actor's work commands most of our attention, overshadowing the considerable contributions of the writer, director, cinematographer, editor, and composer of the score. As Kernodle puts it in *An Introduction to the Theatre:*

> Whether the picture is *Tom Jones, Thunderball, The Sound of Music, Ship of Fools,* or *The Collector,* it is the star that draws the crowds. The audience may be amused, thrilled or deeply moved by the story, fascinated by new plot devices, property gadgets, and camera angles, charmed by backgrounds that are exotic, or captivated by those that are familiar and real, but it is the people on the screen, and especially the faces, that command the center of attention.

Therefore, because we naturally respond to film's most human ingredient, the actor's contribution is extremely important.

Yet in spite of our tendency to focus attention on the actor, there is general agreement among critics and directors that the actor's role in film should be a subordinate one, one of many important elements contributing to a greater aesthetic whole, the film itself. As Alfred Hitchcock states it, "Film work hasn't much need for the virtuoso actor who gets his effects and climaxes himself, who plays directly to the audience with the force of his talent and personality. The screen actor has got to be much more plastic; he has to submit himself to be used by the director and the camera."

144

THE GOAL OF THE ACTOR

The ultimate goal of any actor should be to make us believe completely in the reality of the character. If this goal is to be achieved, actors must either develop or be blessed with several talents. First of all, they must be able to project sincerity, truthfulness, and naturalness, and to project these qualities in such a way that we are never aware that they are only acting a part. In a sense, then, good acting must seem not to be acting at all.

Actors must also possess the intelligence, imagination, sensitivity, and insight into human nature necessary to understand fully the characters they play—their inner thoughts, motivations, and varying emotional reactions. Furthermore, actors must have the ability to express these things convincingly through voice, bodily movements, gestures, or facial expressions, so the qualities seem true to the characters portrayed and the situation in which they find themselves. And actors must maintain the illusion of reality in their characters with complete consistency from beginning to end. It is also important that actors keep their ego under control, so that they can see their roles in proper perspective to the dramatic work as a whole. Actors who do not possess these capabilities must be willing and able to take direction well enough so that they will *appear* to have them.

THE DIFFERENCES BETWEEN FILM ACTING AND STAGE ACTING

Acting for motion pictures and acting for the stage have in common the goals, traits, and skills described above, yet there are important differences in the acting techniques required for the two media. The primary difference involves the relative distance between the performer and the spectator. As mentioned earlier, when acting in the theater, actors must always be sure that every member of the audience can see and hear them distinctly. Thus, stage actors must constantly project the voice, make gestures that are obvious and clear, and generally move and speak so they can be clearly heard and seen by the most remote observer. This is no problem in a small, intimate theater, but the larger the theater and the more distant the spectator in the last row, the further the actor's voice must be projected and the broader the gestures must be. As these adjustments are made, the depth and reality of the performance suffer, since louder tones and wider gestures lead to generalized form and stylization. Therefore, the finer, subtler shades of intonation are lost as the distance between actor and audience increases.

The problem of reaching a remote spectator does not exist in films, since the viewer is moved (in effect) to the best possible locations for hearing and viewing the actor. With the mobility of the recording microphone, the film actor may speak as softly as possible, or even whisper, with full confidence that every word will be heard and every subtle tone of voice perceived. The same holds true for facial expression, gesture, and body movement, for in close-ups even the subtlest facial expressions are clearly visible to the most remote spectator. And the mobility of the camera further assures the actor that the scene will be viewed from the most effective angle. Thus film acting can be, and in fact *must be,* much more subtle and restrained than stage acting.

Actor Robert Shaw put it this way: "Here's the difference: onstage, you have to dominate the audience. You don't have to *think* the way you do when you're in the movies. Stage acting is the art of *domination.* Movie acting is the art of *seduction.*"* This is not to say however, that film acting is less difficult than stage acting. The film actor must be extremely careful in every gesture and word, for the camera and microphone are unforgiving and cruelly revealing, especially in close-ups. Since complete sincerity, naturalness, and restraint are all-important, a single false move or phony gesture or a line delivered without conviction, too much conviction, or out of character will shatter the illusion of reality.

Thus, the most successful film actors either possess or can project, with seeming ease and naturalness, a truly genuine personality, and somehow appear to be completely themselves without self-consciousness or a sense of strain. This rare quality generally seems to depend more on some kind of natural "gift" or talent than on disciplined study and training.

Another difficulty faces film actors because film acting is done in discontinuous bits and pieces to be assembled later rather than in consecutive order. For this reason, assuming the proper frame of mind, mood, and acting style for each segment of the film becomes a problem. For example, an actor required to speak in a dialect remotely removed from his own natural speech patterns may have difficulty capturing the dialect in exactly the same way in each bit of filming, a problem he would not have in a continuous stage performance. A clear advantage also arises from this difference. The performance of the film actor can be made more nearly perfect than that of the stage actor, for the editor and director choose the best and most convincing performance from a series of performances or "takes" of the same sequence and join them into a continuous whole of best performances.

Family Weekly, June 11, 1972.

Another disadvantage in film acting is that actors have no direct link with the audience as stage actors do, and can only act for imagined future spectators. Since they cannot draw on audience reaction for inspiration, whatever inspiration they receive must come from the director, the crew, and the fact that their work will have more permanence than that of the stage actor.

Film is also for the most part a more "physical" medium than drama; that is, film actors must use more nonverbal means of communication than stage actors. Julian Fast discusses this aspect of film acting in his book *Body Language:* "Good actors must all be experts in the use of body language. A process of elimination guarantees that only those with an excellent command of the grammar and vocabulary get to be successful."

The grammar and vocabulary of body language include a vast array of nonverbal communication techniques, but the motion picture is perhaps unique in its emphasis on the plastic human face. Although the face and facial expressions play a part in other story forms, such as fiction and drama, in film the face becomes a medium of communication in its own right. Magnified through projection on the screen, the human face with its infinite variety of expressions can convey both a depth and a subtlety of emotion that cannot be approached through purely rational or verbal means. As Hungarian film critic and theorist Béla Balázs so aptly puts it, "What appears on the face and in facial expression is a spiritual experience which is rendered immediately visible without the intermediary of words."

The human face is a marvelously complex structure, capable of transmitting through slight changes in mouth, eyes, eyelids, eyebrows, and forehead a tremendously wide range of emotions. This helps to explain another important difference between film acting and stage acting: the film's emphasis on shots that show a character "reacting" rather than acting. In this particular type of shot, called a *reaction shot,* the dramatic impact is achieved through a close-up of the emotional reaction registered on the face of the person most affected by the dialogue or the action. Within the brief moment that the actor's face is on the screen, it must register clearly, yet subtly and without the aid of dialogue, the appropriate emotional response. Whereas some of the most powerful moments in film are built around such "facial acting," the stage actor's facial reactions are seldom, if ever, quite so important to a play's dramatic power.

But even in reaction shots the film actor is often assisted by the nature of the medium, for much of the powerful and expressive quality of the human face in film is created by the contexts in which it appears,

66. *The actor's face as a means of communication:* Humphrey Bogart as
67. the paranoid Captain Queeg in *The Caine Mutiny.* In the first picture, the seeds of Queeg's paranoia have been planted. Bogart's eyes
are anxious and worried, and his jaw is a little slack, conveying sub-
tlely Queeg's bewilderment as his self-control slips away. In the second picture (during the storm sequence) all control is gone. Queeg's
psychotic state is revealed in the stark terror in the eyes; the jaw is
slack, and the face is that of a terrified, cornered animal. (Culver
Pictures)

68.   *The reaction shot:* There is no need for the camera to show us the
      scene inside the crash-landed bomber—the gruesome horror of what
      lies inside is clearly reflected on the faces of Robert Wagner and his
      crew. *The War Lover.* (Culver Pictures)

and the "meanings" of many expressions are determined by skillful editing. Thus the actor's face may not be so beautifully expressive as the
visual contexts may make it appear. This phenomenon was demonstrated by an experiment conducted by a young Russian painter, Lev
Kuleshov, and film director V. I. Pudovkin:

> We took from some film or other several close-ups of the well-known
> Russian actor Mosjukhin. We chose close-ups which were static and which
> did not express any feeling at all—quiet close-ups. We joined these close-
> ups, which were all similar, with other bits of film in three different com-
> binations. In the first combination the close-up of Mosjukhin was immedi-
> ately followed by a shot of soup standing on a table. It was obvious and
> certain that Mosjukhin was looking at this soup. In the second combina-
> tion the face of Mosjukhin was joined to shots showing a coffin in which
> lay a dead woman. In the third the close-up was followed by a shot of
> a little girl playing with a funny toy bear. When we showed the three com-
> binations to an audience which had not been let into the secret, the result
> was terrific. The public raved about the acting of the artist. They pointed
> out the heavy pensiveness of the mood over the forgotten soup, were
> touched and moved by the deep sorrow with which he looked on the dead
> woman, and admired the light, happy smile with which he surveyed the
> girl at play. But we knew in all three cases the face was exactly the same.

149

This experiment is not cited to prove that film acting is only an illusion created by editing. But it does show that we are eager to respond to faces, whether those faces are really projecting what we think we see or not.

Film actors must also be able to communicate more with bodily movements and gestures than stage actors. Since the stage actor's chief instrument of expression is the voice, his or her movements are mainly an accompaniment to or an extension of what is said. In film, however, physical movement and gestures may communicate effectively without dialogue. The size of the human image magnified through projection on the screen enables the actor to communicate physically with the viewer by using extremely subtle movements. A slight shrug of the shoulders, the nervous trembling of a hand viewed in close-up, or the visible tensing of the muscles and tendons in the neck may be much more important than anything said. A classic example of the role of body language in film acting is Jack Palance's portrayal of the gunfighter Wilson in *Shane*. Palance plays Wilson as the personification of pure evil: Every movement, every gesture is slow and deliberate yet tense, so that we get the feeling that the man is a rattlesnake, moving slowly and sensuously but always ready to strike in a split second. When he slowly performs the almost ritualistic act of putting on his black leather gloves in order to practice his profession, Palance makes us sense with horror Wilson's cold, cruel indifference to human life.

Film acting is thus an art in itself which, although it shares its basic goals with stage acting, utilizes fundamentally different techniques to achieve these goals.

TYPES OF ACTORS

Film actors can be classified in several ways, but it is perhaps most meaningful for us to view them in terms of how the roles they play relate to their own personalities. In *A Primer for Playgoers,* Edward A. Wright and Lenthiel H. Downs provide a useful breakdown of these types as follows:

1. *Impersonators.* An *impersonator* is an actor who has the talent to completely leave his real identity and natural personality behind to assume the total personality and characteristics of a character with whom he may have few characteristics in common. Such an actor can completely submerge himself in a role, altering his personal, physical, and vocal characteristics to such a degree that he seems to become the

69. *Evil personified:* Jack Palance as the gunfighter Wilson in *Shane.* (Culver Pictures)

character he is playing, and we actually lose sight of his identity as an actor. The roles such actors can perform are almost unlimited.

2. *Interpreters and commentors.* An *interpreter and commentor* is an actor who plays characters bearing a close resemblance to himself in personality and physical appearance, and who interprets these parts dramatically without wholly losing his own identity. Although he may slightly alter himself to fit the role, he does not attempt a radical change in his individual personality traits, physical characteristics, or voice qualities. He chooses instead to color or interpret the role by filtering it through his own best qualities, modifying it to fit his own inherent abilities. The end result is an effective compromise between actor and role, between the real and assumed identity. This compromise adds a unique creative dimension to the character being portrayed, for in his delivery of the lines the actor reveals something of his own thoughts and feelings

151

concerning the character he is playing, but he does so without ever falling out of character. Thus, the actor may simultaneously comment on and interpret the role. Although the range of roles such an actor can play is not as wide as that open to impersonators, it is still relatively wide. If he is cast wisely within this range, he can bring something new and fresh to each role he plays, in addition to his own best and most attractive qualities.

3. *The personality actor.* The actor who plays himself and whose primary "talent" is to be himself and nothing more is called a *personality actor.* He projects the essential qualities of sincerity, truthfulness, and naturalness, and he generally possesses some dynamic and magnetic mass appeal through a striking appearance, a physical or vocal idiosyncrasy, or some other special quality strongly communicated to us on film. This actor, however popular, is incapable of assuming any variety in the roles he plays, for he cannot project sincerity and naturalness when he attempts to move outside his own basic personality. Thus he must either fit exactly the roles in which he is cast, or the roles must be tailor-made to fit his personality.

THE STAR SYSTEM

In the past many personality actors and some interpreter and commentor actors were exploited in what became known as the *star system,* an approach to filmmaking based on the assumption that the average moviegoer is more interested in personalities than in great stories or, for that matter, in film art. The stars were, of course, actors with great mass appeal. The big studios did everything in their power to preserve as carefully and as rigidly as possible all those qualities of the stars that appealed to the public, and created films around the image of the star personality. Since the star's presence in a film was the main guarantee of financial success, such films became nothing more than a suitable background, package, or showcase in which to display and market the attractive wares of the actor, who had only to project the charm of his own personality.

However, once these stars realized the commercial advantages of their presence in a film, they demanded to be paid accordingly. As a result, the star system gradually priced itself out of existence. Producers now usually prefer to use lesser-known actors who have the range and flexibility to play a variety of roles and who, of course, demand less money than established stars. However, there is some evidence that a new star system may be in the making—one in which a certain name on the marquee will promise not the repetition of a tested and tried personality, but the guarantee of a high-level performance in a fresh and exciting role. A great many of the older actors and actresses whose images were created and frozen solid under the star system have broken free of their confining images and proved themselves to be highly capable as interpreters and commentors instead of merely the personalities that the star system required them to become.

This is not to say that familiar personalities have no importance in the modern film. The personality cults that spring up periodically around such actors as Humphrey Bogart or W. C. Fields provide ample evidence to the contrary. We will always be attracted to familiar faces and personalities, for we seem to have a psychological need for the familiar, the predictable, and the comfortable. But possibly because the television weekly series has helped satisfy that need, the modern filmgoer not only demands more flexibility in film acting, but has begun to realize that many actors he once considered the same in every role were actually commenting on and interpreting the roles they played.

CASTING

Acting skills aside, the casting of actors in roles "right" for them is an extremely important consideration. If his physical characteristics, facial features, voice qualities, or the total personality he naturally projects is not suited to the character he is attempting to portray, his performance will probably not be convincing. Thus, in spite of their great ability as impersonators, Alec Guinness or Peter Sellers could not effectively play the roles assigned to John Wayne, for example, nor could Burt Lancaster be very effective in the roles played by Woody Allen, Wally Cox, or Arnold Stang.

Less extreme problems in casting can be solved by sheer genius or camera tricks. For example, in the film *Boy on a Dolphin*, Alan Ladd, who measured 5'6", was cast as leading man opposite Sophia Loren, who at 5'9" towered over him. But in one scene, which showed them walking side by side, Ladd seemed at least as tall or slightly taller than Loren. What the camera didn't show was that the actress was actually walking in a shallow trench especially dug for the purpose. And in the film version of *Who's Afraid of Virginia Woolf?*, the character named Honey (Sandy Dennis), is repeatedly referred to as "slim-hipped" in spite of visual evidence to the contrary. The discrepancy here is obscured by Miss Dennis's acting; she projects a psychological type of "slim-hippedness" that is more convincing than the physical reality.

70.	*Casting problem:* Because Sophia Loren is so much taller than Alan Ladd, she is photographed standing a step below him in this scene from *Boy on a Dolphin*. (Culver Pictures)

Casting decisions involve not only the unique charactersitics of an actor, but the way those characteristics relate to the traits of other members of the cast. Two actors who are very similar in physical appearance, or who have almost identical voices are seldom used in the same film unless the plot clearly calls for such similarities. On the other hand, sharp and striking contrasts between actors may be highly desirable, especially if they are to be played off against each other as foils. Physical characteristics and "natural" personality traits are especially important in casting actors in roles where we have clear mental images of the character before we see the movie, as in the case of films about familiar historical figures or those based on popular novels. We often have a difficult time believing in actors who violate our preconceived notions of such characters, and even outstanding performances seldom overcome this handicap.

Financial considerations also play an important part in casting. A well-known actor may be the perfect choice for a starring role, but may be too high-priced for a film with a limited budget. He may also have other commitments that prevent him from taking the part. Thus casting becomes a matter of selecting the best available talent within the limits of the film's budget and shooting schedule.

Although his methods of casting are perhaps unique because he also writes many of the stories he directs, Billy Wilder provides an excellent example of the importance of casting to a film. Instead of selecting a cast to fit an existing story, Wilder often starts with a story idea alone, and then proceeds to select and sign up his cast. Only after the actors he wants agree to do the film does the actual writing of the script begin. As Wilder himself puts it, "What good is it to have a magnificent dramatic concept for which you must have Sir Laurence Olivier and Audrey Hepburn if they're not available?"

QUESTIONS
ON ACTING

1 Which actors did you feel were correctly cast in their parts? Which actors were not cast wisely? Why?

2 How well were the physical characteristics, facial features, and voice qualities of the actors suited to the characters they were attempting to portray?

3 If a performance was unconvincing, was it because the actor was miscast in the role to begin with, or did he simply deliver an incompetent performance?

      a. If faulty casting seems to be the problem, what actor would you choose for the part if you were directing the film?

      b. If the actor proved incompetent in the part, what were the primary reasons for his failure?

4 Based on your knowledge of their past performances, classify the actors in the major roles as "impersonators," "commentors and interpreters" or "personalities."

5 Try to determine whether the following actors and actresses are impersonators, interpreter/commentors, or personalities: George C. Scott, Cary Grant, Laurence Olivier, Steve McQueen, Robert Duvall, John Wayne, Marlon Brando, Sophia Loren, Elizabeth Taylor, Faye Dunaway, Dustin Hoffman, Anne Bancroft, Shirley MacLaine, Clint Eastwood, Gene Hackman, James Stewart, Racquel Welch, Glenda Jackson, Peter O'Toole, Woody Allen, Diane Keaton, Humphrey Bogart, Doris Day, Joan Crawford, Gary Cooper, Sean Connery, Al Pacino, Mia Farrow, etc. Justify your decision in categorizing each actor or actress by describing the degree of similarities or differences in his or her roles in at least three movies. Which of the actors or actresses are most difficult to categorize and why?

6   Consider the following questions with respect to each of the "starring" actors:

    a.   Does the actor seem to depend more on the charm of his own personality, or does he attempt to "become" the character he is playing?

    b.   Is the actor consistently believable in his portrayal of the character he is playing, or does he occasionally fall out of character?

    c.   If the actor seems unnatural in his part, is it because he tends to be overdramatic, or does he seem wooden and mechanical? Is his unnaturalness more apparent in the way he delivers his lines, or in his physical actions?

7   In which specific scenes is the acting especially effective or ineffective? Why?

8   Where are the actors' facial expressions used in reaction shots? What reaction shots are particularly effective?

chapter 8

THE DIRECTOR'S STYLE

A motion picture is always a cooperative effort, a joint creative interaction of many artists and technicians working on diverse elements, all of which contribute to the finished film. Because of the technical and physical complexity of the task of filmmaking and the large number of people involved, it may seem misleading to talk of any single individual's style. However, since the director generally serves as the unifying force and makes the majority of the creative decisions, it is perhaps proper to equate a film's style with the director's style.

The actual amount of control that directors have over the films they direct can vary widely. At one extreme is the director who functions primarily as a hireling of a big studio. The studio buys a story or an idea, hires a script writer to translate it into film language, and then assigns the script to a director who more or less mechanically supervises the shooting of the film.

At the other extreme is the concept of the director as *auteur* or complete filmmaker. Here the director is in complete control of the entire process from beginning to end, from the first glimmering of a story idea to the finished film. He or she conceives of the idea for the story, writes the script or the screenplay, and then carefully supervises every step in the filmmaking process, from selecting the cast and finding a suitable setting for shooting down to the final editing.

Most directors fall into some gray area between these two extremes, since the degree to which the studio interferes with or controls the effort and the director's dependence on other creative personalities vary considerably. Nevertheless, regardless of the actual degree of control over the film, the director has the greatest opportunity to impart a personal artistic vision, philosophy, technique, and attitude into the film as a whole, thereby dictating or determining its "style." In analyzing or evaluating a director's style, therefore, we assume that he or she has exercised aesthetic control over at least the majority of complex elements that make up a finished film.

A meaningful assessment of any director's style requires the careful study of at least three of his or her films, concentrating on those special qualities of the work that set the individual apart from all other directors. Since some directors can go through a long evolutionary period of stylistic experimentation before they arrive at anything consistent enough to be called a style, the study of six or more films may be necessary to characterize their style.

THE CONCEPT OF STYLE

In simplest terms, a director's style is the manner in which he or she expresses his or her own unique personality through the language of the medium. "Style" is actually an all-embracing term, for it is reflected in almost every decision the director makes. Every single element or combination of elements may reveal a unique creative personality behind the film, shaping, molding, and filtering the film through his own intellect, sensibility, and imagination. If we can assume that all directors strive to communicate clearly with the audience, then we can further assume that directors want to manipulate our responses to correspond with their own, so that we can share that vision. Thus, almost everything the directors do in making a film becomes a part of their style, because in almost every decision they are in some subtle way interpreting or commenting upon the action, revealing their own attitudes, and injecting their own personality indelibly into the film.

Before analyzing the separate elements that reveal style in a film, it is worthwhile to make some general observations about the film as a whole. In this first general overall analysis, we might consider which of the following terms best describe what is stressed or emphasized by the film:

1. Intellectual and rational *or* emotional and sensual.
2. Calm and quiet *or* fast-paced and exciting.
3. Polished and smooth *or* rough and crude-cut.
4. Cool and objective *or* warm and subjective.
5. Ordinary and trite *or* fresh, unique, and original.
6. Tightly structured, direct, and concise *or* loosely structured and rambling.

7. Truthful and realistic *or* romantic and idealized.

8. Simple and straightforward *or* complex and indirect.

9. Grave, serious, tragic, and heavy *or* light, comical, and humorous.

10. Restrained and understated *or* exaggerated.

11. Optimistic and hopeful *or* bitter and cynical.

12. Logical and orderly *or* irrational and chaotic.

An accurate assessment of these values will provide at least a beginning in the analysis of the director's style; a complete analysis must, of course, look into a breakdown of his or her treatment of individual film elements.

SUBJECT MATTER

Perhaps no single element of a director's style is more important than his or her choice of subject matter. If the director is truly an *auteur*—one who conceives of the idea for a film and then writes the script or supervises the writing to conform to his or her own vision of the film—the subject is an essential aspect of his or her style. But even when this is not the case, directors who are free to choose the stories they want to film express their style by their choices of subject. Even studio assignments may reveal the director's style if such assignments are made in accordance with an already-established style.

In studying several films by a single director, the first thing to determine is whether a common thematic thread runs through all these films. One director may be concerned primarily with social problems, another may deal with man's relationship to God, and yet another may be interested primarily in the struggle between good and evil. Directors' choices of subject matter may also be determined by the fact that they try to achieve similar emotional effects or moods in everything they do. Alfred Hitchcock, for example, is clearly identified with the terror-suspense film, in which the mood becomes a kind of "thematic" concern. Similarly, some directors prefer to work with only one genre, such as the western, the historical pageant, or comedy, and others may specialize in adapting novels or plays to film.

The types of conflicts that directors choose to deal with constitute an extremely important thematic thread. Some directors lean toward the serious examination of subtle philosophical problems concerning the complexities of human nature, the universe, or God; others may favor simple stories of ordinary people facing the ordinary problems of life.

Still others may prefer to treat conflict on a purely physical plane, as in the action-adventure film.

The subject chosen may also show some consistency with respect to the concepts of time and space. Some directors may work only in compressed time, and prefer a story that is compressed into a very short time period—a week or less—while others may prefer historical panoramas covering a century or more. Spatial concepts may be equally diverse: some directors specialize in the historical pageant or epic film, with casts of thousands and a broad sweeping landscape as a canvas. Others may restrict themselves to a limited physical setting and keep the number of actors in the cast to a bare minimum.

In some cases, our study of a director's style may reveal a unified world view, a consistent philosophical statement on the nature of man and the universe. Even irony, which is generally thought of as a technique, can take on philosophical implications reflecting the director's world view if it is used enough (see the section on irony in Chapter 3).

CINEMATOGRAPHY

As far as the visual elements of style are concerned, the cinematographer, who actually does the camera work, plays a very significant role. But we cannot be present on the set, and lack the "inside" knowledge necessary to accurately assess the cinematographer's contribution. We can't really know how much of the visual style of *Birth of a Nation* was the work of Billy Bitzer, how much imagery in *Citizen Kane* was conceived by Greg Toland, or how much of *The Seventh Seal* resulted from the creative vision of Gunnar Fischer. Therefore, because directors usually choose the cinematographer they want, we can assume their selections are based on a compatibility of "visual philosophies," and for simplicity's sake we usually attribute the film's visual style to the director.

In analyzing visual style we must first consider the composition. Some directors will use composition very formally and dramatically; others will prefer a more informal or low-keyed effect. One director may favor a certain type of arrangement of people and objects in the frame, while another may place special emphasis on one particular type of camera angle. Important differences may also be noted in "philosophies of camera." For example, some directors stress the *objective camera* (one that views the action as a remote spectator); others may lean toward the other end of the spectrum—the *subjective camera*, which views the scene from the visual or emotional point of view of a participant. Other choices include using a variety of unique stylistic devices (such as unusual camera angles, slow or fast motion, colored or light-diffusing filters, or distorting lenses) to interpret the visual scene in some unique way.

Lighting also expresses directorial style: Some directors prefer to work mostly with high-key lighting, which creates stark contrasts between light and dark and leaves large portions of the set in shadow, while others favor low-key lighting, which is more even and contains many subtle shades of gray. Even the character of the lighting contributes greatly to the director's visual style, since a director may consistently favor either harsh, balanced, or diffused lighting throughout a series of films.

Treatment of color may also be an element of style. Some directors use sharp, clear images with bright, highly contrasting hues dominating the image; some favor soft, muted, pastel shades and dim or even blurred tones.

CAMERA MOVEMENT

Directors also reveal their style through the use of camera movement. The possibilities range from using the static camera, with as little camera movement as possible, to favoring the fixed camera, moving mostly through panning and tilting. Another choice is a slow, liquid, almost floating "poetic" camera movement, with the camera mounted on a dolly or boom crane. And while one director may favor the freedom and spontaneity of the jerky hand-held camera, another may make great use of the zoom lens to simulate movement in and out of the frame. The type of camera movement favored is an important stylistic element, for it creates its own sense of pace and rhythm, and greatly affects the overall impression which the film makes.

Some directors are also more concerned with achieving three-dimensionality in their images than others, and their techniques of achieving this effect automatically become an integral part of their visual style.

EDITING

Editing is also an extremely important stylistic element, especially as it affects the overall rhythm or pace of the film. The most obvious element of editorial style is the average shot length in the film. Generally, the longer the time between editorial cuts, the slower the pace of the film. Editorial cuts that mark time-place transitions also may take on a unique rhythmic character. For example, one director may favor a soft, fluid transition, such as a slow dissolve, where another may simply cut immediately from one sequence to the next, relying on the sound track or the visual context to make the transition clear. When editorial juxtapositions are used creatively, the director's style may also be seen in the nature of the relationships between shots. Directors may stress an intellectual relationship between two shots by using ironic or metaphorical juxtapositions, or emphasize the visual continuity by cutting to similar forms, colors, or textures. They might also choose to emphasize aural relationships by linking the two shots solely through the sound track or the musical score.

Other special tricks of editing, such as the use of parallel cutting, fragmented flash-cutting, and dialogue overlaps are also indicators of style. Editing may also be characterized by whether it calls attention to itself or not; thus, one director may lean toward editing that is clever, self-conscious, and tricky, whereas another may favor editing that is smooth, natural and unobtrusive. Use of montages and the nature of the images employed also help to characterize editing style.

CHOICE OF SETTING AND SET DESIGN

Closely related to the choice of subject or genre in revealing directorial style is the choice of setting and the degree to which it is emphasized. The visual emphasis placed on the setting may be an important aspect of the director's style. One director may lean toward settings that are stark, barren, or drab; another may choose only settings of great natural beauty. Some may use setting to help us understand character, or as a powerful tool to build atmosphere or mood; others may simply allow it to slide by as a backdrop to the action, giving no particular emphasis to the setting at all.

By choosing to photograph certain details in the setting the director may stress the sordid and brutal aspects or the idealized and romantic qualities of the environment. This type of emphasis may be very important in determining the director's style, for it may reflect an overall world view. Other significant factors of setting may also reflect the director's style: for example, the social and economic classes focused on, whether or not the settings are rural or urban, and whether contemporary, historical past, or futuristic time periods are favored. Also, when elaborate sets have obviously been constructed especially for a film, the director's taste will often be apparent in the set design.

SOUND AND SCORE

Directors also make use of the sound track and the musical score in unique and individualistic ways. Whereas one may simply use whatever natural sound is necessary to match the visual image, another may consider sound almost as important as the visual image and use offscreen sound imaginatively to create a sense of total environment. Yet another director may use sound in an impressionistic or even symbolic manner; still another might stress the rhythmic and even musical properties of natural sounds and use them instead of a musical score.

With respect to screen dialogue, some directors want every word to be clearly and distinctly heard, and record with this aim in mind, while others allow lines to overlap and frequent interruptions to occur for the realism these effects produce. Loudness or softness of the sound track as a whole may also reflect something of a director's style. One director may employ silence as a "sound" effect, while another may feel a need to fill every second with some kind of sound. A similar distinction may be made in directors' emphasis on dialogue. Some may use a minimum of dialogue, while others may fill the sound track with it and depend on it to carry the major burden of their film's communication.

Directors also may vary greatly in their utilization of the musical score. One director may be completely dependent on music to create and sustain mood; another may use it only sparingly. One may use music to communicate on several levels of meaning, while another may use music only when it reinforces the rhythms of the action on the screen. Whereas one director may desire the music to be understated or even completely inconspicuous, so we are not even aware of the score, another may employ a strong, emotional score that occasionally overpowers the visual elements. Some favor music scored expressly for the film; others employ a variety of familiar music as it fits their purpose. Instrumentation and size of orchestra used is also an element of style: Some directors prefer a full symphony sound; others find a few instruments or even a single instrument more effective.

CASTING AND ACTING PERFORMANCES

Most directors have a hand in selecting the actors they work with, and it must be taken for granted that they can have a strong influence on individual acting performances. In the choice of actors, one director may take the safe, sure way, by casting established stars in roles very similar to those they have played before; another may prefer to try relatively unknown actors who do not already have an "image" established; another director may like to cast an established star in a role entirely different from anything he has played before. Some directors never work with the same actor twice, while others employ the same "stable" of actors in almost every film they make.

In their choice of actors, directors may also reveal an emphasis on certain qualities. For example, a director can have a remarkable "feel" for faces, and choose stars and even bit players who have faces with extremely strong visual character, that is, faces that may not be beautiful or handsome, but are strikingly powerful on the screen. On the other hand, a director might prefer to work with only what are called the "beautiful people." Whereas one director may seem to stress the actors' voice qualities, another may consider the total body, or the "physical presence" of the actor more important.

The director may have a tremendous influence on the acting style of the actors in the cast, although this may be difficult to determine even in a study of several films. Thus an actor who has a tendency to overplay for one director may show more subtlety and restraint with another. Whether a director has the ability to influence the acting style of each actor under his or her direction is of course impossible to detect, but in some cases the director's influence may be obvious. Almost every aspect of an actor's performance can be influenced by the director—the subtlety of the facial expressions, the quality of the voice and physical gestures, and the psychological depth of the interpretation of the role.

QUESTIONS
ON THE DIRECTOR'S STYLE

1   After viewing several films by a single director, what kinds of general observations can you make about his or her style? Which of the adjectives listed below are descriptive of his or her style?
   1. Intellectual and rational *or* emotional and sensual.
   2. Calm and quiet *or* fast-paced and exciting.
   3. Polished and smooth *or* rough and crude-cut.
   4. Cool and objective *or* warm and subjective.
   5. Ordinary and trite *or* fresh, unique and original.
   6. Tightly structured, direct, and concise *or* loosely structured and rambling.
   7. Truthful and realistic *or* romantic and idealized.

8. Simple and straightforward *or* complex and indirect.
9. Grave, serious, tragic, and heavy *or* light, comical, and humorous.
10. Restrained and understated *or* exaggerated.
11. Optimistic and hopeful *or* bitter and cynical.
12. Logical and orderly *or* irrational and chaotic.

2 What common thematic thread is reflected in the director's choice of subject matter? How is this thematic similarity revealed in the nature of the conflicts he or she deals with?

3 In the films you have seen, what consistencies do you find in the director's treatment of space and time?

4 Is a consistent philosophical view of the nature of man and the universe found in all the films studied? If so, attempt to describe the director's world view.

5 How is the director's style revealed by the following visual elements: composition and lighting, "philosophy of camera," the nature of the camera movement, and methods of achieving three-dimensionality?

6 How does the director use special visual techniques (unusual camera angles, fast motion, slow motion, distorting lenses, and so on) to interpret or comment on the action, and how do these techniques reflect his or her overall style?

7 How is the director's style reflected in the different aspects of the editing in the films, such as the rhythm and pacing of editorial cuts, the nature of transitions, montages, and other creative juxtapositions? How does the style of the editing relate to other elements of the director's visual style, such as the "philosophy of camera" or the point of view emphasized?

8 How consistent is the director in using and emphasizing setting? What kind of details of the natural setting does the director emphasize, and how do these details relate to his or her overall style? Is there any similarity in the director's approach to entirely different kinds of settings? How do the sets constructed especially for the film reflect the director's taste?

9 In what ways are the director's use of sound effects, dialogue, and the musical score unique? How are these elements of style related to his or her visual style?

10 What consistencies can be seen in the director's choice of actors and in the performances they give under his or her direction? How does the choice of actors and acting styles fit in with the style in other areas?

**DIRECTORS'
VISUAL
STYLES**

A.   Director: Ingmar Bergman, *The Seventh Seal.* (Culver Pictures)

B.   Director: Ingmar Bergman, *The Seventh Seal.* (Culver Pictures)

C.   Director: Ingmar Bergman, *Wild Strawberries*. (Culver Pictures)

D.   Director: Ingmar Bergman, *Through a Glass Darkly*. (Culver Pictures)

**See questions
on pages 182–83**

G.   Director: Alain Resnais, *Last Year at Marienbad.* (Culver Pictures)

H.   Director: Alain Resnais, *Last Year at Marienbad.* (Culver Pictures)

See questions on pages 182–83

**DIRECTORS'
VISUAL
STYLES**

I.   Director: John Ford, *The Grapes of Wrath.* (Culver Pictures)

J.   Director: John Ford, *The Grapes of Wrath.* (Culver Pictures)

K.   Director: John Ford, *The Informer*. (Culver Pictures)

See questions on pages 182–83

L.   Director: John Ford, *Rio Grande*.

**DIRECTORS'
VISUAL
STYLES**

M. Director: Federico Fellini, *La Dolce Vita.* (Culver Pictures)

N. Director: Federico Fellini, *La Dolce Vita.* (Culver Pictures)

O.   Director: Federico Fellini, *8 1/2.* (Culver Pictures)

P.   Director: Federico Fellini, *La Strada.* (Culver Pictures)

**See questions
on pages 182–83**

S.   Director: Alfred Hitchcock, *Lifeboat*. (Copyright © 1944 Twenti-
      eth Century-Fox Film Company Ltd. All Rights Reserved)

**See questions
on pages 182–83**

T.   Director: Alfred Hitchcock, *Psycho.*

DIRECTORS' VISUAL STYLES

U. *Couples.* Director: Robert Rossen, *Lilith.* (Culver Pictures)

V. *Couples.* Director: John Ford, *Stagecoach.* (Culver Pictures)

W. *Couples.* Director: Jack Cardiff, *Sons and Lovers.* (Copyright © Twentieth Century-Fox Film Company Ltd. All Rights Reserved)

See questions on page 183

X. *Couples.* Director: Josef Von Sternberg, *The Devil Is a Woman.*

Y.   *Setting.*   Director: John Ford, *The Grapes of Wrath.*   (Culver Pictures)

Z.   *Setting.*   Director: Ingmar Bergman, *Wild Strawberries.*   (Culver Pictures)

AA. *Setting.* Director: Orson Welles, *The Trial.* (Culver Pictures)

BB. *Setting.* Director: Federico Fellini, *8 1/2.* (Culver Pictures)

**See questions
on pages 183–84**

DIRECTORS' VISUAL STYLES

CC. *Groups.* Director: Alfred Hitchcock, *Notorious.* (Culver Pictures)

DD. *Groups.* Director: John Ford, *Stagecoach.* (Culver Pictures)

EE. *Groups.* Director: Robert Rossen, *All the King's Men.*
(Culver Pictures)

See questions
on page 184

FF. *Groups.* Director: Orson Welles, *Citizen Kane.* (Culver Pictures)

QUESTIONS
ON THE DIRECTORS' VISUAL STYLES

The pictures on the preceding pages represent films by several different directors. Although it is difficult, if not impossible, to "capture"a director's visual style in a limited number of still pictures, most of the pictures here contain strong stylistic elements. Study the pictures listed below as representative of each director's style, and try to answer the questions which follow about each director.

> *Ingmar Bergman:* Illustrations A, B, C, D, and Z.
> *Alain Resnais:* Illustrations E, F, G, and H.
> *John Ford:* Illustrations I, J, K, L, V, Y, and DD.
> *Federico Fellini:* Illustrations M, N, O, P, and BB.
> *Alfred Hitchcock:* Illustrations Q, R, S, T, and CC.

1   What does each set of pictures reveal about the director's visual style, as reflected in such things as composition and lighting, "philosophy of camera" or point of view, use of setting, methods of achieving three-dimensionality, and choice of actors?

2   With the exception of Alain Resnais, whose style is represented by four pictures from a single film (*Last Year at Marienbad*), the pictures represent three or more films by each director. Study the pictures *from each film* and see what you can deduce about the nature of the film.

    a.   What do the pictures reveal about the general subject matter of the film or the kind of cinematic theme being treated?

    b.   Characterize as clearly as possible the mood or emotional quality suggested by the stills from each film.

    c.   If you are familiar with other films by the same director, how do these thematic concerns and emotional qualities relate to his other films?

3   Considering all the stills from each director, characterize each director as to how he fits the following descriptive sets:

    a.   Intellectual and rational *or* emotional and sensual.

    b.   Naturalistic and realistic *or* romantic, idealized, and surreal.

    c.   Simple, obvious, and straightforward *or* complex, subtle, and indirect.

    d.   Heavy, serious, and tragic *or* light, comical and humorous.

4   Which directors represent *extremes* of each of the descriptive sets above?

5 Which director seems most formal and structured in composition? Which director seems most informal and natural in composition?

6 Which director seems to be trying to involve us emotionally in the action or dramatic situation portrayed in the stills? How does he attempt to achieve this effect? Which director's viewpoint seems most objective and detached, and why do the pictures have that effect?

7 Which director relies most on lighting for special effects, and what effects does he achieve?

8 Which director places the most emphasis on setting to create special effects or moods?

9 Compare the visual styles of the foreign directors (Bergman, Fellini, and Resnais) with the styles of the American directors (Ford and Hitchcock). Can you see any basic differences between the foreign and American directors' styles? If so, what is the nature of those differences?

10 Based on your answers to all the preceding questions, what general observations can you make about each director's style?

11 *Couples:* The four-picture set U, V, W, and X shows four different directors' treatment of couples. Three additional pictures from the Directors' Series also feature couples: E and F from *Last Year at Marienbad* and Q from *North by Northwest.* Study these seven pictures carefully, and answer the following questions:

    a. What basic stylistic differences do you see in these pictures?

    b. What does each picture tell about the relationship of the couple portrayed? How is this information conveyed?

    c. What are the basic differences in the two romantic love scenes (from *Sons and Lovers* and *The Devil Is a Woman*)? How can you explain these differences?

12 *Use of Setting:* The four-picture set Y, Z, AA, and BB shows four different directors' use of setting. Four additional pictures from the Directors' Series also place emphasis on setting: G and H from *Last Year at Marienbad*, L from *Rio Grande*, and T from *Psycho.* Study these eight pictures carefully and answer the following questions:

    a. What special quality does the setting add to each of the pictures? How are these qualities emphasized by the way the setting is photographed?

    b. What kinds of interrelationships between the characters and the setting are implied in each picture?

    c. What seems to be the primary function of setting in each picture? Is it used primarily for sheer visual impact, for realism, to create emotional atmosphere or mood, or to reflect something about the characters? Is there any evidence within the picture to suggest that the setting may have symbolic importance?

13 *Groups:* The four-picture set CC, DD, EE, and FF shows four directors' treatments of groups. Two additional pictures from the Directors' Series also feature groups: J from *The Grapes of Wrath* and S from *Lifeboat*. Study these six pictures carefully and answer the following questions:

a. Which character is the object of primary interest in each picture, and what methods does the director use to direct our attention toward that person?

b. What does each picture show about interrelationships between the different characters in the group? How are these interrelationships conveyed?

c. In which of the pictures is the character of primary interest also the dominant figure in the group? If the dominant figure is not the object of primary interest, how is his dominance revealed?

d. In which pictures are we made to feel almost a part of the group? In which pictures do we feel separate from the group? How are these effects achieved?

chapter 9

SPECIAL PROBLEMS
OF FILM ANALYSIS

THE PROBLEMS OF ADAPTATION

REASONABLE EXPECTATIONS

One of the most difficult problems of film analysis arises when we see a film adaptation of a play we have seen or a novel we have read, for we generally approach such films with completely unreasonable expectations. Usually we expect the film to duplicate exactly the experience we had in seeing the play or in reading the novel, which is, of course, completely impossible. Since we have already experienced the story once, and are familiar with the characters and events, the adaptation is bound to lack some of the freshness of the original. But there are a great many other factors which should be considered if we are to approach an adaptation with the proper frame of mind. To know what we can reasonably expect from the film adaptation of either a play or a novel requires foresight into the kinds of changes that will occur, as well as an understanding of the relative strengths and weaknesses of the mediums involved.

CHANGE OF MEDIUM

First of all, we must expect some changes, since the medium in which a story is told has a very definite effect on the story itself. Since each medium has its own strengths and limitations, any adaptation from one medium to another must take these factors into account and adapt the subject matter to fit the strengths of the new medium. Thus, if we are to judge a film adaptation fairly, we should recognize that a novel, a play, or a film may tell generally the same story, but that each is a distinct work of art representing a different medium. And in spite of the fact that some properties are shared by all three, each medium has its own distinctive techniques, conventions, consciousness, and viewpoint. We do not expect an oil painting to have the same effect as a statue or a woven tapestry picturing the same subject, and we should look on the film adaptation of a novel or a play in much the same manner.

CHANGING CREATIVE ARTISTS

The influence that any change in creative talents will have upon a work of art must certainly be considered. No two creative minds are alike, and once the reins have been turned over to another creative hand the end product will be different. Some kind of change in creative personnel occurs in almost any kind of adaptation: Even when the novelist writes the screenplay or the playwright adapts his or her own play for the screen, changes, and sometimes rather drastic changes, are sure to be made. Some of these changes may be required by the new medium. For example, the average novel contains more material than a film could ever hope to include, so the screenwriter or director must be highly selective in choosing what to include in the film and what to leave out. Because the novel cannot be translated intact, its emphasis may have to be changed, even if the novelist is writing the screenplay. The most significant changes, however, will come about because the novelist or playwright must surrender some of his or her artistic control to the director and the actors.

To expect an exact carry-over from one medium to another where different creative artists are involved seems especially irrational when we consider our attitudes toward different versions of the same vehicle within the same medium. For example, we fully expect the same play staged or filmed by different directors and with different actors to differ vastly in emphasis and interpretation. Consider Olivier's *Hamlet,* Burton's *Hamlet,* Williamson's *Hamlet,* and even Chamberlain's *Hamlet* (the latter made for television). All are different and all are praised for being different, for we expect and perhaps even demand that they be different. As filmgoers, we must develop an equally tolerant attitude toward all film adaptation, and freely grant the new creative talent some poetic license.

Of course, there are limits to which poetic license can justifiably be carried. If a work is changed so much that it is almost unrecognizable, it should probably not even bear the same title as the original. It has been said, perhaps with justification, that Hollywood frequently distorts the meaning of a novel so thoroughly that nothing is left but the title. Two brief examples may illustrate the validity of that statement, though it probably does not apply to the two films mentioned.

John Ford, when asked about his indebtedness to the novel in making *The Informer* supposedly replied, "I never read the book." In a similar vein, Edward Albee was once asked whether or not he was pleased with the screen adaptation of *Who's Afraid of Virginia Woolf?* He replied ironically that, although it omitted some things he felt were important, he was rather pleased with the adaptation, especially in light of the fact that a friend had called him to pass on the rumor that filmmakers were seeking someone to cast in the role of George and Martha's nonexistent son.

CINEMATIC POTENTIAL
OF THE ORIGINAL WORK

Renata Adler wrote, "Not every written thing aspires to be a movie." And, indeed, some plays and novels are more adaptable to the film medium than others. The style in which a novel is written for example, certainly affects its adaptability to film. Randall Stewart and Dorothy Bethurum point out important differences in the novelistic styles of Ernest Hemingway and Henry James:

> It is interesting to observe that two such influential prose writers as Hemingway and Henry James should be at the opposite poles of style: one (Hemingway) giving us the rhythms of speech, the other (James) literary convolutions found only on the printed page, one (Hemingway) elemental and sensuous, the other (James) complex and infinitely qualifying. Each style is admirably fitted for the purpose for which it is intended. James is concerned primarily with the intellectual analysis of experience. Hemingway's aim is the sensuous and emotional rendering of experience.

Because of these differences in their style, a Hemingway novel would be more easily adapted to the screen than a novel by Henry James. The last point made is especially important: Hemingway's sensuous and emotional rendering of experience is cinematic; James's intellectual analysis of experience is not. The difference in the two writers' styles and their adaptability to the screen can be observed in the following samples of their work:

Mrs. Gereth had said she would go with the rest to church, but suddenly it seemed to her that she should not be able to wait till church-time for relief: breakfast, at Waterbath, was a punctual meal, and she had still nearly an hour on her hands. Knowing the church to be near, she prepared in her room for the little rural walk, and on her way down again, passing through corridors and observing imbecilities of decoration, the aesthetic misery of the big commodious house, she felt a return of the tide of last night's irritation, a renewal of everything she could secretly suffer from ugliness and stupidity. Why did she consent to such contacts, why did she so rashly expose herself? She had had, heaven knew, her reasons, but the whole experience was to be sharper than she had feared. To get away from it and out into the air, into the presence of sky and trees, flowers and birds was a necessity of every nerve. The flowers at Waterbath would probably go wrong in color and the nightingales sing out of tune; but she remembered to have heard the place described as possessing those advantages that are usually spoken of as natural. There were advantages enough it clearly didn't possess. It was hard for her to believe that a woman could look presentable who had been kept awake for hours by the wall-paper in her room; yet none the less, as in her fresh widow's weeds she rustled across the hall, she was, as usual, the only person in the house incapable of wearing in her preparation the horrible stamp of the exceptional smartness that would be conspicuous in a grocer's wife. She would rather have perished than to have looked *endimanchee*.

Opening paragraph from The Spoils of Poynton,
by Henry James

Nick stood up. He was all right. He looked up the track at the lights of the caboose going out of sight around the curve. There was water on both sides of the track, then tamarack swamp.

He felt of his knee. The pants were torn and the skin was barked. His hands were scraped and there were sand and cinders driven up under his nails. He went over to the edge of the track down the little slope to the water and washed his hands. He washed them carefully in the cold water, getting the dirt out from the nails. He squatted down and bathed his knee.

First two paragraphs of "The Battler,"
by Ernest Hemingway*

Although the problems of adapting a play to the screen are not generally as great as those presented by the James novel, playwrights also have styles that affect the ease with which their plays can be adapted to

---

**Reprinted from "The Battler" by Ernest Hemingway with permission of Charles Scribner's Sons.

film. Tennessee Williams, for example, is a more cinematic playwright than Edward Albee, basically because his verbal imagery is more concrete and sensual, and because his plays contain speeches that lend themselves to visual flashbacks—such as the one describing Sebastian's death in *Suddenly Last Summer.*

PROBLEMS CREATED BY THE VIEWER

When we see a film adaptation of a favorite play or novel, we as viewers create many problems that work against our enjoyment of the film. First, our own experience of the play or novel is itself a creative process. We have locked very vividly in our minds strong visual images and impressive bits of dialogue from the play or novel. In a play, we may even remember the inflections with which the actors delivered the lines. Because we experienced them first, these images or bits of dialogue become the standard by which we measure all second efforts. Furthermore, we are not aware of the degree of our own selectivity. Because remembering is a very selective process, it is also a creative act. Unconsciously and a bit unfairly perhaps, we demand that the adaptation single out for emphasis or at least treat all of those things which are important to us—that is, everything our memory has selected from the original. We do not always mind if things are left out so long as they are not our favorite things. In a sense, we have the same reaction to many film adaptations that we might have toward a friend we haven't seen for a long time, and who has changed greatly over the intervening years. Mentally prepared to meet an old friend, we meet a stranger, and take the changes as a personal affront, as though the friend had no right to undergo them without our knowledge or permission.

FILM ADAPTATIONS OF NOVELS

The general problems discussed above influence our reactions to film adaptations of both novels and plays. But a complete understanding of the problems involved requires a deeper examination of the specific difficulties posed by the nature of the medium being translated into film. Therefore, to fully grasp the difficulties of translating a novel into film, we must look specifically at several characteristics of the novelistic form.

NOVELISTIC VERSUS CINEMATIC
POINT OF VIEW

The problem of point of view. Point of view is an extremely important factor in any novel, for the fictional point of view controls and dictates the form and shape the novel takes, and determines its area of emphasis, tone, strengths, and limitations. A change in point of view is almost as important in a work of fiction as a change from one medium to another, for the point of view in a novel determines to a large degree what the novelist can and cannot do. To appreciate the difficulties the filmmaker faces in translating a novel into film requires some familiarity with literary viewpoints. A basic understanding of each of the five fictional viewpoints should be provided by the brief descriptions and examples which follow.

1. *First person.* A character who has participated in or observed the action of the story gives us an eye-witness or first-hand account of what happened and his or her responses to it.

> Yes sir. Flem Snopes has filled that whole country full of spotted horses. You can hear folks running them all day and all night, whooping and hollering, and the horses running back and forth across them little wooden bridges ever now and then kind of like thunder. Here I was this morning pretty near halfway to town, with a team ambling along and me setting in the buckboard about half asleep, when all of a sudden something come swurging up outen the bushes and jumped the road clean, without touching hoof to it. It flew right over my team big as a billboard and flying through the air like a hawk. It taken me thirty minutes to stop my team and untangle the harness and the buckboard and hitch them up again.

> *Opening paragraph of "Spotted Horses,"*
> *by William Faulkner**

2. *Omniscient narrator point of view.* An all-seeing, all-knowing narrator, capable of reading the thoughts of all the characters and capable of being several places at once if need be, tells us the story.

> There was a woman who was beautiful, who started with all the advantages, yet she had no luck. She married for love, and the love turned to dust. She had bonny children, yet she felt they had been thrust upon her, and she could not love them. They looked at her coldly, as if they were finding fault with her. And hurriedly she felt she must cover up

*William Faulkner, "Spotted Horses" from *The Faulkner Reader* (New York: Random House, Inc.).

some fault in herself. Yet what it was that she must cover up she never knew. Nevertheless, when her children were present, she always felt the center of her heart go hard. This troubled her, and in her manner she was all the more gentle and anxious for her children, as if she loved them very much. Only she could not feel love, no, not for anybody. Everybody else said of her: 'She is such a good mother. She adores her children." Only she herself, and her children themselves, knew it was not so. They read it in each other's eyes.

There was a boy and two little girls. They lived in a pleasant house, with a garden, and they had discreet servants, and felt themselves superior to anyone in the neighborhood.

Although they lived in style, they felt always an anxiety in the house. There was never enough money.

Opening paragraphs of "The Rocking-Horse Winner,"
by D. H. Lawrence*

3. *Third-person limited point of view.* The narrator is omniscient except for the fact that his or her powers of mind-reading are limited to or at least focused on a single character. This character's thoughts are extremely important to the novel, for he or she becomes the central intelligence through which we view the action.

Although Bertha Young was thirty she still had moments like this when she wanted to run instead of walk, to take dancing steps on and off the pavement, to bowl a hoop, to throw something up in the air and catch it again, or to stand still and laugh at nothing—at nothing, simply.

What can you do if you are thirty and, turning the corner of your own street, you are overcome, suddenly, by a feeling of bliss—absolute bliss!—as though you'd suddenly swallowed a bright piece of that late afternoon sun and it burned in your bosom, sending out a little shower of sparks into every particle, into every finger and toe? . . .

Oh, is there no way you can express it without being "drunk and disorderly"? How idiotic civilization is! Why be given a body if you have to keep it shut up in a case like a rare, rare fiddle?

Opening paragraphs of "Bliss,"
by Katherine Mansfield†

4. *Dramatic point of view (also called the concealed- or effaced-narrator point of view).* We are not conscious of a narrator, for the au-

---

*From "The Rocking-Horse Winner," *The Complete Short Stories of D. H. Lawrence,*© 1961 by Angelo Ravagli & C. M. Weekley, Executors of the Estate of Frieda Lawrence Ravagli.

†Copyright 1920 by Alfred A. Knopf, Inc. and renewed 1948 by John Middleton Murry. Reprinted from *The Short Stories of Katherine Mansfield,* by permission of the publisher.

thor does not comment on the action, but simply describes the scene, telling us what happens and what the characters say, so we get a feeling of being there, observing the scene as we would in a play.

> The door of Henry's lunchroom opened and two men came in. They sat down at the counter.
> "What's yours?" George asked them.
> "I don't know," one of the men said. "What do you want to eat, Al?"
> "I don't know," said Al. "I don't know what I want to eat."
> Outside it was getting dark. The street light came on outside the window. The two men at the counter read the menu. From the other end of the counter Nick Adams watched them. He had been talking to George when they came in.
> "I'll have a roast pork tenderloin with apple sauce and mashed potatoes," the first man said.
> "It isn't ready yet."
> "What the hell do you put it on the card for?"
> "That's the dinner," George explained. "You can get that at six o'clock."
> George looked at the clock on the wall behind the counter. "It's five o'clock."
> "The clock says twenty minutes past five," the second man said.
> "It's twenty minutes fast."
> "Oh, to hell with the clock," the first man said. "What have you got to eat?"

> *Opening paragraphs of "The Killers,"*
> *by Ernest Hemingway**

5. *Stream of Consciousness or Interior Monologue.* This is a kind of first-person narrative, except the participant in the action is not consciously narrating the story. What we get instead is a unique kind of inner view, as though a microphone and a movie camera in the fictional character's mind were recording for us every thought, image, and impression that passes through his brain, without the conscious acts of organization, selectivity, or narration.

> *Stay mad. My shirt was getting wet and my hair. Across the roof hearing the roof loud now I could see Natalie going though the garden among the rain. Get wet I hope you catch pneumonia go on home Cowface. I jumped hard as I could into the hog-wallow the mud yellowed up to my waist stinking I kept on plunging until I fell down and rolled over in*

---

*Reprinted from "The Killers" by Ernest Hemingway with permission of Charles Scribner's Sons.

it. "Hear them in swimming, sister? I wouldn't mind doing that myself." If I had time. When I have time. I could hear my watch. *Mud was warmer than the rain it smelled awful. She had her back turned I went around in front of her. You know what I was doing? She turned her back I went around in front of her the rain creeping into the mud flatting her bodice through her dress it smelled horrible. I was hugging her that's what I was doing. She turned her back I went around in front of her. I was hugging her I tell you.*

I don't give a damn what you were doing

From The Sound and the Fury,
by William Faulkner*

Of the five points of view possible in a novel, three require of the narrator an ability to look inside a character's mind to "see" what he or she is thinking. Omniscient, third-person limited, and stream of consciousness all stress the thoughts, concepts or reflections of a character—elements that are difficult to depict cinematically. The basic problem is that these three fictional points of view have no natural cinematic equivalents. George Bluestone discusses this problem in *Novels into Film:*

> The rendition of mental states—memory, dream, imagination—cannot be as adequately represented by film as by language . . . . The film, by arranging external signs for our visual perception, or by presenting us with dialogue, can lead us to infer thought. But it cannot show us thought directly. It can show us characters thinking, feeling, and speaking, but it cannot show us their thoughts and feelings. A film is not thought; it is perceived.

Another problem arises from the fact that in three of the viewpoints—first person, omniscient, and third-person limited—we are aware of a narrator, of someone telling a story. The sense of a narrator, or a novelistic point of view, can be imposed (or superimposed) upon a film through voice-over narration added to the sound track. But this is not a natural cinematic quality, and it is rarely completely successful in duplicating or even suggesting the novelistic viewpoints. In film we usually simply see the story unfold. The dramatic point of view, then, is the only novelistic viewpoint that can be directly translated into cinema. The problem here is that few if any novels are written in the strict dramatic point of view, because this viewpoint requires so much concentration of the reader; he or she must read between the lines for the sig-

---

*William Faulkner, *The Sound and the Fury* (New York, Random, House, Inc.).

nificance or meaning. Thus this viewpoint is usually restricted to short stories.

The usual "solution" to these problems of adaptation is to ignore the problem of point of view, omit the prose passages stressing thought or reflection, and simply duplicate the novel's most dramatic scenes. The problem, of course, is that such prose passages and the point of view often contain much of the essence of the novel. This means that even though the filmmaker attempts to capture the novel's essence cinematically, it cannot always be done. The following examples of specific problems of adapting a novel into film should help to illustrate this point.

FIRST-PERSON POINT OF VIEW

The first-person point of view also has no true cinematic equivalent. The completely consistent use of the subjective point of view (with the camera recording everything from the point of view of a participant in the action) does not really work effectively in film. Even if it did, it would not really be an equivalent to the fictional first-person viewpoint. With the subjective camera, we feel that we are involved in the action, seeing it through a participant's eyes. But a fictional first person does not equate reader with participant; rather, the narrator and the reader are two separate entities. The reader "listens" while the first-person narrator "tells" the story.

In novels with a first-person point of view, such as *Huckleberry Finn* or *The Catcher in the Rye,* the reader has an intimate relationship with the narrator, who tells the story as a participant in the action. The writer "speaks" directly to the reader and forms emotional ties with him. The reader feels that he knows the narrator, that they are intimate friends. This kind of tie or emotional bond between narrator and reader is much closer than any a remote, unseen director who "shows" us a story in pictures might be able to create. The intimacy of the warm, comfortable relationship between a first-person narrator and the reader can rarely be achieved in film, even with the help of voice-over narration.

Furthermore, the unique personality of the narrator is often extremely important in the first-person novel, and much of this personality may be impossible to show in action or dialogue, for it is the aspect of his personality revealed by the way he tells a story, not the way he looks, acts, or speaks in dialogue, that comes across in the novel. This quality, which would certainly be missing from the film, might be called the narrator's essence, a quality of personality that gives a certain flair or flavor to the narrative style and that, although essential to the tone of the book, cannot really be translated into film. Consider, for example, the verbal flavor of Holden Caulfield's first-person narration from *The Catcher in the Rye:*

> Where I want to start telling is the day I left Pencey Prep. Pencey Prep is this school that's in Agerstown, Pennsylvania. You probably heard of it. You've probably seen the ads, anyway. They advertise in about a thousand magazines, always showing some hotshot guy on a horse jumping over a fence. Like as if all you ever did at Pencey was play polo all the time. I never once saw a horse anywhere near the place. And underneath the guy on the horse's picture, it always says: "Since 1888 we have been molding boys into splendid, clear-thinking young men." Strictly for the birds. They don't do any damn more molding at Pencey than they do at any other school. And I didn't know anybody there that was splendid and clearthinking at all. Maybe two guys. If that many. And they probably came to Pencey that way.

Because of the unique personality of the narrator, the first-person point of view affects the tenor of the novel not as a way of seeing but as a way of telling, a verbal essence which sets the tone and style for the whole novel. Thus it is virtually impossible to imagine a film version of *The Catcher in the Rye* without a great deal of voice-over narration running throughout the film. Although such approaches have been tried in film (one example is Henry Miller's *Tropic of Cancer,* which also has a distinctly flavorful first-person narrative style), for the most part such extensive use of voice-over is not very effective in films.

One fairly successful attempt in which the flavor of the first-person narrator was suggested by the voice-over narration was *To Kill a Mockingbird.* The voice-over, however, was used with restraint, so that the feeling of unnaturalness that often results when someone tells us a story while we are watching it unfold was avoided. And the personality of the narrator here was not as unique as Holden Caulfield's in *The Catcher in the Rye* or Miller's narrator's in *Tropic of Cancer,* so the burden of style and tone did not rest so much on the narrator's verbal essence.

THE PROBLEM OF LENGTH AND DEPTH

Because of the rather severe limitations imposed upon the length of a film and the amount of material it can successfully treat, a film is forced to suggest pictorially a great many things that a novel could explore in depth. In many ways, the film adaptation of a novel is like Ernest Hemingway's image of the iceberg:

> If a writer of prose knows enough about what he is writing about he may omit things that he knows and the reader, if the writer is writing truly enough, will have a feeling of those things as strongly as though the author had stated them. The dignity of movement of an iceberg is due to only one-eighth of it being above water.

At best, the film version can capture one-eighth of the novel's depth. It is doubtful that it can ever capture the seven-eighths which lie beneath the surface, but the filmmaker must nevertheless attempt to suggest the hidden material. The filmmaker's task will, of course, be much easier if he or she can assume that we have read the novel. But we still must accept the fact that there are dimensions to the novel that are inaccessible to film.

The long novel creates an interesting dilemma: Should the filmmaker content him- or herself with doing a part of the novel by dramatizing a single action which can be thoroughly treated within cinematic limits, or should he or she attempt to capture a sense of the whole novel by hitting the high points and leaving the gaps unfilled? If the latter is attempted, complex time and character relationships may wind up being implied rather than clearly stated. Usually the filmmaker must limit not only the depth to which a character can be explored, but also the actual number of characters treated. This may result in a necessity to create composite characters, who combine the plot functions of two or even more characters from the novel into one. Furthermore, in adapting the long novel to film, complex and important subplots might have to be completely eliminated.

Generally, then, the shorter the novel, the better the chances for effective adaptation to the screen. In length perhaps the short story is really better suited than most novels, for many short stories have been translated into film with little or no expansion.

Philosophical Reflections. Often, the most striking passages in a novel are those in which we sense an inner movement of the author's mind toward some truth of life, and are aware that our own mind is being stretched by his contemplation and reflection. Such passages do not stress external action, but rather lead to an internal questioning on the meaning and significance of events, taking the reader on a kind of cerebral excursion into a gray world where the camera cannot go. The following passage from *All the King's Men,* for example, could not really be effectively treated in film:

Two hours later I was in my car and Burden's Landing was behind me, and the bay, and windshield wipers were making their busy little gasp and click like something inside you which had better not stop. For it was raining again. The drops swung and swayed down out of the dark into my headlights like a bead portiere of bright metal beads which the car kept shouldering through.

There is nothing more alone than being in a car at night in the rain. I was in the car. And I was glad of it. Between one point on the map and another point on the map, there was the being alone in the car in the rain. They say you are not you except in terms of relation to other people. If there weren't any other people there wouldn't be any you, and not being you or anything, you can really lie back and get some rest. It is a vacation from being you. There is only the flow of the motor under your foot spinning that frail thread of sound out of its metal gut like a spider, that filament, that nexus, which isn't really there, between the you which you have just left in one place and the you which you will be when you get to the other place.

You ought to invite those two you's to the same party sometime. Or you might have a family reunion for all the you's with barbecue under the trees. It would be amusing to know what they would say to each other.

But meanwhile, there isn't either one of them, and I am in the car in the rain at night.*

Because *All the King's Men* is full of such passages, this one could not be singled out for treatment in voice-over narration. It is also highly improbable that the dramatic scene described here (the narrator, Jack Burden, driving alone in the rain at night) could suggest his thoughts even to a viewer who had read the novel.

When a visual image in the novel is more closely related to the philosophical passage, and serves as a trigger to the reflection, there is a greater probability that the filmmaker would be able to suggest the significance of the image to those who have read the novel, but even this is by no means certain. In the two passages quoted below (both from *All the King's Men*), the first gives us a rather clear visual image and could be effectively treated on film. The second passage is primarily the narrator's reflection on the significance of the visual image, and could at best be only suggested in a film:

In a settlement named Don Jon, New Mexico, I talked to a man propped against the shady side of the filling station, enjoying the only patch of shade in a hundred miles due east. He was an old fellow, seventy-five if a day, with a face like sun-brittled leather and pale-blue eyes under the

*Excerpted from *All the King's Men,* copyright 1946, 1974 by Robert Penn Warren. Reprinted by permission of Harcourt Brace Jovanovich, Inc.

brim of a felt hat which had once been black. The only thing remarkable about him was the fact that while you looked into the sun-brittled leather of the face, which seemed as stiff and devitalized as the hide on a mummy's jaw, you would suddenly see a twitch in the left cheek, up toward the pale-blue eye. You would think he was going to wink, but hc wasn't going to wink. The twitch was simply an independent phenomenon, unrelated to the face or to what was behind the face or to anything in the whole tissue of phenomena which is the world we are lost in. It was remarkable, in that face, the twitch which lived that little life all its own. I squatted by his side, where he sat on a bundle of rags from which the handle of a tin skillet protruded, and listened to him talk. But the words were not alive. What was alive was the twitch, of which he was no longer aware.

*   *   *

We rode across Texas to Shreveport, Louisiana, where he left me to try for north Arkansas. I did not ask him if he had learned the truth in California. His face had learned it anyway, and wore the final wisdom under the left eye. The face knew that the twitch was the live thing. Was all. But, having left that otherwise unremarkable man, it occurred to me, as I reflected upon the thing which made him remarkable, that if the twitch was all, what was it that could know that the twitch was all? Did the leg of the dead frog in the laboratory know that the twitch was all when you put the electric current through it? Did the man's face know about the twitch, and how it was all? And if I was all twitch how did the twitch which was me know that the twitch was all? Ah, I decided, that is the mystery. That is the secret knowledge. That is what you have to go to California to have a mystic vision to find out. That the twitch can know that the twitch is all. Then, having found that out, in the mystic vision, you feel clean and free. You are at one with the Great Twitch.

Summarizing a character's past.   In the novel, when a character first appears, the novelist often provides us with a quick thumbnail sketch of his or her past, as illustrated by the summary of the origins and past history of Billy, the deaf mute boy from Larry McMurtry's novel, *The Last Picture Show:*

> While the boys worked Sam stood by the stove and warmed his aching feet. He wished Sonny weren't so reckless economically, but there was nothing he could do about it. Billy was less of a problem, partly because he was so dumb. Billy's real father was an old railroad man who had worked in Thalia for a short time just before the war: his mother was a deaf and dumb girl who had no people except an aunt. The old man cornered the girl in the balcony of the picture show one night and begat Billy. The sheriff saw to it that the old man married the girl, but she died when Billy was born and he was raised by the family of Mexicans who helped the old man keep the railroad track repaired. After the war the

71. *Character without a past:* Sam Bottoms as Billy, the deaf-mute boy
     in *The Last Picture Show.* (Culver Pictures)

hauling petered out and the track was taken up. The old man left and got
a job bumping cars on a stockyards track in Oklahoma, leaving Billy with
the Mexicans. They hung around for several more years, piling prickly pear
and grubbing mesquite, but then a man from Plainview talked them into
moving out there to pick cotton. They snuck off one morning and left
Billy sitting on the curb in front of the picture show.

From then on, Sam the Lion took care of him. Billy learned to sweep,
and he kept all three of Sam's places swept out: in return he got his keep
and also, every single night, he got to watch the picture show. He always
sat in the balcony, his broom at his side: for years he saw every show that
came to Thalia, and so far as anyone knew, he liked them all. He was never
known to leave while the screen was lit.*

Here McMurtry summarizes a character's whole background in two
brief paragraphs. In the film version, no background on Billy is provided
whatsoever. Such information could not be worked into the film's dialogue without bringing in an outsider, some character who didn't know

*Excerpted from *The Last Picture Show* by Larry McMurtry. Copyright©1966 by Larry
McMurtry. Reprinted by permission of The Dial Press.

Billy, to ask about his past. But having characters spend a great deal of time talking about the backgrounds of other characters does not make for good cinema—it becomes too static, too talky. The only alternative is to dramatize such paragraphs visually. But this type of material not only lacks the importance to justify such treatment, it would also have to be forced into the main plot structure in a very unnatural manner. Thus, the kind of background information in the passages above is simply not suited to a natural cinematic style, and the past history of many film characters therefore remains a mystery. Because novels can and do provide this kind of information, they possess a dimension of depth in characterization that films usually don't have.

Cinematic compression of time versus novelistic summary. Cinematic techniques are capable of giving us the impression that time is passing; even relatively long periods of time can be suggested by a well-made transition or even a montage. But film is severely limited by its inability to summarize what happens in that span of time. This kind of summary is not a cinematic art, for it does not always lend itself to images and dialogue. In *All the King's Men,* Robert Penn Warren summarizes seventeen years of a woman's life as follows:

> As for the way Anne Stanton went meanwhile, the story is short. After two years at the refined female college in Virginia, she came home. Adam by this time was in medical school up East. Anne spent a year going to parties in the city, and got engaged. But nothing came of it. After awhile there was another engagement, but something happened again. By this time Governor Stanton was nearly an invalid, and Adam was studying abroad. Anne quit going to parties, except an occasional party at the Landing in the summer. She stayed at home with her father, giving him his medicine, patting his pillow, assisting the nurse, reading to him hour by hour, holding his hand in the summer twilights or in the winter evenings when the house shook to the blasts off the sea. It took him seven years to die. After the Governor had died in the big tester bed with a lot of expensive medical talent leaning over him, Anne Stanton lived in the house fronting the sea, with only the company of Aunt Sophonisba, a feeble, grumbling, garrulous, and incompetent old colored woman, who combined benevolence and a vengeful tyranny in the ambiguous way known only to old colored women who have spent their lives in affectionate service, in prying, in wheedling, and chicanery, in short-lived rebelliousness and long irony, and in second-hand clothes. Then Aunt Sophonisba died, too, and Adam came back from abroad, loaded with academic distinctions and fanatically devoted to his work. Shortly after his return, Anne moved to the city to be near him. By this time she was pushing thirty.

She lived alone in a small apartment in the city. Occasionally she had lunch with some woman who had been a friend of her girlhood but who now inhabited another world. Occasionally she went to a party, at the house of one of the women or at the country club. She became engaged for a third time, this time to a man seventeen or eighteen years older than she, a widower with several children, a substantial lawyer, a pillar of society. He was a good man. He was still vigorous and rather handsome. He even had a sense of humor. But she did not marry him. More and more, as the years passed, she devoted herself to sporadic reading—biography (Daniel Boone or Marie Antoinette), what is called "good fiction," books on social betterment—and to work without pay for a settlement house and an orphanage. She kept her looks very well and continued, in a rather severe way, to pay attention to her dress. There were moments now when her laugh sounded a little hollow and brittle, the laughter of nerves, not of mirth or good spirits. Occasionally in a conversation she seemed to lose track and fall into self-absorption, to start up overwhelmed by embarrassment and unspoken remorse. Occasionally, too, she practiced the gesture of lifting her hands to her brow, one on each side, the fingers just touching the skin or lifting back the hair, the gesture of a delicate distraction. She was pushing thirty-five. But she could still be good company.

The scene above, comprising only two pages of a 602-page novel could make an entire film by itself if treated in detail. Some of what happens to Anne Stanton could be *suggested* by a transitional montage, but no form of cinematic shorthand is capable of really filling in or summarizing a seventeen-year period the way the novelist can. Thus, film is capable of making clear transitions from one time period to another and suggesting the passage of time, but is not so effective at filling in the events that take place between the two periods.

NOVELISTIC PAST TENSE VERSUS CINEMATIC PRESENT TENSE

Regardless of the point of view, most novels are written in the past tense, giving the reader a very definite sense that the events happened in the past, and are now being remembered and recounted. In the novel, there is a distinct advantage to using the past tense. It gives us a clear impression that the novelist has had time to think over the events, to measure their importance, reflect on their meaning, and understand their relationship to each other.

On the other hand, even though it may be set in a framework of the past or take us into the past by way of flashback, a film unfolds before

72. *Cinematic past tense:* A voice-over narration serves to provide a structural framework for the film version of *To Kill a Mockingbird.* Since the voice is that of the adult Scout (at left) recalling the events of a childhood experience, the technique helps to give the film a sense of novelistic past tense.

our eyes, creating a strong *sense* of present tense, a "here and now" experience. The events in a film are not things that once happened and are now being remembered and recalled—they are happening right now, as we watch. Various techniques have been employed to overcome this limitation. Special filters have been used to create a sense of a past time, as with the Rembrandt effect in *The Taming of the Shrew,* the hazy and rather faded "memory" images from the *Summer of '42,* or the sepia-toned snapshot stills in *Butch Cassidy and the Sundance Kid.* In *To Kill a Mockingbird*, voice-over narration was used to capture the past tense, the sense of experience remembered. This was accomplished by a narrator's voice, obviously that of an adult, recalling childhood experiences.

Another important distinction is the time spent in experiencing a novel versus that spent in watching a film. If the novel is long, the reader may linger in its world for days or even weeks. He can control the pace and stretch the experience out as much as he likes; he can even reread passages that interest him greatly. He can take time out from the reading process, stopping or freezing the novel's flow to reflect on the writer's ideas at a certain point. In film, however, the pace is pre-determined. The visual flow, the sparkling stream of images moves on. Beautiful images, significant truths, strong lines of dialogue cannot be replayed. Thus the very quickness with which a film sweeps by—its quality of cinematic restlessness—distinguishes it from the novel.

OTHER FACTORS INFLUENCING
ADAPTATIONS OF NOVELS

Commercial considerations also play an extremely important role in determining whether or not a novel will be made into a film. A best-selling novel may virtually assure the producing agency that it will profit from making a film version, whether the novel in question has real cinematic potential or not. A unique commercial interrelationship exists between film and novel. The film version of a best-selling novel will profit at the box office from the public's familiarity with the novel. In turn, a screen version that is a box-office success will further increase sales of the novel. A first-class film adaptation of an unknown novel may even make such a novel a best-seller.

In recent years, there has been a steadily increasing trend toward the *spin-off novel,* a novel which is written *after* the screenplay. Such novels as *2001: A Space Odyssey, Last Tango in Paris,* and *Love Story* were written after the screenplays were completed. Spin-off novels not only sell well because they are based on popular films, but if released while the films are still playing, they help to promote box-office success as well. One of the best of these novels, Herman Raucher's *Summer of '42,* was released before the film and became a best-seller.

The popularity of a novel may also influence the filmmaker in the adaptation. If filmmakers know that a large percentage of their audience will be familiar with the novel, they can make creative decisions based on this assumption. Ideally, film adaptations of such novels should be fairly true to the novel: Creative tampering with the basic plot should be kept to a minimum, and the most important characters should be left unchanged and carefully cast. Most importantly perhaps, the director should attempt to capture the over-all emotional spirit or tone of the novel. If creative and selective choices are carefully made in terms of a true understanding and appreciation of the novel, the filmmaker can remind viewers who have read the novel of the weight and depth of the emotional and philosophical material submerged beneath the surface and make them feel its presence.

Occasionally an outstanding film, such as *To Kill a Mockingbird,* may even be able to communicate or at least suggest the meaning that lies beneath the surface to those who haven't read the novel.

Some filmmakers seem to make the opposite assumption: that very few filmgoers will know the novel. These filmmakers totally disregard the basic spirit or essence of the novel in "adapting" it to film, thus destroying the film completely for those familiar with the novel. In such cases, the film must be judged as a completely distinct work of art. This type of film, a very loose adaptation, may actually be better suited to the medium than the close adaptation, and may seem a better film to those not familiar with the novel. Thus, a viewer who reads the novel before seeing a film may have a distinct advantage when the film depends on the viewer's knowledge of the novel. But when the filmmaker so deviates from the essence of the novel as to create an entirely different work, reading the novel before seeing the film is a real disadvantage. By not knowing the novel, the filmgoer will be able to judge the film without preconceived notions, simply as a film.

It is often advantageous to see the film before reading the novel, for the film may provide a great aid to our visual imagination, and we may then read the novel with relatively clear-cut ideas of how the characters look and sound.

QUESTIONS
ON ADAPTATIONS OF NOVELS

After reading the novel, but before seeing the film, consider the following questions concerning the novel.

1 How well is the novel suited for adaptation to the screen? What natural cinematic possibilities does it have?

2 Judged as a whole, does the novel come closer to stressing Hemingway's sensuous and emotional rendering of experience, or James's intellectual analysis of experience?

3 How essential is the author's verbal style to the spirit or essence of the novel? Could this verbal style be effectively translated into a pictorial style?

4 What is the novel's point of view? What will necessarily be lost by translating the story into film?

5 If the novel is written in the first-person point of view (as told by a participant in the action), how much of the spirit of the novel is expressed through the narrator's unique narrative style—that is, the particular flair or flavor built into his *way of telling* the story rather than the story itself? Could this verbal style be suggested through a minimum of voice-over narration on the sound track, so that the device would not seem unnatural? Is the feeling of a warm, intimate relationship between reader and narrator established by the novel, as though the story is being told by a very close friend? How could this feeling be captured by the film?

6 Is the novel's length suited to a close adaptation, or must it be drastically cut to fit the usual film format? Which choice would seem most logical for the filmmaker in adapting this novel:

    a. Should he try to capture a sense of the novel's wholeness by hitting the high points without trying to fill in all the gaps? What high points do you think must be dramatized?

    b. Should he limit himself to a thorough dramatization of just a part of the novel? What part of the novel could be thoroughly dramatized to make a complete film? What part of the story or what subplots should be left out of the film version?

7 How much of the novel's essence depends on the rendition of mental states: memories, dreams, or philosophical reflections? How effectively can the film version be expected to express or at least suggest these things?

8 How much detail does the author provide on the origins and past history of the characters? How much of this material can be conveyed cinematically?

9 What is the total time period covered by the novel? Can the time period covered be adequately compressed into a normal-length film?

After seeing the film version, reconsider your answers to the questions above, and also answer those following.

10 Is the film version a close or a loose adaptation of the novel? If it is a loose adaptation, is the departure from the novel due to the problems caused by changing from one medium to another, or by the change in creative personnel?

11 Does the film version successfully capture the spirit or essence of the novel? If not, why does it fail?

12   What are the major differences between the novel and the film, and how can you explain the reasons for these differences?

13   Does the film version successfully suggest meanings that lie beneath the surface and remind you of their presence in the novel?   In which scenes is this accomplished?

14   Did having read the novel enhance the experience of seeing the film, or did it take away from it?   Why?

15   How well do the actors in the film fit your preconceived notions of the characters in the novel?   Which actors exactly fit your mental image of the characters?   How do the actors who don't seem properly cast vary from your mental image?   Can you justify, from the director's point of view, the casting of these actors who don't seem to fit the characters in the novel?

FILM ADAPTATIONS OF PLAYS

We can, of course, expect more similarity in a film adaptation of a play than a novel. To begin with, the problems of length and point of view are minimized. The actual running time for a play (not including time between acts or scenes) is seldom longer than three hours. Although some cutting in length generally occurs, and some selectivity and change may be apparent, these changes are usually not drastic.

The difference in point of view is primarily that theatergoers are bound to a single point of view because they must stay in their seats while the film version can use any one of the four cinematic viewpoints, spiriting the viewers back and forth, around and about, so that they see the action from a variety of viewpoints. Through the use of close-ups, the filmmaker can give us a sense of physical and emotional closeness, and of being involved in the action. This kind of closeness can sometimes be achieved in the small or intimate theater, but the point of view and the physical distance between theatergoer and actors remain essentially the same throughout the play.

In both mediums the director is able to comment on or interpret the action for the audience, but the film director probably has more options and techniques available for expressing subjective-interpretive views. Stage directors must rely primarily on lighting for these effects, while screen directors have at their command such additional techniques as fast motion, slow motion, distorting lenses, changes from sharp to soft focus, and so on. Some carry-over exists between the two media, however, for some stage productions have begun simulating certain cinematic effects. For example, a flashing strobe light on actors in motion gives the effect of the fast, jerky motion of the early silent comedies, and such devices are used by stage directors for this effect.

STRUCTURAL DIVISIONS

Films and plays differ, however, in the fact that plays have clear-cut structural divisions called acts or scenes, which influence the positioning of peaks of dramatic power and intensity. The end of an act, for example, may build to a roaring emotional peak, setting up a strong dramatic echo to carry over into the next act. Although film has *sequences,* which roughly correspond to acts in plays, the flow is continuous. One sequence flows smoothly into the next. Sometimes there are similarities even here, however, for the *freeze frame* gives a sequence a sense of ending in much the same way the end of an act might. The cinematic device also approximates the old effect of the *tableau,* where the actors froze themselves in dramatic postures for a few seconds before the curtain in order to etch the scene deeply in the audience's memory.

Such structural divisions may in some cases work well in both mediums, but sometimes an end of a stage act builds up to too high a pitch for a cinema sequence, and its power may seem unnatural or out of place. A perceptive critic such as Renata Adler can spot such problems, as she does in her review of *The Lion in Winter:* "The film is far too faithful to the play. It divides neatly into acts, has a long sag in the middle, is weakest in its climaxes."

SENSE OF SPACE

The change most certain to occur in a film adaptation of a play is the breaking out of the tight confining physical bonds and limitations imposed by the stage setting. Some kind of movement in space is almost essential to film, and to keep the image moving, the filmmaker will usually expand the concepts of visual space involved. He or she may find some excuse to get the action moved outdoors for a while at least, or will introduce as much camera movement and editorial cuts between different viewpoints as possible to keep the image "alive." In the film version of *Who's Afraid of Virginia Woolf?* for example, Mike Nichols moved the camera about constantly, dollying it down hallways and around corners for cinematic effect. He also extended space by adding the scene in the roadhouse, which required a wild car ride for getting there and back, whereas in the play, this scene was confined to the living room set. The film of *Long Day's Journey into Night* did not go to such extremes, but it employed camera movement and editing effectively to keep the image alive in what was essentially a very confining set.

Such changes may actually alter a play's total effect significantly. The fact that the movement in a play is narrowly confined and restricted may serve a powerful end. By keeping the physical action and movement static, by narrowing the physical boundaries in which the characters operate and bottling up the dramatic scene, the director is often able to intensify the conflict. The dramatic tension among characters in psychological conflict seems more explosive when it is tightly confined. For example, in the stage version of *Virginia Woolf* the guests, Nick and Honey, are virtually prisoners in the home of George and Martha. The narrow confines of the set stress this feeling. While the trip to the roadhouse in the film version adds a cinematic quality, it also relaxes this tension of confinement to some degree. Thus, dramatic tension created by psychological conflicts and developed through verbal means is often more potentially explosive because its physical setting is narrow and confined.

> 73.   *Four characters on a powder keg:* The tightly confined set of *Who's Afraid of Virginia Woolf?* makes the psychological conflicts at work even more explosive.

Film is simply better and more naturally suited to action and movement, the kind provided by physical conflicts on an epic scale. The restless need for motion in the nature of the film medium results in film's difficulty in coping with static, confined dramatic tension. Film builds its tension best through rhythmic physical action and especially by physical movement toward resolution. A typical example of cinematic tension and its emphasis on movement occurs in *Shane.* The tension is established through violent conflict in a prolonged fistfight between Shane (Alan Ladd) and Joe Starret (Van Heflin) to see who will ride into town for the big showdown. The movement and rhythm of Shane's ride to town further add to the building tension cinematically. It might be pointed out, also, that film can handle physical conflict much better than the stage. Camera angles, sound effects, and the ability to draw the viewer into close emotional involvement make a fistfight much more real than it could ever appear on the stage.

FILM LANGUAGE VERSUS STAGE LANGUAGE

John Howard Lawson wrote, "The nature of film is opposed to the modes of speech that are accepted in the theatre." Thus we can expect film dialogue to differ from stage dialogue. Generally, film dialogue is simpler than that used on the stage. Because the visual image carries so much more weight in film than on the stage, much that might require dialogue on the stage is stated pictorially in film. When the plot can be developed by showing what happens instead of having someone tell what happens, the filmmaker generally chooses the former. Because of the additional burden carried by the visual element, film dialogue may be simpler, more casual, and even less poetic. Poetic dialogue is much better suited to the stage than to the film.

To some degree, differences in dialogue may be related to other differences in the medium. For example, the more the concept of physical space is expanded, the more dominant action and movement become, and the less natural poetic dialogue becomes. Consider for example, Renata Adler's review of Zefferelli's *Romeo and Juliet:*

> The prose suffers a bit, sounding more like *West Side Story* than perhaps it ought to. In the classic speeches, one begins to worry about diction and wish the modern world would recede and let Shakespeare play through.

But Miss Adler has failed to take into account the basic difference between film language and stage language. Stage language—ornate, com-

74.   *Stage convention into film:* Sir Laurence Olivier as Hamlet during
the "Frailty, thy name is woman. . . ." soliloquy. (Culver Pictures)

plex, refined, and poetic—carries the major burden of communication
in a Shakespeare play. But in Zefferelli's *Romeo and Juliet,* we see a new
Shakespeare, a more cinematic Shakespeare than has ever been produced before, created by a director who understands his medium well
enough to recognize its limitations and utilize its strengths without holding the usual worshipful attitude toward the language of another medium.   Zefferelli's *Romeo and Juliet* is a visual, cinematic experience
rather than a verbal and "dramatic" one; the director captures the spirit
and essence of Shakespeare's play without using the entire text. The result is what Zefferelli intended it to be: good cinema, not good Shakespeare.

Thus language which is too refined, too elaborate, or too poetic is
generally out of place and unnatural in film. If film is to "speak" poet-
ically, it must do so through its primary element—the visual image, not
the spoken word.

STAGE CONVENTIONS VERSUS
CINEMA CONVENTIONS

Certain conventions that are perfectly acceptable on the stage cannot always be reproduced in cinematic form. Among these is the Shakespearean soliloquy. In Sir Laurence Olivier's adaptation of *Hamlet,* for example, the "to be or not to be" soliloquy is filmed in the following manner: Through some parts of the speech, Hamlet's face is pictured in tight close-up without lip movement, while Olivier's voice speaks the lines on the sound track as an interior monologue. At times, however, Hamlet's lips move, perhaps to show the intensity of his thought. Whatever the intention, the point is that the Shakespearean soliloquy, with its ornate, poetic language and structure, does not translate effectively as a cinematic interior monologue, and it seems equally artificial if done as it would be on the stage.

Another stage convention that cannot always be translated in cinematic or visual terms is retrospective narrative, the recounting of past events in stage dialogue. Under some conditions such material is ideally suited for the cinematic flashback, but not in all cases. In Universal's 1968 version of *Oedipus the King,* for example, the "official" story of the murder of King Laius, that he was killed by a band of robbers, is recounted and accompanied by a flashback showing the murder as described. The problem is that we know that Oedipus himself killed Laius and his escorts singlehandedly. Our difficulty with the flashback is that it pictures an event that did not really happen. When we see the scene in flashback, therefore, we are confused. We have seen a false version of the event take place before our eyes, but it has a semblance of truth that the *telling* of an event does not necessarily have. For this reason, the cinematic flashback does not work well with past events that are not recounted accurately or truthfully in dialogue. The fact that a later flashback may show the event as it actually happened does little to overcome the fact that the untrue flashback is not a natural for the cinema.

Surrealistic and expressionistic renderings of the stage set also cause difficulties in translation to the film. To some degree, they can be represented or suggested through the use of special camera techniques, such as unusual points of view and distorting lenses. But for the most part we expect the physical setting and background in film to be realistic, and we reject as noncinematic the kind of stage unreality or distortion of the set such as that in, for example, the *Cabinet of Dr. Caligari.* If *Caligari* were being filmed today, it would probably achieve its strange effects solely through the use of special filters and distorting lenses.

75.   *Expressionist distortion of the set: The Cabinet of Dr. Caligari,* 1919.

Whereas the stage audience expects and accepts the stage set or some part of it to suggest or represent reality without being real, the film audience is conditioned to real settings, and will accept no substitute.

These and many other conventions of the stage do not carry over into cinematic form, or at least cannot be replaced with an exact cinematic equivalent.

OTHER CHANGES

Several other types of changes can be expected in an adaptation from a play. Even if the actors were available, the screen version may not use the same cast as the stage play, either because some of the stage actors cannot be convincing in front of a camera, or because a big name is needed as a box-office attraction.

Because the big-city theater audience is more sophisticated than the nationwide movie audience, some changes may also be made with this

76.   *Poetic justice:* Sweet little Rhoda (Patty McCormack), shown here charming her mother (Nancy Kelly) in a scene from the film version of *The Bad Seed*, died in the end of the film but survived in the play. (Culver Pictures)

difference in mind. Some effort may be made to simplify the play in the film version, and harsh language may be censored to some degree. Endings may even be changed to conform to expectations of the mass audience. The stage version of *The Bad Seed*, for example, ends chillingly with little Rhoda, the beautiful but evil child-murderess who has killed at least three people, alive and well, still charming her naive and unsuspecting father. In the ending of the film version, however, she is struck with lightning; thus, the demands of the mass audience for poetic justice are satisfied. Such changes, of course, are less frequent since the motion picture rating code went into effect in the late 1960s.

QUESTIONS
ON ADAPTATIONS OF PLAYS

1   How does the film version differ from the play in terms of its concept of physical space? How does this affect the overall spirit or tone of the film version?

2   How cinematic is the film version? How does it use special camera and editing techniques to keep the visual flow of images in motion and to avoid the static quality of a filmed stage play?

3   What events does the filmmaker "show" happening that are only described in dialogue during the play? How effective are these added scenes?

4   Are the play's structural divisions (into acts and scenes) still apparent in the film, or does the film successfully blend these divided parts into a unified cinematic whole?

5   What stage conventions employed in the play are not translatable into cinematic equivalents? What difficulties and changes does this bring about?

6   How does the acting style of the film differ from that of the play? What factors enter into these differences?

7   What basic differences can be observed in the nature of the dialogue in the two versions? Are individual speeches generally longer in the play or in the film? In which version is the poetic quality of the language most apparent?

8   What other important changes have been made in the film version? Can you justify these in terms of change of medium, change in creative personnel, or differences in moral attitudes and sophistication of the intended audiences?

THE SILENT FILM

The silent film presents us with several problems with respect to film analysis. First of all, we seldom have the opportunity to see a silent film as it was intended to be shown; instead we see copies of these films that are duped, decayed, and corrupted, with much of their original brightness and impact lost forever.

Furthermore, most silent films are shown today without the musical accompaniment that normally was provided for the audiences of the silent era. Sometimes a complete score was distributed along with the film and played by a complete orchestra, as was the case with *Birth of a Nation.* Usually, a single piano or organ player simply improvised as the film was shown. Such music filled a definite vacuum, and the silent film without it has a ghostly kind of incompleteness. Thus, many of the silent film's best moments lose their impact because their rhythmic qualities and emotional moods are not underscored as was intended.

Even more important is the fact that we are not "tuned in" to silent films as a unique means of expression. Used to the levels of communication conveyed by the sound film, and conditioned to "half-watch"everything by the ever-present television, we have lost our ability to concentrate on purely visual elements. If we are to fully appreciate the silent film, we must master a new set of watching skills, and become more sensitive and responsive to the language of the silent film, especially its most expressive vehicles: the human face and body.

In the last years of the silent film, the expressive qualities of the human face and body had developed into a complex and subtle art; the slightest bodily movement, gesture, or facial expression could express the deepest of passions or the tragedy of a human soul. The actors of the later silent films thus were able to "speak" clearly and distinctly to their audience, not through the voice, but through a pantomime of eyes, mouth, hands, and bodily movement. With this highly developed art of pantomime, the silent film possessed an expressive means that was self-sufficient and capable of conveying a narrative through purely pictorial means with a minimum of subtitles.

The mass audience of the silent era learned the art of reading faces, gestures, and bodily movements by constant conditioning, but we must work a little harder at mastering this art. We are exposed to it in the modern film in "reaction" shots, but they are generally of short duration and often lack the subtlety of the best silent films. At its best, the "language" of the silent film could express some things that words cannot express, as Béla Balázs passionately points out:

> The gestures of visual man are not intended to convey concepts which can be expressed in words, but such inner experience, such non-rational emotions which would still remain unexpressed when everything that can be told has been told. Such emotions lie in the deepest levels of the soul and cannot be approached by words that are mere reflections of concepts: just as our musical experiences cannot be expressed in rationalized concepts, what appears on the face and in facial expression is a spiritual experience which is rendered immediately visible without the intermediary of words.

If we are to respond properly to silent films, we must become aware of the subtlety and the power of the silent film language—a language capable of both silent soliloquy (a single face "speaking" the subtlest shades of meaning) and mute dialogue (where a conversation takes place between two human beings through facial expressions and gestures). The silent film language can, through the close-up, reveal not only what is visibly written on a face, but also something between the lines, and it is sometimes even capable of capturing contradictory expressions simultaneously on the same face.

The language of the silent film is not restricted to the face, however, for the hands, the arms, the legs, and the torso of the actor also become powerful instruments of expression. The language of the expressive face and body is perhaps more individual and personal than the language of words. As each actor in the sound film has distinct voice qualities that are unique to his or her means of verbal expression, each actor in the silent film has a personal style of facial and physical expression of emotion.

One of the most powerful means of expression involving the whole body is the actor's walk. In the silent film, because it is usually a natural and unconscious type of expression of emotion, the walk becomes an important aspect of each actor's own unique screen personality or style. When used consciously for expression, it can be changed to express such varying emotions as dignity, strong resolution, self-consciousness, or modesty.

We should also recognize that the silent film is a product of another age and must be judged, at least to some extent, as a reflection of the society and culture of that day. Although these films express the mentality of their own age adequately, anything old-fashioned usually strikes us as comic at first, until we become accustomed to the older fashion or style. Then the strangeness recedes into the background, allowing us to see the more universal elements present.

Full appreciation of the *earlier* silent film is often made difficult by the broad and exaggerated gesturing and grimacing of the actors, who were still using the melodramatic techniques of the stage acting of that day. These unnatural and forced gestures and expressions seem ridiculous when seen in microscopic close-up. As the art of film acting evolved, actors realized the necessity for restraint in gesture and subtlety of expression, but a great many otherwise memorable films remain seriously handicapped by the older acting style.

All things considered, however, the silent film has much to offer us if we are willing to learn its special language and understand its own unique "sophistication." We can observe a different kind of acting skill, and see its evolution from over-blown exaggeration to the restraint and subtlety of a polished art. We can learn to appreciate the effectiveness of a narrative told clearly and quickly through purely pictorial means or with a minimum of subtitles. The absence of dialogue can make us more sensitive to film's visual rhythmic qualities. And, finally, we can learn to appreciate an art form that soars above the formidable barriers of language differences, for the silent film's greatest power is that it speaks a universal world language.

QUESTIONS
ON THE SILENT FILM

1   Is the acting style melodramatic, with broad and exaggerated gestures and facial expressions, or is it subtle, refined, and even understated?
2   What is unique about the acting styles of each of the major actors? Which actors depend most on facial expression, and which ones depend more on gestures and bodily movements?
3   How many different emotions are expressed by actors through their walks? Which actors in the film have unique walks that become a part of their acting style and the total personality they project?
4   How effective is the film in telling its story without words? How much does the film need to rely on subtitles to make the action absolutely clear?

77.   *Exaggerated gestures and expressions* in the early silent film, *Birth of a Nation.*

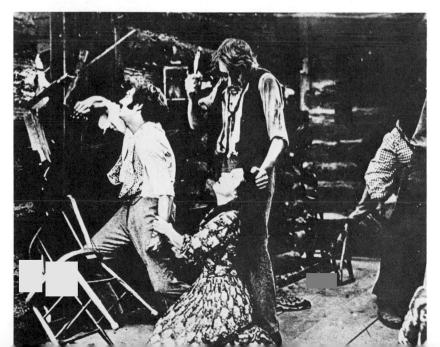

THE FOREIGN-LANGUAGE FILM

The most difficult problem, of course, in analyzing the foreign-language film is the language barrier itself. In spite of the fact that the visual image carries the major burden of communication in film, the spoken word still plays an important role. Therefore, some method must be used to help us understand the dialogue. There are two basic methods of translating dialogue in the foreign-language film: voice dubbing and the use of printed subtitles.

VOICE DUBBING

In the case of a French film which will also play in America, the voice-dubbing process works as follows: The actor speaks the lines of dialogue in his native language (French), and this dialogue is recorded and becomes a part of the sound track for the French version. For the American market, however, the dialogue sound track in French is replaced by an English sound track, where voices in English are recorded to correspond to the mouth and lip movements of the French actors whose images are on the screen. To match image and sound track, the translator very carefully selects English words that phonetically approximate the French words being spoken, so that the visual image of the French actor and the spoken words in English give the impression of being synchronized with each other. Perhaps the clearest advantage of voice dubbing is that it enables us to watch the film in the usual way, and, because the actors seem to be speaking English, the film does not seem so foreign.

But the disadvantages and limitations of the voice-dubbing process are numerous. Perhaps the primary flaw in dubbing is the effect that results from separating actors from their voices, often making the acting seem stiff and wooden. Renata Adler, a strong opponent of voice dubbing, states, "The process is hopeless, destroying any illusion of life, and leaving the actor somewhere between a mouthing fish and a blubbering grotesque."

Another problem is that perfectly accurate lip synchronization is never really possible. For example, although the French phrase *mon amour* might closely approximate the lip movements of a translation such as *my dearest,* the French word *oui* does not come close to the lip movements of the English word *yes.* Even if perfect lip synchronization were possible, another very formidable obstacle would remain: Each language has its own emotional character, rhythmic patterns, and accompanying facial expressions and gestures, all of which seem unnatural when another language is dubbed in. French facial expressions, for example, simply do not correspond to English words. Schools of acting are certainly influenced by the nature of the language spoken, especially by its general emotional character. Consider for example, the difference between the Italian acting style, with its emphasis on elaboration, and the Swedish style, which is much more restrained. Thus, because of the impossibility of perfect synchronization and the differences in national emotional temperaments reflected in acting styles, dubbing can never really capture the illusion of reality. A certain artificial quality often permeates the entire film and becomes a gnawing irritation to the viewer.

Furthermore, the process of voice dubbing eliminates the natural power, character, and unique emotional quality of the original language, the very sound of which, understandable or not, may be essential to the spirit of the film. The sense of reality that is lost in the voice-dubbing process returns when the original language is spoken, and the foreign film in its own language has a resonance and an authenticity that is impossible to achieve through dubbing.

If the voices are not carefully chosen for dubbing, another difficulty may exist. When the dubbed voices do not fit the actors and the general tone of the film, the illusion of reality suffers even more. For example, in the Russian film of *War and Peace,* the dubbing, according to Renata Adler, makes the inhabitants of Moscow sound as if they came from Texas. In such situations, a certain degree of authenticity might be saved by having the dubbed voices speak English with a Russian accent.

SUBTITLES

When voice dubbing is not employed, the foreign-language film makes use of printed subtitles. Here a concise English translation of the French dialogue appears in printed form at the bottom of the screen while the dialogue is being spoken. By reading this translation, we have a fairly clear idea of what is being said by the French actors speaking in their own native language.

The use of subtitles has several advantages over the use of voice dubbing. First, and perhaps most importantly, it does not interfere with the illusion of reality to the same degree as dubbing, even though the appearance of writing at the bottom of the screen is not completely natural. Because the actors are not separated from their voices, their performances seem more real and human, as well as more powerful. Furthermore, by retaining the voices of the actors speaking in their native language, the subtitled film keeps the power, character, and unique emotional quality of the culture that produced it. The importance of this last point cannot be overestimated. To quote Renata Adler on the subject once more,

> One of the essential powers and beauties of the cinema is that it is truly international, that it makes language accessible in a highly special way. Only in movies can one hear foreign languages spoken and—by the written word in sub-titles—participate as closely as one ever will in a culture that is otherwise closed to one.

Thus, subtitles interfere less with the viewer's overall aesthetic experience of the film, with the film's cultural integrity, and with its essential reality. Since much of the film's reality comes through to us intuitively even in a language we cannot understand, it is more important that the voice-image link remain intact than that we clearly understand every word of dialogue.

This is not to say that the use of subtitles does not also have its disadvantages. One of the most obvious is that our attention is divided between watching the visual image on the screen and reading the subtitles. If we read slowly or if the editing is fast-paced, we may miss important parts of the visual image and lose a sense of the film's continuity. Furthermore, most subtitles are so concise that they are oversimplified and incomplete. They are designed to convey only the most basic level of meaning in the dialogue, and do not even attempt to capture the full flavor and quality of the dialogue in the original language.

Another problem often arises from the fact that subtitles are printed in white. The white letters appear on the bottom of the screen, and if the visual image on the part of the screen behind the subtitles is white or light in color, the subtitles become completely illegible. This was the case, for example, in *Tora, Tora, Tora!,* where the white subtitles were often placed against the white background of Japanese naval officers' uniforms. Although it would seem to be a relatively easy matter to change the color of the subtitle letters so they stand out in contrast against the background, this is never done.

In spite of these disadvantages, the use of subtitles is still perhaps the best solution to the language barrier, especially in the slow-paced film that is edited in such a way that the viewer-listener-reader can perform all his or her tasks before the visual image changes completely through an editorial cut from one shot to another. In a fast-paced film, where editorial cuts occur at a very high frequency and full attention to the visual image is demanded, voice dubbing may be the only answer.

CULTURAL PREJUDICE

"If you think this picture's no good, I'll put on a beard and say it was made in Germany. Then you'll call it art." So read a subtitle from Will Rogers's *The Ropin' Fool,* made in 1922. The statement reflects another problem in the analysis of the foreign-language film. Because of some kind of long-standing American sense of cultural inferiority, we are much too prone to bow down and worship almost anything European. Thus, in the 1950s, many films that were not above the standards of American Grade B movies were lavishly praised by American critics and film buffs simply because they were made in France, Germany, or Italy. This is not to say that there were not some great films produced by these countries during that period, but a tendency existed to praise them all. At the same time, American filmgoers turned a somewhat jaundiced eye toward the films produced in their own country. Thus, any film made in Europe was automatically considered a highly serious and artistic statement, while the American film was generally ignored or dismissed as slick commercial trash.

The shoe also fits the other foot, for Europeans often appreciate certain aspects of American films that Americans cannot see or appreciate. For example, French critics were much more lavish in their praise of *Bonnie and Clyde* than were American critics. Jerry Lewis is also appreciated more by the French than by Americans. This phenomenon cannot easily be explained, but it is perhaps related to several factors. First, the language barrier may cause the audience to read things between the subtitles which are not there. At any rate, a more subjective and creative viewing is required when meanings are suggested rather than spelled out clearly. Also, a foreign director's cinematic style may have greater power and fascination because of its strangeness to the viewer, who is so used to home-grown varieties that they fail to move him in the same way.

Since a film gives us a reflection of the culture and society that produced it, the overreaction to a foreign film may actually be caused by the same kind of desire that makes us want to travel. Often we simply want a change of scene, a brief escape from the ordinary and the familiar, or we are curious about other people in faraway places, about their similarities to us and their differences. And sometimes we are simply fascinated by the different flavor, essence, or spirit of another country, by its dominant lifestyle. All of these factors play a part in our reaction to the foreign-language film, and serve to make our analysis and evaluation more subjective.

QUESTIONS
ON THE FOREIGN-LANGUAGE FILM

1 Which method is used to translate the dialogue into English—subtitles or voice dubbing? Was this the best way to solve the language problem for this particular film? Why?

2 If subtitles are used, how well do they seem to capture the essence of what is being said by the actors? Are the subtitles ever difficult to read because of light-colored backgrounds? Is the film's pace slow enough to allow for both reading the subtitles *and* following the visual image?

3 If voice dubbing is used, how closely do the English words spoken on the sound track correspond to the mouth and lip movements of the foreign actors? Do you get used to the fact that the voices are dubbed, or is it a constant irritation? How well-suited are the voice qualities and accents on the sound track to the actors with which they are matched? Does the overall emotional quality of the English translation match the facial expressions and gestures of the foreign actors?

4 How does the foreign director's style differ from American cinematic styles? What effect does this have on your response to the film?

5 How does the film reflect the culture of the country that produced it? How is this culture or lifestyle different from what we know in America? How is it similar? What different aspects of this foreign culture do you find most fascinating, and why?

THE HISTORICALLY IMPORTANT FILM

Another serious problem facing the modern viewer is the analysis and evaluation of the historically important film. This type of film, which proves to be significant in the years following its release because of the innovations in cinematic technique or style it introduces, must not be approached with the same expectations we have for the modern film. In many cases, the historically important film is neither effective aesthetically, nor as an immediate sensual experience. Such a film must be viewed and evaluated in a very specialized way, in terms of its historical context.

To place such a film in the proper perspective, we should consider it from at least two different viewpoints. First, we should be familiar with the films produced prior to the film being viewed, so that we can see it in relationship to what has been done before. In this way we will be able to appreciate the innovations in style or cinematic technique that the film introduces, and understand the significance of the film's contribution to the development of the medium. Next, we should examine it in terms of the modern film, to determine which of these innovations in style or technique have been assimilated by contemporary filmmakers.

It is in comparison to the modern film that the historically important film often suffers most, for it is likely to seem time-worn and full of cinematic clichés. Ironically, often the more time-worn and out of date a film of this type seems, the more significant it is historically, for such an effect generally means that the film's innovations had such a strong impact on later directors that they have become standard practice. The difficulty in appreciating such films lies in the fact that the power, freshness, and originality of the innovations are often lost between the time they are introduced and the time we see the film, not because the innovations are not effective, but because they have become commonplace.

Some historically important films, even those that are most frequently imitated, somehow retain their original power and freshness. When such films prove themselves to be great in their own right, and appeal equally to viewers in any time period, they are known not only as historical groundbreakers or milestones, but as classics, the power of which no amount of imitation can really destroy.

Sometimes, however, we may encounter a film that might be called a "false classic," which retains its appeal over a fairly long period of time and then suddenly loses it because other works in the medium suddenly surpass it. According to Dwight Macdonald, this is what happened to Cocteau's *Blood of a Poet:* "It suddenly showed its age, looking mannered rather than stylized, more affected than affecting, terribly thin in content and slow in movement."

A very different type of historical significance may be seen in films that are so unique that the innovations they introduce are never really imitated or assimilated generally into the medium. Such a film is *The Cabinet of Dr. Caligari,* which Dwight Macdonald calls "a unique anti-movie that came close to perfection by breaking all the rules." Such a film may be interesting to study because of its "one-of-a-kindness," or because of the rebellious spirit which produced it, but its value as a part of any evolutionary study of the medium is very limited, for it is really a stepping stone to nowhere.

QUESTIONS
ON THE HISTORICALLY IMPORTANT FILM

1 Based on your knowledge of the films produced prior to this film, what innovations in cinematic style or technique did this film introduce? Which of these innovations are still being used in the modern film?
2 Does the film seem crude, time-worn, or full of clichés when compared to the modern film, or is it still fresh and powerful? What specific elements or qualities in the film led to your decision?
3 What is the film's contribution to the overall development of the motion picture? What would the modern film be like if the innovations introduced by this film had never been tried? How have the innovations introduced by this film been polished and refined in the modern film?

THE FEATURE FILM ON TELEVISION

Watching a feature film on television presents a variety of problems that seriously hamper the processes of analysis and evaluation.

THE SIZE OF THE IMAGE

The most obvious of these problems is the reduced size of the visual image. Movies are intended to be shown in movie theaters on screens that are often enormous. Therefore, the drastic reduction in size that occurs when movies are shown on television greatly diminishes the effect of the visual image. For example, in a typical long shot, a lone human figure projected life-size may take up a relatively small space on the theater screen. When this image is reduced to the size of the average television image, the actor may not even be recognizable. When the wide-screen films are shown on television, the difference between the shape of the theater-projected image and the television picture tube means that between one-third and one-fourth of the image cannot be shown. A special editing device insures that the most significant part of each frame is seen on the television tube, but the cinematographer's art suffers nevertheless. In some cases, the reduced size of the image actually interferes with clear communication of the story, especially in situations where we must keep a clear picture of the actor's relationship to the setting, and the reduced image makes it impossible for us to get our bearings.

The reduced size of the image on television also adds to the difficulty of reading the subtitles of foreign films. In addition to the white letters on light background that caused problems even in the theater, we now find letters or words cut off at the bottom or at the sides of the television screen. The reduction of sharpness in the television image compounds the problem, making the reading of subtitles on television next to impossible. For these reasons, voice dubbing is probably the best means for translating the foreign language film on television.

MISSING SEGMENTS

Of equal importance is the problem of fitting the feature film into a shortened time period. When the film is too long for the time allotted by the television station or network, segments are simply cut out to make it fit the scheduled period. Since the original creators of the film, the director and the editor, have no control over what is cut, the cutting is seldom done with much concern about its effect on the artistic structure of the film as a whole. Thus, what the viewer sees on television may be a badly butchered shell of the film the director intended. Directors such as Otto Preminger have complained about the distortion of their art caused by such butchering, and some have even threatened legal action against the networks, but no real solution has yet been worked out.

COMMERCIAL BREAKS

The quality of the film experience on television is also seriously hampered by the fact that commercial breaks come at regularly scheduled intervals. This means that the film must be interrupted at such points, whether these times fall at a suitable place for a break in the film's continuity or not. Thus, the film's dramatic structure (its peaks and valleys of dramatic power, intensity, or tension) is fragmented in such a way that its effects are either weakened or distorted.

NETWORK VERSUS LOCAL STATIONS

The editing and commercial scheduling in network films should perhaps be expected to be better than that done by local stations. In many cases, however, the best films on television are the late-night movies aired by local stations. There are fewer commercial breaks in the late time slots and no definite time period is set for ending, so the film can be shown in its entirety. Even network films now often run over the rigid two-hour time slot, so that there is probably less butchering of films on television than in the past.

Other methods are used for showing an entire film on television. Sometimes, for example, longer films are broken in half and shown on successive nights or a week apart in the same time slot. This is certainly not the best way to get a feeling for the whole, but it may be preferable to mindless butchering.

A partial solution to several problems that affect the feature film on television is provided through the innovation of the *made-for-television film*. As the term implies, these films are designed for showing on television instead of in theaters. In watching such films, we should be able to detect at least four kinds of improvements in using them rather than the regular theater film on television:

1. The film should be structured with some regard for the timing of interruptions, so that the film breaks for commercials at dramatically appropriate times. Thus, each unbroken portion of the film should be roughly equivalent to an act or a scene in a stage play.

2. Since it is designed and written for the two-hour time slot, the made-for-television film should exist as an integrated and complete whole, exactly as the director intended it.

3. The problems caused by the small size of the television screen discussed above should be solved by the fact that the film is visually composed and shot with the size and shape of the television screen in mind. Since television is essentially a "close-up" medium, these films will make more use of close-up shots than would a film intended for wide-screen projection in a movie theater.

4.   Censorship has caused problems for many feature films shown on television. In the standard feature film, objectionable segments were simply cut out so they would not be seen by the television audience. With the made-for-television film, there should be no real problems with censorship, since the film is designed with the mass audience in mind.   Some experiments have been made with shooting two versions of the same film: one for the theater market, which can restrict its audience through the movie rating code, and a pre-censored version for the television market, which cannot restrict its audience. The television version of such films may differ radically from the theater version in such aspects as treatment of sexual material, nudity, coarseness of language, and violence. Plot changes may be so extensive that the two versions really have little in common, as was the case with one of these experiments, *Secret Ceremony*.

QUESTIONS
ON THE FEATURE FILM ON TELEVISION

1   To what degree is the film's continuity destroyed by commercial breaks? Which of these breaks occur at appropriate times in terms of the film's dramatic structure, and which breaks weaken the dramatic tension appreciably?
2   If you saw the film in a theater, can you remember portions that were cut out of the television showing? How important were these segments to the spirit or plot of the film? Can you justify these deletions in terms of the new medium or its mass audience? Were these segments cut out for reasons of time limits or censorship?
3   If the film is a made-for-television film, how successful is it in solving the problems of the theater film on television?

THE SOCIAL-PROBLEM FILM

The social-problem film is perhaps even more difficult to evaluate than the film of historical importance. The problem presented by both, however, is essentially the same—that of becoming out-dated or time-worn. But with the social-problem film, the aging process can occur very rapidly; the film can become not only dated, but completely irrelevant in just a few short years. This happens any time the social problem being attacked by the film is eliminated or corrected. Thus, in a sense the social-problem film can enjoy a long and happy life only by failing in its purpose, for its impact is generally lost as soon as the problem being dealt with no longer exists. This is especially true for the film that treats a narrow, topical, and very contemporary problem. On the other hand, the more universal the problem, the more widespread its effects, and the more resistant it is to reform, the longer the life span of a social-problem film directed against it. So long as the social problem exists, the film will still have relevance.

Once in a while, if a social problem film is artistically done it becomes more than a mere vehicle to encourage social reform, and may also outlive the problem it attacks. Such durability depends on the enduring qualities of the characters or character types involved, and on the quality of the story. Strong memorable characters and a good story will carry the social-problem film a long way, even after the specific problem dealt with no longer has relevance.

QUESTIONS
ON THE SOCIAL-PROBLEM FILM

1   Does the social problem being attacked by the film have a universal and timeless quality, affecting all people in all time periods, or is it restricted to a relatively narrow time and place?
2   Is the film powerful enough in terms of a strong story line, enduring characters, good acting, artistic cinematography, and so on, to outlive the social problem it is attacking? In other words, how much of the film's impact is caused by its relevance to a current problem and its timing in attacking that problem?
3   If the immediate social problems on which the film focuses were permanently corrected tomorrow, what relevance would the film have to the average viewer twenty years from now?

VIEWER-CENTERED PROBLEMS IN FILM ANALYSIS

In addition to the special problems presented by specific film types, serious obstacles to objective analysis and maximum enjoyment are often created by prejudices and misconceptions in the viewers themselves and by the particular set of circumstances under which they watch the film. A conscious awareness of the nature of these problems should encourage us to try to overcome them or at least minimize their effect.

CATEGORICAL REJECTION

One of the most difficult types of prejudice to overcome is that which forces us to approach certain types of films with a grim determination to dislike them. While it is natural to prefer some types of films over others, most of us can appreciate or enjoy some aspects of almost any film. We should also keep in mind that some films simply do not fit our preconceived notions of the standard categories. For example, one person might stay away from *Bonnie and Clyde* because he or she does not like gangster movies, another may shun *Patton* out of a dislike for war movies, and a third may ignore *Blazing Saddles* because it's a western. All would lose a memorable film experience in the process, for all three films are more than simple genre pieces. Even professional critics are subject to this form of prejudice, but they must see all kinds of films and are often pleasantly surprised, as illustrated by the following excerpt from Rex Reed's *Holiday* review of *Patton* and *M*A*S*H:*

> When Hollywood goes to war, it usually drops nothing but bombs. The movies rarely use the theater of war as a theater of ideas; most war films are, in fact, only mere excuses for various studio technical departments to flex their muscles with the latest developments in scar tissue, heavy machinery, and explosions. It was with more than a fair degree of sound loathing, therefore, that I approached the screenings of both *Patton* and *M*A*S*H.* Two new 20th Century Fox war flicks, I moaned, from the studio that bored us all to death with *The Longest Day?* Now I'm eating crow. They are both extraordinarily fine pictures that do more to raise the artistic level of the war-movie genre in the direction of serious filmmaking than anything I've seen in quite some time.*

Perhaps even narrower in their outlook are those filmgoers who have an inflexible attitude about what movies are supposed to be. This type of categorical rejection might be illustrated by two extreme cases. One is the filmgoer who says, "I just want to be entertained," and is offended if he sees a film which is grim and depressing. (Ironically, this same filmgoer may desire and even expect a stage play to be grim and depressing, but he feels that the motion picture's only function should be light entertainment.) The viewer at the other extreme is equally nar-

*Holiday Magazine (April 1970), vol. 47, no. 4.

row in his outlook; he expects every film to make some deep, serious, profound, and highly artistic statement on the human condition, and is often disappointed if the film is *not* grim and depressing, for a film which is not grim and depressing may be *entertaining,* and for him that is not the motion pictures' proper function.

Closely related to those who reject films categorically are those who set up their own rigid ground rules for certain films and ignore the intentions and artistic aims of the director. This kind of narrowness can easily be seen in *Time's* first review of *Bonnie and Clyde,* where the reviewer condemned the film purely on the grounds that it was not an historically accurate portrayal of the career of Bonnie and Clyde. In making such a judgment, he simply ignored the intentions of the director, Arthur Penn, and judged the film according to his own narrow critical framework.

Others may reject films because of equally ridiculous minor reasons. Some may stay away from black and white films because of their preference for color; others may shun foreign-language films because they have difficulty reading subtitles or because they cannot get used to dubbing that is not perfectly synchronized with mouth movement.

MISTAKING THE PART FOR THE WHOLE

Almost as detrimental to perceptive film evaluation as categorical rejection is the blindness caused by overresponding to individual elements rather than the film as a whole. An extreme example of this prejudice is the viewer who is infected with a near fatal case of actor worship or antipathy: "I just love all Roddy McDowell pictures!" or "I can't stand Doris Day movies!" Such extreme reactions are very common with some viewers, who fail to see the actor as subordinate to the film.

Less extreme examples of this same blindness include the overresponse to certain film elements, especially those elements capable of causing a strong audience response. The two ingredients most likely to cause this kind of reaction are sex and violence. Although some films are certainly guilty of exploiting these ingredients, and of overemphasizing them to the point of the ridiculous, this is not always the case; some films may demand the use of nudity and/or violence to tell honestly the story they have to tell. The point is simply that the use of sex or violence should not be condemned *per se*, without considering the film as a whole, and the perceptive filmgoer should neither reject nor praise a film simply with respect to its treatment of sex or violence. For example, the violent ending of *Bonnie and Clyde* did not, by itself, determine the overall quality of that film. And such films as *The Fox* or *The Virgin and the Gypsy* actually require some emphasis on sexual encounters to honestly tell their stories.

Filmgoers may also overrespond to such elements as the musical score or the visual beauties of the natural landscape. In *Dr. Zhivago,* for example, the song *Lara's Theme* and the beautiful ice palace made vivid and lasting impressions, and perhaps convinced many viewers that the film was better than it actually was.

GREAT EXPECTATIONS

Another subjective factor that greatly influences film evaluation is simply expecting too much from a film. We may develop great expectations for a film from a variety of influences. It may be that the film has received a lot of publicity for winning awards from such prestigious groups as the Academy of Motion Picture Arts and Sciences, the New York Film Critics, or the Cannes Film Festival. Even if the film has not won any awards, we may be aware that it has generally won widespread critical acclaim. We may also base our high expectations on the past performances or achievements of the film's actors or its director, or simply on their reputations if we have not seen their work before. And perhaps the most difficult factor to ignore is the word-of-mouth raves of our friends. The result is that our expectations are built up so high that the film can't possibly measure up, and our disappointment causes a negative reaction to a film we would have liked immensely if we had never heard of it until we saw it. Expectations may also run too high if we are particularly fond of a novel that is later adapted to film. Film can never completely reproduce the experience of a novel, and the more we like a novel the more likely we are to be disappointed with the film version.

Our own memory may even play tricks on us, and influence our reactions to a film that may have been a favorite many years before. With the passage of time, we sometimes build the remembered experience up in our minds to the point that the actual film, when viewed, seems rather drab by comparison. Although this self-indulgent nostalgia and glorification of the past is a rather natural human trait, we might simply try to see the wisdom of the man who was told that "*Gone With the Wind* just isn't as good as it used to be," and replied, "It never was."

AN EXCESS OF EXPERTISE (OR, THE MAN WHO KNEW TOO MUCH)

Although filmmakers go to great pains to make their films as realistic in every detail as possible, and usually hire technical advisors to help with special problems, there will still be a relatively small number of us who simply know too much for our own good, at least inasmuch as our reaction to a given film is concerned. If we possess special technical skills or inside knowledge about subjects dealt with, we are often unable to enjoy the film because of minor technical errors to which most viewers would be completely oblivious. Take for example a concert violinist viewing a film about a great violinist. The actor playing the part could be trained to finger the violin well enough to convince the average viewer, but the concert violinist would see at a glance how awkward or inept the actor's fingering actually was. More likely than not, his reaction to this minor detail would completely destroy his chances of enjoying the film. In such a case, the solution is simple: The expert viewer should not expect such a high degree of realism, and should try to enjoy other aspects of the film as much as possible.

THE INFLUENCE OF EXTERNAL FACTORS

Our response to any film is also determined to a large degree by external factors that have nothing to do with either our own prejudices or the film itself. Some of these factors can be controlled to some degree, while others lie completely beyond our power. To begin with, our mood, mental attitude, and physical condition at the time we see a film have a great deal to do with our response to it. If we are tired or sleepy, have eaten too much, or had a few drinks, we may lack the concentration required to understand or appreciate the film fully. If we have had to stand in line for an extended period, we may develop a grim set to our jaws and a "This better be worth it!" attitude, a prejudice which no film ever made could overcome.

Once inside the theater, other external factors come into play. We may find ourselves in uncomfortable seats, located directly behind the world's tallest man and directly in front of the world's loudest popcorn box rattlers. A bad sound track may make the dialogue difficult to hear, and a scratchy print may take something away from the visual effect. Waiting for the drunken or nearsighted projectionist to focus the image may also be very taxing. For the most part, however, the theater-goer has it over the film student, who must often watch films in hard classroom seats located in the worst acoustical environment imaginable. In either case we have little choice but to try to make the best of the situation.

Another factor that cannot be overlooked is the reaction we have to the audience around us. A crying baby or a talkative group nearby can certainly keep us from becoming totally immersed in the story on the screen. On the other hand, the reactions of the audience around us may have certain positive effects that are capable of actually intensifying our pleasure in the film. This is especially true with comedy; laughter is contagious, and we enjoy laughing more in a group than we do alone. Imagine the difference between seeing such a picture as *Tom Jones* in an almost empty theater, and seeing it in a theater packed with a highly responsive audience. This kind of community response or herd instinct may also work to some degree with fear and pathos, but if members of the audience overreact it may have adverse effects. One who laughs too hard at things that really aren't funny may make some viewers self-consious about their own responses, and loud sobbing or sniffling may cause others to resort to the defense mechanism of laughter.

When watching films either on television or at a drive-in theater, we lose the positive effects of the theater audience's reactions, and must face different types of external obstacles. Complete immersion in the film experience is impossible with television; if the drastically reduced size of the image and the frequent commercial interruptions can be tolerated, there are generally enough normal household distractions to make television film viewing somewhat less than satisfactory.

The facts that the drive-in screen is larger and there are no commercial interruptions do not make up for the drawbacks of drive-in viewing. Although the drive-in theater must certainly be recognized as a great American institution, and certain arts can be practiced there, it leaves much to be desired as a place to practice the art of watching films. Dirty windshields, fog, rain, insects flying through the projection light, carlights occasionally fading out the image on the screen, ridiculously poor-quality in-car speakers, discomforts caused by various weather conditions, and a multitude of other distractions all work against the drive-in as an ideal place for watching movies. Still, it must be admitted that seeing a great movie on television or at the drive-in is better than not seeing it at all.

Since the drive-in theaters still specialize in double features, we might consider how one feature may affect our response to the other. Although the drive-ins usually schedule two films of the same genre in their double features (two horror films, two comedies, and so on) studies have shown that such programming weakens the effect of the second feature. The less alike the two films are, the stronger our reaction will be to the second feature. In other words, ideally a light comedy and a horror show should be shown on the same bill so that we will have not only a fresh but also a contrasting emotional reaction to the second feature. If both films are of the same type, we will be drained of whatever emotional response is called for by the first feature, and our response to the second feature will be weakened.

The art of watching films, therefore, involves increased awareness of ourselves as uniquely individual and complex response mechanisms, reacting to forces both internal and external that are completely beyond the filmmaker's control. Although such forces lie outside the film itself, they play a part in a large number of our film experiences. We owe it to ourselves to recognize their effect on our responses to any film, and do everything in our power to overcome or minimize the negative effects such factors may produce.

QUESTIONS
ON VIEWER-CENTERED PROBLEMS

1 Do you have any strong prejudices against this particular type of film? If so, how did these prejudices affect your response to the film? Does this film have any special qualities which set it apart from other films of the same genre?

2 How much do your personal and highly subjective responses to the following aspects of the film affect your judgment: actors and actresses in the film, treatment of sexual material, and scenes involving violence? Can you justify the sex and violence in the film aesthetically, or are these scenes included strictly for box-office appeal?

3 What were your expectations before seeing the film? How did these expectations influence your reaction to the film?

4 Do you have some specialized knowledge about any subject dealt with by the film? If so, how does it affect your reaction to the film as a whole?

5 Was your mood, mental attitude, or physical condition while seeing the movie less than ideal? If so, how was your reaction to the film affected?

6 If the physical environment in which you watched the film was less than ideal, how did this influence your judgment?

---

chapter 10

ANALYSIS OF THE WHOLE FILM

In the previous chapters, we broke the film down into its separate parts, and considered several questions after each section to help us reach a better understanding of each separate film element. Now we must attempt to put the separate parts together, to relate them to and consider them in terms of their contribution to the whole film. Before we begin to put the pieces back together, however, we need to consider the whole process involved in the art of watching films, because the process begins in most cases long before we see the film.

PRECONCEPTIONS: REVIEWS AND OTHER SOURCES

How much should we know about the film before we see it? There is, of course, no simple answer to this question. Sometimes we have little control over how much we know about a movie before we see it, but some general guidelines on how to prepare for seeing a film might be helpful.

To begin with, we don't usually go to see a film that we know absolutely nothing about, for several sources exist from which we pick up general ideas and attitudes about each film. If we handle this information properly and do not let it overinfluence us, it can greatly enhance our viewing experience. On the other hand, if we allow these influences to completely dominate our thinking, the richness of our experience may be diminished.

One of the most common ways to gain some knowledge about a film before seeing it is to read reviews. In addition to helping us decide what films we want to see, reviews provide us with several different kinds of information and opinions. One of the most valuable functions of a review is to provide us with some essential factual information about the film. It gives us the name of the film, its director, the actors in leading roles, a brief summary of its subject matter and its plot, and even whether it's in color or black and white.

In addition to this factual information, most reviews mention or single out those elements in the film that are most significant and most worthy of special attention. They may also help us place the film in context by relating it to similar films past or present, or by relating it to other films by the same director. The review may even employ analysis, breaking the film into its parts and examining the nature, proportions, functions, and interrelationship of these parts. The review will almost always include some kind of value judgment on the film, some negative or positive opinions on its overall worth or merit. But we must watch very carefully how we read reviews at this point.

Before seeing the film, we should be primarily interested in a single question: whether the film will be interesting and enjoyable enough to be worth seeing. To answer this question, all we need to do is read several reviews of the film in a very superficial way, looking for the basic kinds of information all reviews provide, such as who directed the film, who the major actors are, what the basic plot or subject matter is. We will also pick up a very general picture of the reviewers' reactions to the film—that is, generally speaking, whether the critics liked the film. If we are interested in seeing the film, we should also take note of those elements or high points that the reviewers singled out as worthy of special attention, as well as how they place the film in context with other films, past and present. But we should generally ignore or forget the other ideas, opinions, analyses, interpretations, and subjective reactions presented in the reviews. Most importantly, we should not look too deeply into any single critic's evaluation or subjective reactions to the film. To do so may seriously hamper or limit our own response, so that we see the same things that the critic has seen, but nothing more. Not only does taking a critic's opinion too seriously restrict our personal and subjective response, it often destroys the independence of our judgment on the film's worth and weakens our critical perception in the process. Thus, we should prepare ourselves for seeing a film by reading some reviews before we go, but we should not overprepare to the point that our personal response to the film is overly influenced by the opinions of others.

Imagine how our view of *Bonnie and Clyde* would be distorted and limited if we paid serious attention to *Time*'s first review of that film, and restricted ourselves to seeing what the reviewer has seen.

... Producer Beatty and Director Arthur Penn have elected to tell their tale of bullets and blood in a strange and purposeless mingling of fact and claptrap that totters uneasily on the brink of burlesque. Like Bonnie and Clyde themselves, the film rides off in all directions, and ends up full of holes.

... Faye Dunaway's Sunday-social prettiness is at variance with any known information about Bonnie Parker. The other gang members struggle to little avail against a script that gives their characters no discernible shape.

The real fault with *Bonnie and Clyde* is its sheer, tasteless aimlessness. Director Penn has marshalled an impressive framework of documentation: a flotilla of old cars, a scene played in a movie theater while *Gold Diggers of 1933* runs off on the screen, a string of dusty, fly-bitten Southwestern roads, houses and farms. (One booboo: the use of post 1934 dollar bills.) But repeated bursts of country-style music punctuating the bandits' grisly adventures and a sentimental interlude with Bonnie's old Maw photographed through a hazy filter, aims at irony and misses by a mile. And this, if you please, was the U.S. entry in this year's Montreal Film Festival.*

Viewers who followed this reviewer's lead could end up focusing their attention on the historical inaccuracies, and miss the real experience of that film. Too much emphasis on the trees (or the post–1934 dollar bills) may cause us to miss the entire forest.

A similar phenomenon occurs in John McCarten's *New Yorker* review of *Shane,* in which the critic becomes so upset about the fact that Shane sides with the homesteaders that he builds his review around his defense of the cattlemen, mentioning them three different times in the review and thus neglecting more important elements in the film:

High among Hollywood's articles of faith . . . is the doctrine that the gentlemen running cattle in the Old West were somehow criminal because they objected to having their grazing land invaded by homesteaders, bean patches, and Monday workers. I was moved to reflect on these beliefs, all of which strike me as cockeyed. . . .

* * *

Stevens [the director] deals with the entirely orthodox notion that the homesteaders in Wyoming were given a highly unfair shake by the cattlemen. I'm not at all sure that he really believes this, however, because he takes so much pleasure in filming the cattlemen's noble, unfenced demesne.

* * *

. . . My original feeling about the glorification of homesteaders and the vilification of their betters on the range still holds, however tenuously.

*Reprinted by permission from TIME, The Weekly Newsmagazine; Copyright Time Inc. 1967.

It is certainly an odd thing when pictures about the cow country do their best to eliminate their principal ingredient.†

In reading reviews, we must always remember that criticism is a highly subjective process, and if we take any single review or series of reviews too seriously before seeing a film we will restrict our ability to judge the film independently. Also, if we rely too much on the reviews, we may completely lose faith in our own judgment and end up in a tug-of-war between critical opinions. Consider the dilemma we might face if we took all the reviews on *Bonnie and Clyde* seriously before seeing the film. *Time* summarizes the critical views on *Bonnie and Clyde* as follows:

> *Bonnie and Clyde* also stirred up a battle among movie critics that seemed to be almost as violent as the film itself. Bosley Crowther of the *New York Times* was so offended by it that he reviewed it—negatively— three times. "This blending of farce with brutal killings is as pointless as it is lacking in taste," he wrote. *Time's* review made the mistake of comparing the fictional and the real Bonnie and Clyde, a totally irrelevant exercise. *Newsweek* panned the film, but the following week returned to praise it.
>
> The *New Yorker* ran a respectful appreciation by Guest Critic Penelope Gilliatt, followed nine weeks later with an ecstatic 9,000 word analysis by another guest critic, Pauline Kael. In Chicago, the *Tribune's* reviewer sided with the nay-sayers. He called it "stomach churning"; the *American* said it was "unappetizing." But the *Daily News* acclaimed it as one of the most significant motion pictures of the decade; the *Sun Times* said it was "astonishingly beautiful." It seemed as if two different Bonnie and Clydes were slipping into town simultaneously.*

Reviews, of course, are not the only source of information and attitudes about films. The great amount of publicity released on almost every film can often influence our reactions. Television talk shows frequently feature interviews with actors or directors of recently released films. A great deal of important information is also picked up from the grapevine, the word-of-mouth "reviews" by friends who' have seen the movie. We should certainly consider all this information before seeing a film, but none of it should be taken too seriously.

Although it is almost impossible to do, and often highly impractical even when it is possible, seeing a movie "cold"—without knowing any-

---

†From a review in *The New Yorker*. Reprinted by permission;© 1953 The New Yorker Magazine, Inc.

*Reprinted by permission from TIME, The Weekly Newsmagazine; Copyright Time Inc. 1967.

thing at all about it—can be highly desirable. Without any kind of information about the film, we can watch it completely free of others' opinions about it and judge it purely on its own merits. But given the increased price of movies, few of us can simply walk into a theater on impulse, saying, "I think I'll take in a movie." If we get a chance at all to see a film this way, it is usually when the theater schedules an unannounced sneak preview of a newly released film along with something we want to see anyway.

THE BASIC APPROACH: WATCHING, ANALYZING, AND EVALUATING THE FILM

When we actually enter the theater to watch the film, we need to keep certain things in mind. The first of these is that we cannot freeze the film for analysis—only in its continuous flowing form is it truly a motion picture. Therefore, we must concentrate most of our attention on responding sensitively to what is happening on the screen—the simultaneous interplay of image, sound, and motion. Yet at the same time, in the back of our minds, we must be storing up impressions of another sort, asking ourselves "How?" "Why?" and "How effective is it?" about everything we see and hear. We must make an effort to become totally immersed in the "reality" of the film, and at the same time maintain some degree of objectivity and critical detachment.

As discussed earlier, if we can see the film twice, our analysis will be a much easier task. The complexity of the medium makes it difficult to consider all the elements of a film in a single viewing; too many things happen on too many levels to allow for a complete analysis. Therefore, we should try to see the film twice whenever possible. In the first viewing, we can watch the film in the usual manner, concerning ourselves primarily with plot elements, the total emotional effect, and the central idea or theme. Ideally, after the first viewing, we will have some time to reflect on and clarify the film's purpose and its theme in our minds. Then, in a second viewing, since we are no longer caught up in the suspense of "what happens," we can focus our full attention on the hows and whys of the filmmaker's art. The more practice we have in the double-viewing technique, the easier it will become for us to combine the functions of both viewings into one.

It is sometimes possible in film classes to view the entire film and then screen selected segments that illustrate the function and interrelationship of the different elements to the film as a whole. Then the film can be viewed again in its entirety so that the parts can be seen in the continuous stream of the whole. This practice can be very helpful in developing the habits and skills of film analysis.

Double viewing not only helps with our analysis, but in the cases of exceptional films, it should also increase our appreciation. Many critics, for example, strongly advocate seeing a film twice. For example, Dwight Macdonald wrote, in regard to Fellini's *8½*, "the second time I saw *8½*, two weeks after the first, I took more notes than I had the first time, so many beauties and subtleties and puzzles I had overlooked."

However, regardless of which option we have, single viewing, double viewing, or breaking the film into segments, we can follow basically the same procedure in approaching the film for analysis.

THEME AND THE DIRECTOR'S INTENTIONS

The first step in analysis should be to get a fairly clear idea of the film's primary concern, focus, or "theme" and to establish the director's intentions. To begin with we might try to classify the film in terms of its primary concern. Is the film structured around its action or plot, a single unique character, the creation of a specialized mood or feeling, or is it designed to convey an idea or make a statement? Once this decision has been made, we can move on to a clearer and more specific statement of theme or central focus, trying to pinpoint it and state it as concisely as possible. What we really want to know here, is: *What is the director's purpose or primary aim in making the film, what is the true subject of the film, and what kind of statement, if any, does the film make about that subject?*

THE SEPARATE ELEMENTS
AND THEIR RELATIONSHIP TO THE WHOLE

Once we have tentatively made our decision about the film's theme or central concern and the director's intentions in the film, and have stated the theme as concisely and precisely as possible, we should move on to see how well our decisions stand up under a complete analysis of all film elements. After we have tried to answer all the applicable and relevant questions relating to each separate element, we are prepared to relate each element to the whole. The basic question here is this: *How do all the separate elements of the film relate to and contribute to the theme, central purpose, or total effect?* Answering this question involves at least some consideration of all the elements in the film, although the contribution of some will be much greater than others. Every element should be considered at this point: story, dramatic structure, symbolism, characterization, conflict, setting, title, irony, cinematography, editing, film type and size, sound effects, dialogue, the musical score, the acting, and the film's overall style.

If we can see clear and logical relationships between each element and the theme or purpose, then we may assume that our decision on the film's theme was valid. If we cannot see these clear relationships, however, we may need to reassess our original understanding of the theme and modify it to fit the patterns and interrelationships we see among the individual film elements.

Once our analysis at this level is complete and we have satisfied ourselves that we understand the film as a unified work of art, ordered and structured around a central purpose of some kind, we are almost ready to move on to an evaluation process. In other words, once we feel that we understand the director's intentions and have a pretty clear idea of how he went about carrying those intentions out, we are free to make some kind of judgment on whether he succeeded or failed in his purpose, and to what extent he accomplished what he set out to do.

THE FILM'S LEVEL OF AMBITION

Because it is closely related to the director's intention, however, there is one factor to consider before beginning an objective evaluation: the film's level of ambition. It is grossly unfair to judge a film that seeks only to entertain as though it were intended as the ultimate in serious cinematic art. Thus, we must adjust our expectations for the film to the level of communication at which the film is aimed. Renata Adler describes the need for this adjustment as follows:

> . . . If a movie stars Doris Day, or if it is directed by John Wayne, the reviewer tries to put himself in a Day or Wayne sympathetic frame of mind and argue, on other grounds, that the film is better Day or lesser Wayne, but once the ingredients are fairly named, the reader knows and is freed to his taste. The same with Luis Buñuel. Of course, if you have a film that stars Doris Day *and* is directed by Luis Buñuel—and comparable situations with great directors do arise the critical inventory part gets complicated.

I think it is absolutely essential in a review to establish the level of ambition that a film is at, to match it, if possible with the level of your own, and then to adjust your tone of voice. There is no point in admiring an Elvis Presley film in the same tone of voice as a George C. Scott—or in treating simple lapses of competence with the same indignation one has for what seem to be failures of taste and integrity.*

This is not to say that we should give up our own standards or ground rules for what makes a good film. But we should make some attempt to judge the film in terms of what the director was trying to do and the level on which he was trying to communicate before we apply our own yardsticks of evaluation. Therefore, before we make any kind of objective evaluation we must consider this question: *What is the film's "level of ambition"?*

OBJECTIVE EVALUATION OF THE FILM

Once we have clearly established the theme, the director's intentions, and the level of ambition, and have seen how the elements function together to contribute to the theme, we are ready to begin our objective evaluation of the film. The overall question to consider is simply this: *In terms of the director's intentions and the film's level of ambition, how well does the film succeed?* After considering this question, we must review our earlier assessment of the effectiveness of all individual film elements to determine the effect each element has on our answer to this question. Once we have done this, we can proceed to the next question: *Why does it succeed or fail?* In attempting to answer this question, we should be as specific as possible, determining not only "why?" but "where?" Here we should look into individual elements for strengths and weaknesses, deciding which parts or elements of the film contribute the most to the film's success or failure: *Which elements or parts make the strongest contribution to the theme and why? Which elements or parts fail to function effectively in carrying out the director's intentions? Why do they fail?* We must be careful here to weigh each strength and weakness in terms of its overall effect on the film, avoiding petty nit-picking such as concentrating on slight technical flaws and the like.

And, since we are making an objective evaluation of the film, we should be prepared to defend each decision with a logical argument,

---

*From *A Year in the Dark* by Renata Adler. © 1969 by The New York Times Company. Reprinted by permission.

based on or supportable by our analysis as a whole. We must explain *why* something works well or *why* a given scene fails to achieve its potential. In every part of this evaluation we should be as logical and rational as possible, defending each value judgment with a just argument. When called for, these judgments should always be made in terms of acceptable critical standards, value systems, or criteria of measurement.

SUBJECTIVE EVALUATION OF THE FILM

Up to this point, we have been using a systematic and reasonable critical methodology. But hopefully, we have done so with the full awareness that we cannot reduce art to reason, or make it a simple matter of $2 + 2 = 4$. Our reaction to films is much more complex than this, for we are human beings, not analytical computers, and we know that much of art is intuitive, emotional, and personal. Thus our reaction to it will include strong feelings, prejudices, and biases. It will be colored by our own experiences in life, by our moral and social conditioning, our degree of sophistication, our age, the time and place in which we live, and by every other unique aspect of our personality. Now that we have completed our objective analysis and evaluation, we are ready to allow ourselves the luxury of leaving the rationally ordered framework and describe the nature and intensity of our own response to the film. *What were your personal reactions to the film? What are your personal reasons for liking it or disliking it?*

QUESTIONS
ON ANALYSIS OF THE WHOLE FILM

Overall Analysis and Evaluation

1 What is the director's purpose or primary aim in making the film?
2 What is the true subject of the film, and what kind of statement, if any, does the film make about that subject?
3 How do all the separate elements of the film relate to and contribute to the theme, central purpose, or total effect?
4 What is the film's "level of ambition"?
5 In terms of the director's intentions and the film's level of ambition, how well does the film succeed in what it tries to do? Why does it succeed or fail?

6   What elements or parts make the strongest contribution to the theme and why?   What elements or parts fail to function effectively in carrying out the director's intentions?   Why do they fail?

7   What were your *personal* reactions to the film;   What are your *personal* reasons for liking it or disliking it?

OTHER APPROACHES TO ANALYSIS, EVALUATION, AND DISCUSSION

Once we have completed our personal and subjective evaluation of the film's worth, we may want to approach the film from several rather specialized angles or critical perspectives.   These exercises in criticism might be especially meaningful as guidelines for classroom discussion. Each of the approaches described has its own focus, bias, perspective and intentions, and each looks for something a little different in the film.

THE FILM AS A TECHNICAL ACHIEVEMENT

If we have sufficient understanding of the film medium and the techniques of filmmaking, we may want to focus our attention on the technical devices that the filmmaker uses and the importance of these techniques to the film's overall impact.   In evaluating the film in this manner, we are more concerned with *how* the director communicates, not what he or she communicates or why.   By these standards, the most perfect film is that which best utilizes the potential of the medium.   Films such as *Citizen Kane* and *2001: A Space Odyssey* both rate very high in this respect.   Questions that we should consider with this kind of focus in mind follow:

  1.   How well does the film utilize the full potential of the medium?

  2.   What inventive techniques are employed, and how impressive are the effects they create?

  3.   Judged as a whole, is the film technically superior or inferior?

  4.   Technically speaking, what are the film's strongest points and what are its weakest?

THE FILM AS A SHOWCASE FOR THE ACTOR—
THE PERSONALITY CULT

If our primary interest is in actors, acting performances, and screen personalities, we may want to focus our attention on the performances of the major actors in the film, especially the established "stars" or film personalities. In this approach, we assume that the leading actor has the most important effect on the quality of the film, that he "carries" the film on the basis of his acting skill or personality. Judged through this framework, the best film is that in which the basic personality, acting style, or personal idiosyncrasies of the leading actor in the cast are best projected. In this approach, then, we look on the film as a showcase for the actor's talent, and think of it as a "John Wayne movie," or a "Bogart movie." To give this approach validity, we must of course be familiar with a number of other films starring the same actor, so that we can evaluate his performance in comparison with the roles he has played in the past. To evaluate a film through this approach, we might consider the following questions:

1. How well are the actor's special personality traits or acting skills suited to the character he plays and to the action of the film?

2. Does this role seem tailored to fit his personality and skills, or does he "bend" his personality to fit the role?

3. How powerful is his performance in this film compared with his performance in other starring roles?

4. What similarities or significant differences do you see in the character he plays in this film and the characters he has played in other films?

5. Judging in terms of past performances, how difficult and demanding is this particular role for the actor?

THE FILM AS A PRODUCT OF A SINGLE
CREATIVE MIND—THE AUTEUR APPROACH

In this approach we focus on the style, technique, and philosophy of the film's dominant creative personality—the director who acts as an *auteur* (author), a complete filmmaker whose genius, style, and creative personality are reflected in every aspect of the film. Since all truly great directors impose their personalities on every aspect of their films the film is viewed not as an objective work of art, but as a reflection of the person who made it, especially in terms of his or her artistic vision or style. A good movie according to this theory is therefore one which bears the trademark of the director and reflects the personality of a single creative genius in every element—the story, the casting, the cinematography, the lighting, the music, the sound effects, the editing, and so on. And the film itself must not be judged alone, but as a part of the whole canon of the director's works. In evaluating a film from this approach, then, we should consider the following questions:

1.   In terms of this film and other films by the same director, how would you describe the directorial style?

2.   How does each element of this film reflect the director's artistic vision, style, and overall philosophy of film or even his or her philosophy of life itself?

3.   What basic similarities does this film have to other films by the same director? How is it significantly different?

4.   Where in the film do we get the strongest impressions of the director's personality showing through, of his or her unique creative intelligence being imposed on the material?

5.   What is the special quality of this film as compared to the other works in the director's canon? As compared to the other films, how well does this film reflect the philosophy, personality, and artisitic vision of the person who made it?

6.   Does this film suggest a growth in some new direction away from the other films? If so, describe that new direction.

THE FILM AS A MORAL, PHILOSOPHICAL, OR SOCIAL STATEMENT

In this approach, often called the *humanistic approach,* we focus our attention on the statement the film makes, and in this respect the best films are those built around a statement that teaches us something. In this kind of evaluation, we must determine if the action and the characters have significance or meaning beyond the context of the film itself—significance in a moral, social, or philosophical sense—that helps us to gain a clearer understanding of some aspect of life, human nature, the human experience, or the human condition. In the humanistic approach, therefore, we judge the film for the most part on its power as an idea with intellectual, moral, social, or cultural importance, and on how effectively it moves us to a different belief or action that will somehow influence our lives for the better. Acting, cinematography, lighting, editing, sound, and so on, are all judged in terms of how effectively they contribute to the communication of the film's message, and the overall value of the film depends on the significance of its theme. We might consider the following questions in evaluating a film by the humanistic approach:

1. What is the statement the film makes, and how significant is the lesson or "truth" we learn from it?

2. How effectively do the different film elements function to get the film's message across?

3. How does the film attempt to influence our lives for the better? What changes in our beliefs and actions does it attempt to bring about?

4. Is the message stated by the film universal, or is it restricted to our own time and place?

5. How relevant is the theme to our own experience?

THE FILM AS AN EMOTIONAL OR SENSUAL EXPERIENCE

In this approach, which is the opposite of the more intellectual humanistic approach, we judge a film in terms of the reality and intensity of its impact on the viewer. The stronger the emotional or sensual experience provided by the film, the better the film is. Generally, with this approach the preference is for films that stress fast-paced action, excitement, and adventure. Since a strong physical or visceral response is desired, a film is judged good if it is simple, hard-hitting, and direct, like a punch in the jaw. Those who favor this approach show a clear anti-intellectual bias, for they want no messages in their films, no significance beyond the immediate experience. They prefer pure action, excitement, and the simple, direct, unpretentious telling of a story. If the experience provided by the film is extremely realistic, vivid, and intense, the film is considered good. In evaluating a film by these standards, we might consider the following questions:

1. How powerful or intense is the film as an emotional or sensual experience?

2. Where in the film are we completely wrapped up and involved in the reality of the film? Where is the film weakest in emotional and sensual intensity?

3. What role does each of the film elements play in creating a hard-hitting emotional and sensual response?

It would be impractical to approach every film we see from the same narrow critical framework drawn strictly from one or another of the approaches discussed here. To do so would severely hamper our evaluation. To be fair in any approach, we must consider the director's intentions and attempt to match our approach to them. Consider the result, for example, if we were to apply the humanistic approach to a James Bond film or an Alfred Hitchcock film.

Vincent Canby's *New York Times* review of Hitchcock's *Frenzy* demonstrates the difficulty of judging a Hitchcock film through a humanistic frame of reference:

> Alfred Hitchcock is enough to make one despair. After 50 years of directing films, he's still not perfect. He refuses to be serious, at least in any easily recognizable way that might win him the Jean Hersholt Award, or even an Oscar for directorial excellence. Take, for example, his new film, "Frenzy," a suspense melodrama about a homicidal maniac, known as the Necktie Killer, who is terrorizing London, and the wrong man who is chased, arrested and convicted for the crimes. What does it tell us about the Human Condition, Love, the Third World, God, Structural Politics, Environmental Violence, Justice, Conscience, Aspects of Underdevelopment, Discrimination, Radical Stupor, Religious Ecstasy or Conservative Commitment? Practically nothing.
>
> It is immensely entertaining, yet it's possible to direct at "Frenzy" the same charges that have been directed at some of his best films in the past, meaning that it's "not significant," that "what it has to say about people and human nature is superficial and glib," that it "does nothing but give out a good time," that it's "wonderful while you're in the theater and impossible to remember 24 hours later."*

Because Hitchcock is a strong personality and a strong director, who imposes his own stylistic trademark on every film he makes, his films can be profitably discussed from the *auteur* viewpoint, and "the film as emotional or sensual experience" approach would be equally if not more appropriate to the Hitchcock film. Because he stresses the subordinate role of the actor to the film, ("all actors should be treated

---

*From "Hitchcock: The Agony Is Exquisite" by Vincent Canby. ©1972 by The New York Times Company. Reprinted by permission.

like cattle"), the "personality cult" approach would be totally worthless, and, as seen above, the humanistic approach leads nowhere. Again, the point here is that the most valid of these approaches is the one that best matches the director's intentions.

THE ECLECTIC APPROACH

One approach to film evaluation, however, is more valid than any one of the narrow critical approaches described above. This is the *eclectic approach,* which accepts the fact that all five approaches have some validity, and simply uses whatever aspects of these approaches are appropriate and useful for the evaluation of a film under consideration. In the eclectic evaluation, we might begin by asking ourselves simply whether the film is good or not, and then trying to support our decision with our answers to several of these questions:

1. How technically sound and sophisticated is the film, and how well does it utilize the full potential of the medium?

2. How powerful is the star's performance?

3. How well does the film reflect the philosophy, personality, and artistic vision of the person who made it?

4. How worthwhile or significant is the statement made by the film, and how powerfully is it stated?

5. How effective is the film as an emotional or sensual experience?

QUESTIONS
ON OTHER APPROACHES TO THE FILM FOR
ANALYSIS, EVALUATION, AND DISCUSSION

The Film as a Technical Achievement

1 How well does the film utilize the full potential of the medium?
2 What inventive techniques are employed, and how impressive are the effects they create?
3 Judged as a whole, is the film technically superior or inferior?
4 Technically speaking, what are its strongest points and what are its weakest?

The Film as a Showcase for the Actor—the Personality Cult

1 How well are the actor's special personality traits or acting skills suited to the character he plays and to the action of the film?
2 Does this role seem tailored to fit his personality and skills, or does he "bend" his personality to fit the role?
3 How powerful is his performance in this film. compared to his performance in other starring roles?
4 What similarities or significant differences do you see in the character he plays in this film and the characters he has played in other films?
5 Judging in terms of past performances, how difficult and demanding is this particular role for the actor?

The Film as a Product of a Single Creative Mind—the Auteur

1 In terms of this film and other films by the same director, how would you describe his style?
2 How does each element of this film serve to reflect the director's artistic vision, his style, and his overall philosophy of film or even his philosophy of life itself?
3 What basic similarities does this film have to other films by the same director? How is it significantly different?
4 Where in the film do we get the strongest impressions of the director's personality showing through, imposing his unique creative intelligence on the material?
5 What is the quality of this film compared to the other works in his canon? As compared to his other films, how well does this film reflect the philosophy, personality, and artistic vision of the man who made it?
6 Does this film suggest a growth in some new direction from his other films? If so, describe that new direction.

The Film as a Moral, Philosophical, or Social Statement

1 What is the statement the film makes, and how significant is the lesson or "truth" we learn from it?
2 How effectively do the different film elements function to get the film's message across?
3 How does the film attempt to influence our lives for the better? What changes in our beliefs and actions does it bring about?

4   Is the message stated by the film universal, or is it restricted to our own time and place?

5   How relevant is the theme to our own experience?

The Film as an Emotional or Sensual Experience

1   How powerful or intense is the film as an emotional or sensual experience?

2   Where in the film are we completely wrapped up and involved in the reality of the film? Where is the film weakest in emotional and sensual intensity?

3   What role does each of the film elements play in creating a hard-hitting emotional and sensual response?

The Eclectic Approach

1   How technically sound and sophisticated is the film, and how well does it utilize the full potential of the medium?

2   How powerful is the star's performance?

3   How well does the film reflect the philosophy, personality, and artistic vision of the man who made it?

4   How worthwhile or significant is the statement made by the film, and how powerfully is it stated?

5   How effective is the film as an emotional or sensual experience?

REREADING THE REVIEWS

Now we are ready to return to the reviews. We have seen the film, analyzed it, and interpreted it for ourselves. We have formed our own opinions on its worth, and have noted our own very personal and subjective reactions to it. Now the review takes on another function, and should be read in an entirely different way from that in which we read it before seeing the film. Now we can read all parts of the review in depth, entering into a mental dialogue (perhaps even an argument) with the reviewer, as we compare our mental notes and opinions on the film with the written review. Here we may agree with the critic on many points, and disagree completely on others. Reader and critic may analyze or interpret the film in the same way, and yet reach opposite conclusions as to its worth. In essence, what results here is a learning experience, with two separate minds coming together on the same work, seeking agreement perhaps but also relishing argument. While we should be open-minded, and try to see the critic's points and understand his or her analysis, interpretation, and evaluation, we must be independent enough not to be swayed by them or be subservient to them.

EVALUATING THE REVIEWER

We might also evaluate the reviewers we read, determining how well we think they have carried out their duties. The key function of the reviewer is to lead us toward a better understanding and a keener appreciation of specific films and of the medium in general. Pauline Kael puts it this way:

> He is a good critic if he helps people understand more about the work than they could see for themselves; he is a great critic, if by his understanding and feeling for the work, by his passion, he can excite people so that they want to experience more of the art that is there, waiting to be seized.

Therefore, after rereading the review in depth, we might first ask ourselves how well the reviewer succeeds in carrying out this function. *Does the critic succeed in helping you understand more about the film than you could see for yourself? Does he or she make the film medium itself seem exciting, so that you want to experience its art more deeply and intensely?*

After answering these basic questions, we can move on to a thorough evaluation of the review itself by considering the following questions:

1. In what parts of the review is the critic merely providing factual information, things which cannot possibly be argued with? How thorough is this information, and how clear an idea does it give of the nature of the film?

2. In what parts of the review does the critic serve as an objective interpreter or guide, pointing out elements of the film that are worthy of special attention, explaining the director's intentions, placing the film in context, or describing the techniques employed? Does he try to analyze or interpret the film objectively?

3. In what part of the review does the critic make relatively objective value judgments on the film's worth? How does he support his

judgments with critical ground rules? Does he make his critical ground rules clear in his support? Does he provide a logical, convincing argument in support of his evaluation, or does he judge the film dogmatically?

4. Where in the review does the critic leave attempts at objectivity and reveal his subjectivity, his prejudices, and his biases? How much does he reveal about his own personality in this part of the review? How valuable are these subjective parts of the review in stimulating your interest in the film or providing material for mental dialogue or argument? What critical weaknesses, limitations, or narrow attitudes are reflected in the review? Does the critic bother to warn us about his prejudices?

5. Which critical method or approach does the critic emphasize? Does he place his emphasis on how the film was made (film as technical achievement), who stars in the film (film as showcase for the actor), who made the film (the *auteur* approach), what the film says (the humanistic approach), or the reality and intensity of the experience of the film (the film as an emotional or sensual experience)?

6. Does the critic carefully consider the director's intentions and the level of ambition of the film and then select his approach and adjust his expectations for the film accordingly? If not, how does this affect his review?

So that we will not be overly influenced by the critics' opinions, we need to develop the discipline of independent thinking, which requires confidence in our skills of observation and analysis, and some degree of faith in our own critical judgment. This is extremely important in developing the confidence to know what we like and the ability to tell why we like it.

Above all, we must develop enough confidence in our own taste, our own insight, our own perception, and our own sensitivity so that, although we may be influenced by the critics' opinions or their arguments, we will never be intimidated by them. We must continually question and weigh every opinion the critics state, and we may even question their personalities—their intelligence, emotional balance, judgment, and even their humanity. For the fact is that, in spite of the valuable services provided by the critics, criticism remains a very secondary and subjective art. No work of criticism ever written has provided the last word on a film, and none should be accepted as such.

DEVELOPING PERSONAL CRITERIA

In achieving confidence in our critical abilities, it might be very helpful to develop some kind of personal criterion for film evaluation. The difficulty of this task is illustrated by the fact that few professional critics have a hard and fast set of rules to judge films by that they have any real faith in. Dwight Macdonald discusses this in the introduction to his collected reviews, *On Movies:*

> I know something about cinema after forty years, and being a congenital critic, I know what I like and why. But I can't explain the *why* except in terms of the specific work under consideration, on which I'm copious enough. The general theory, the larger view, the gestalt—these have always eluded me. Whether this gap in my critical armor be called an idiosyncrasy or, less charitably, a personal failing, it has always been most definitely there.
>
> But people, especially undergraduates hot for certainty, keep asking me what rules, principles or standards I judge movies by—a fair question to which I can never think of an answer. Years ago, some forgotten but evidently sharp stimulus spurred me to put some guidelines down on paper. The result, hitherto unprinted for reasons which will become clear was:
>
> 1. Are the characters consistent, and in fact, are there characters at all?
> 2. Is it true to life?
> 3. Is the photography cliché, or is it adapted to the particular film and therefore original?
> 4. Do the parts go together; do they add up to something; is there a rhythm established so that there is form, shape, climax, building up tension and exploding it?
> 5. Is there a mind behind it; is there a feeling that a single intelligence has imposed his own view on the material?

The last two questions rough out some vague sort of meaning, and the third is sound, if truistic. But I can't account for the first two being there at all, let alone in the lead-off place. Many films I admire are not "true to life" unless that stretchable term is strained beyond normal usage: *Broken Blossoms, Children of Paradise, Zero de Conduite, Caligari, On Approval,* Eisenstein's *Ivan the Terrible.* And some have no "characters" at all, consistent or no: *Potemkin, Arsenal, October, Intolerance, Marienbad, Orpheus, Olympia.* The comedies of Keaton, Chaplin, Lubitsch, the Marx Brothers and W. C. Fields occupy a middle ground. They have "consistent" characters all right, and they are also "true to life." But the consistency is always extreme and sometimes positively compulsive and obsessed (W. C., Groucho, Buster), and the truth is abstract. In short, they are so highly stylized (cf. "the Lubitsch touch") that they are constantly floating up from *terra firma* into the empyrean of art, right before my astonished and delighted eyes.

*   *   *

. . .Getting back to general principles, I can think offhand (the only way I seem able to think about general principles) of two ways to judge the quality of a movie. They are mere rules of thumb, but they work—for me anyway:

    A. Did it change the way you look at things?
    B. Did you find more (or less) in it the second, third, Nth time?
    (Also, how did it stand up over the years, after one or more "periods" of cinematic history?)

    Both rules are *post facto* and so, while they may be helpful to critics and audiences, they aren't of the slightest use to those who make movies. This is as it should be.*

Although Macdonald has little faith in *rigid* principles or guidelines, guidelines of some sort seem necessary for a foundation on which to build and develop the complex art of watching, analyzing, interpreting, and evaluating films.

The basic problem with set ground rules or guidelines for judging art is that they are often inflexible, and fail to expand or contract to fit the work being evaluated. What we need is a general but flexible set of guidelines or critical principles that apply to most films. But any such guidelines must provide for exceptions. A highly innovative or ground-breaking film may come along which does not conform to any of the basic guidelines, even though it is a great film. If we are equipped with a very flexible, wide-ranging set of guidelines, in which absolute consistency of approach is seen as neither necessary nor desirable, we may modify our old guidelines to cover its greatness or create new ones to include it. Since we are constantly experiencing new types of films, our guidelines must be constantly changing and growing to meet our needs.

In developing our personal criteria for film evaluation, we might begin (as Dwight Macdonald did), by trying to formulate a series of questions to ask ourselves about each movie that we see. Or we may simply try to list those qualities we think are essential to any good movie. Whichever course we choose, the task is not an easy one. But just making the effort should add to our understanding of why some movies are better than others. Even if we do come up with a set of guidelines we

*Reprinted from *Dwight Macdonald on Movies* (Prentice-Hall, 1969).

consider adequate, however, we should resist the temptation to carve them into stone. The cinema is a dynamic, evolving art form, still capable of providing us with new films that won't fit the old rules. It is equally important that we keep our minds and eyes open for discovering new things in old films.

Perhaps most importantly of all, we must keep our hearts open to films of all sorts, so that we may continue to respond to movies emotionally, intuitively, and subjectively. Watching films is an art, not a science. The analytical approach should complement or deepen our emotional and intuitive responses, not replace or destroy them. Used properly, the analytical approach will add rich, new levels of awareness to our normal emotional and intuitive responses, and help us to become more proficient in the art of watching films.

QUESTIONS
ON DEVELOPING PERSONAL CRITERIA
FOR FILM EVALUATION

1 Try to construct a set of five to ten questions that *you* think should be answered in judging the merits of a film, *or* list the five to ten qualities *you* think are essential to a good movie.

2 If you fall short on the questions asked for above, or lack confidence in the validity of your essential qualities, try another approach: List those ten films which you consider to be your personal all-time favorites.

3 Now answer the following questions about your list, and see what your answers reveal about your personal criteria for film evaluation:

    a. Consider each film on the list carefully, and decide what three or four things you liked best about the film. Then decide which of these played the most important role in making you like or respect the film.

    b. How many of the films on your list share these qualities which most appeal to you? Which films seem to be most similar in the characteristics you like best?

    c. Do the qualitites you pick out show an emphasis on any single critical approach, or are you eclectic in your tastes? To decide this, answer the following:

    (1) How many of the films listed do you respect primarily for their technique?

    (2) Do several of the films you chose feature the same actor?

    (3) How many of your favorite films are done by the same director?

    (4) Which of the films listed make a significant statement of some kind?

    (5) Which of the films have a powerful, intense, and very real emotional or sensual effect?

d. What do your answers to questions (1) through (5) above reveal about your personal preferences? How narrow and restricted are your tastes?

e. How does your list of favorite films measure up against your first attempt at establishing a personal criterion for evaluation? How can your standards be changed or added to in order to better match your list of film favorites?

appendix

EXERCISE
IN FILM ANALYSIS

Read the brief summaries and excerpts from the final scene of the stage version of *Suddenly Last Summer,** and then look carefully at the pictures from the film version of the same sequence. With the aid of the questions at the end of this section, analyze the sequence as thoroughly as possible. (The picture sequence begins on page 264.)

Catherine (Elizabeth Taylor in the film) has suffered a nervous breakdown, and is a patient in a state asylum. To get her to reveal the traumatic experience which led to her breakdown, the young psychiatrist, Doctor Cukrowicz (Montgomery Clift), gives her a truth serum injection and begins to question her about the experience which occurred "last summer." In the film version, her description of the events becomes a voice-over narration for a series of visual flashbacks.

As Catherine's narration gets under way, she reveals that her cousin Sebastian, whom she loved, was a homosexual who used her considerable female charms to attract men for himself.

> CATHARINE: And before long, when the weather got warmer and the beach so crowded, he didn't need me any more for that purpose. The ones on the free beach began to climb over the fence or swim around it, bands of homeless young people that lived on the free beach like scavenger dogs, hungry children. . . . So now he let me wear a decent dark suit. I'd go to a faraway empty end of the beach, write postcards and letters and keep up my—third-person journal till it was—five o'clock and time to meet him outside the bathhouses, on the street. . . . He would come out, *followed*.
>
> DOCTOR: Who would follow him out?

CATHARINE: The homeless hungry young people that had climbed over the fence from the free beach that they lived on. He'd pass out tips among them as if they'd all—shined his shoes or called taxis for him. . . . Each day the crowd was bigger, noisier, greedier!—Sebastian began to be frightened.— At last we stopped going out there. . . .

DOCTOR: And then? After that? After you quit going out to the public beach?

CATHARINE: Then one day, a few days after we stopped going out to the beach—it was one of those white blazing days in Cabeza de Lobo, not a blazing hot *blue* one but a blazing hot *white* one.

DOCTOR: Yes?

CATHARINE: We had a late lunch . . . [a] five o'clock lunch at one of those fish-places along the harbor of Cabeza de Lobo, it was between the city and the sea, and there were naked children along the beach which was fenced off with barbed wire from the restaurant and we had our tables less than a yard from the barbed wire fence that held the beggars at bay. . . . There were naked children along the beach, a band of frightfully thin and dark naked children that looked like a flock of plucked birds, and they would come darting up to the barbed wire fence as if blown there by the wind, the hot white wind from the sea, all crying out, *"Pan, pan, pan!"*

DOCTOR [*quietly*]:   What's *pan?*

CATHARINE: The word for bread, and they made gobbling noises with their little black mouths, stuffing their little black fists to their mouths and making those gobbling noises, with frightful grins!—Of course we were sorry that we had come to this place but it was too late to go. . . .

DOCTOR [*quietly*]:   Why was it "too late to go"?

CATHARINE: I told you Cousin Sebastian wasn't well. He was popping those little white pills in his mouth. I think he had popped in so many of them that they had made him feel weak. . . . His, his!—eyes looked—dazed, but he said: "Don't look at those little monsters. Beggars are a social disease in this country. If you look at them, you get sick of the country, it spoils the whole country for you. . . ."

DOCTOR: Go on, Miss Catherine, what comes next in the vision?

CATHARINE: The, the the!—band of children began to—serenade us. . . .

She describes their instruments: tin cans strung together, tin cans flattened into cymbals, coarse paper bags with something on a string inside the bag which, when pulled up and down, made a sound like a tuba.

DOCTOR: Your Cousin Sebastian was *entertained* by this—*concert?*

CATHERINE: I think he was *terrified* of it!

DOCTOR: Why was he terrified of it?

CATHARINE: I think he recognized some of the musicians, some of the boys, between childhood and—older. . . .

DOCTOR: What did he do? Did he do anything about it, Miss Catharine?— Did he complain to the manager about it?

CATHARINE: *What* manager? *God?* Oh, *no!*—The manager of the fish-place on the beach? Haha!—No!—You don't understand my cousin!

DOCTOR: What do you mean?

CATHARINE: *He!—accepted!—all!*—as—how!—things!—are!—And thought nobody had any right to complain or interfere in any way whatsoever, and even though he knew that what was awful was awful, that what was wrong was wrong, and my Cousin Sebastian was certainly never sure that anything was wrong!—He thought it unfitting to ever take any action about anything whatsoever!—except to go on doing as something in him directed. . . .

DOCTOR: What did something in him direct him to do?—I mean on this occasion in Cabeza de Lobo.

CATHARINE: After the salad, before they brought the coffee, he sudden-ly pushed himself away from the table, and said, "They've got to stop that! Waiter, make them stop that. I'm not a well man, I have a heart condition, it's making me sick!"—This was the first time that Cousin Sebastian had ever attempted to correct a human situation!—I think perhaps that *that* was his fatal error. . . . It was then that the waiters, all eight or ten of them, charged out of the barbed wire wicket gate and beat the little musicians away with clubs and skillets and anything hard that they could snatch from the kitchen!—Cousin Sebastian left the table. He stalked out of the restaurant after throwing a handful of paper money on the table and he fled from the place. I followed. It was all white outside. White hot, a blazing white hot, hot blazing white, at five o'clock in the afternoon in the city of—Cabeza de Lobo. It looked as if—

DOCTOR: It looked as if?

CATHARINE: As if a huge white bone had caught on fire in the sky and blazed so bright it was white and turned the sky and everything under the sky white with it!

DOCTOR: —White. . .

CATHARINE: Yes—white. . .

DOCTOR: You followed your Cousin Sebastian out of the restaurant on-to the hot white street?

CATHARINE: Running up and down hill. . . .

DOCTOR: You ran up and down hill?

CATHARINE: No, no! *Didn't!*—move either *way!*—at first, we were—
[*During this recitation there are various sound effects. The percussive
sounds described are very softly employed.*] I rarely made any suggestion but *this* time I *did.* . . .

DOCTOR: What did you suggest?

CATHARINE: Cousin Sebastian seemed to be paralyzed near the entrance
of the cafe, so I said, "Let's go." I remember that it was a very wide and
steep white street, and I said, "Cousin Sebastian, down that way is the
waterfront and we are more likely to find a taxi near there. . . . Or why
don't we go back in?—and have them *call* us a taxi! Oh, let's do! Let's do
that, that's better!" And he said, "*Mad*, are you *mad?* Go back in that
filthy place? Never! That gang of kids shouted vile things about me to the
waiters!" "Oh," I said, "then let's go down toward the docks, down there
at the bottom of the hill, let's not try to climb the hill in this dreadful
heat." And Cousin Sebastian shouted, "Please shut up, let me handle this
situation, will you? I want to handle this thing." And he started up the
steep street with a hand stuck in his jacket where I knew he was having
a pain in his chest from his palpitations. . . . But he walked faster and
faster, in panic, but the faster he walked the louder and closer it got!

DOCTOR: What got louder?

CATHARINE: The music.

DOCTOR: The music again.

CATHARINE: The oompa-oompa of the—following band.—They'd somehow gotten through the barbed wire and out on the street, and they were
following, following!—up the blazing white street. The band of naked
children pursued us up the steep white street in the sun that was like
a great white bone of a giant beast that had caught on fire in the sky!—Sebastian started to run and they all screamed at once and seemed to fly in
the air, they outran him so quickly. I screamed. I heard Sebastian scream,
he screamed just once before this flock of black plucked littled birds that
pursued him and overtook him halfway up the white hill.

DOCTOR: And you, Miss Catharine, what did *you* do, then?

CATHARINE: Ran!

DOCTOR: Ran where?

CATHARINE: Down! Oh, I ran down, the easier direction to run was
down, down, down, down!—The hot, white, blazing street, screaming out
"Help" all the way, till—

DOCTOR: What?

CATHARINE: —Waiters, police, and others—ran out of buildings and rushed back up the hill with me. When we got back to where my Cousin Sebastian had disappeared in the flock of featherless little black sparrows, he—he was lying naked as they had been naked against a white wall, and this you won't believe, nobody *has* believed it, nobody *could* believe it, nobody, nobody on earth could possibly believe it, and I don't *blame* them!—They had *devoured* parts of him.
   [*Mrs. Venable cries out softly.*]

Torn or cut parts of him away with their hands or knives or maybe those jagged tin cans they made music with, they had torn bits of him away and stuffed them into those gobbling fierce little empty black mouths of theirs. There wasn't a sound any more, there was nothing to see but Sebastian, what was left of him, that looked like a big white-paper-wrapped bunch of red roses had been *torn, thrown, crushed!*—against that blazing white wall. . . .
   [*Mrs. Venable springs with amazing power from her wheelchair, stumbles erratically but swiftly toward the girl and tries to strike her with her cane. The Doctor snatches it from her and catches her as she is about to fall. She gasps hoarsely several times as he leads her toward the exit.*]

MRS. VENABLE [*offstage*]: *Lion's View! State asylum, cut this hideous story out of her brain!*
   [*Mrs. Holly sobs and crosses to George, who turns away from her, saying:*]

GEORGE: Mom, I'll quit school, I'll get a job, I'll—

MRS. HOLLY: Hush son! Doctor, can't you say something?
   [*Pause. The Doctor comes downstage, Catharine wanders out into the garden followed by the Sister.*]

DOCTOR [*after a while, reflectively, into space*]: I think we ought at least to consider the possibility that the girl's story could be true. . . .

QUESTIONS
FOR EXERCISE IN FILM ANALYSIS
SUDDENLY LAST SUMMER (See pictures on pages 264–268)

1 Judging from the sequence of drawings from the film, what differences do you find in the stage version and the film version of this scene?

2   Analyze each shot in terms of cinematic composition, explaining how the director (Joseph L. Mankiewicz) focuses our attention on the object of greatest significance or interest, how he achieves three-dimensionality, how he keeps the screen "alive," and so on.

3   Analyze each shot as to its dramatic purpose—that is, identify what the director (Joseph L. Mankiewicz) is seeking to accomplish with each shot. What kind of information is he communicating with each shot, and how does he go about it?

4   Try to determine which of the four cinematic viewpoints is being used in each shot, and explain the purpose of using that viewpoint. In terms of the sequence as a whole, are we observers or participants? In which shots are we most involved? In which are we most objective? What determines our degree of involvement?

5   In addition to the voice-over narration, what will the sound track contribute in each shot? Will music be employed? If so, what kind of music and for what purpose? At what points will the sound track volume be loudest? Softest?

6   How important is setting in this sequence? In which shots is it most important or effective?

7   Analyze each shot as to its relative length or running time. Which shots would be the longest? Which would be the shortest? Why?

8   There is usually no *single* right way to assemble a sequence of shots in editing a film. Although chronological ordering of events cannot be altered in a short sequence, there is some flexibility of choice in the shot order in this sequence. How could the shots be restructured without interfering with the chronological flow of events? Which shots could be moved, and to which new position? How does moving a shot from one place to another affect our interpretation of the meaning of the shot?

9   In which shots do the actors communicate most convincingly? What are the actor's primary means of communication in each shot, the face or the body? In which shot is the acting most subtle? In which shot is it most open and obvious?

10   Based on the sequence of pictures shown here, plus the picture of Katharine Hepburn (as Mrs. Venable) feeding the Venus Flytrap (page 37), what generalizations can you make about director Mankiewicz's style?

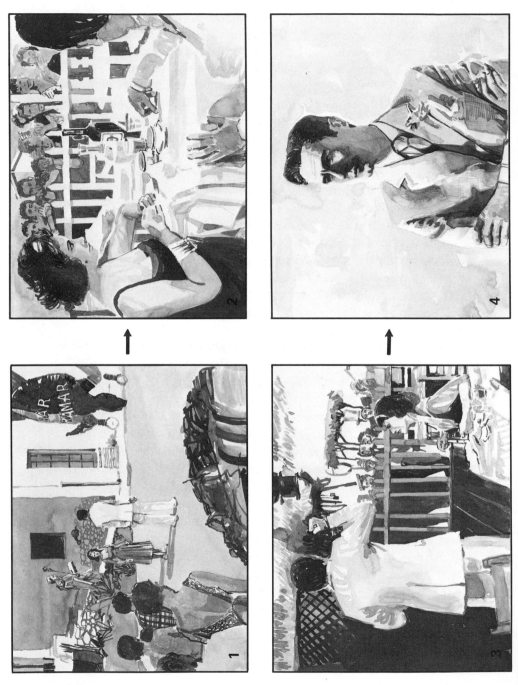

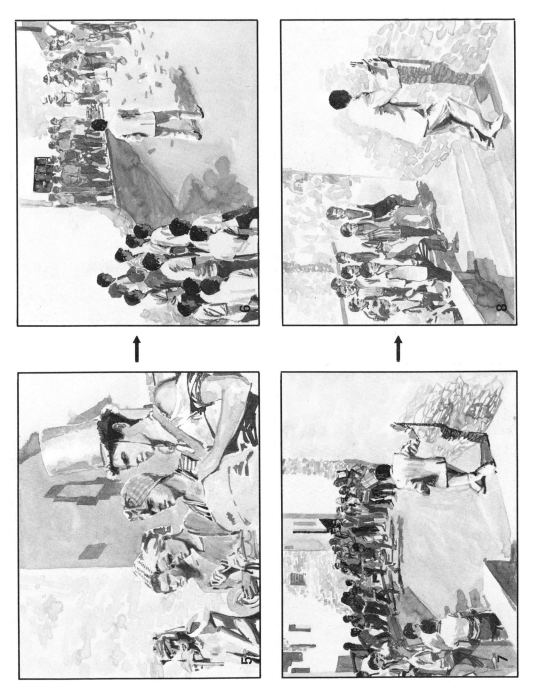

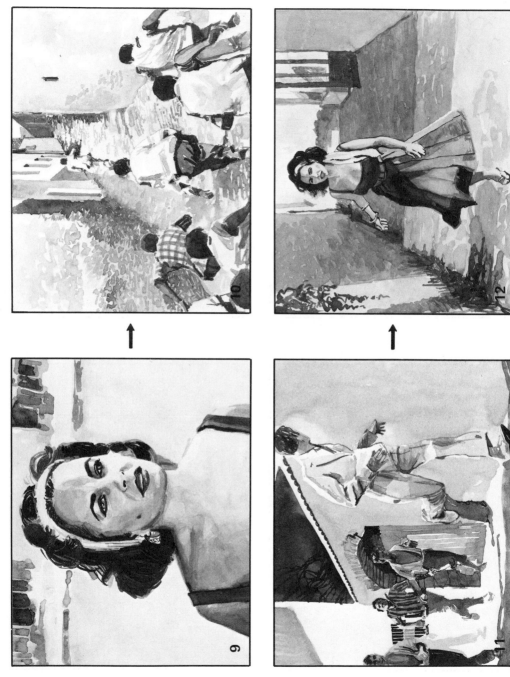

14

13

16

15

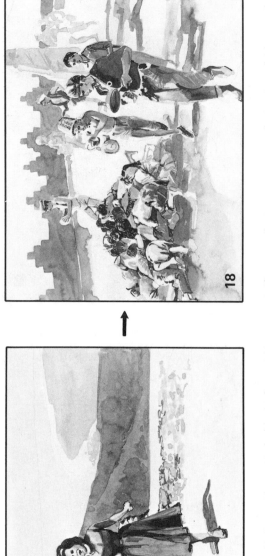

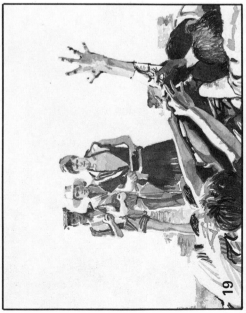

17

18

19

20

COMPREHENSIVE LIST OF QUESTIONS FOR ANALYSIS

Each subsection of questions is given a letter identification so that the instructor may simply assign questions by letter and number. The page numbers beside the lettered heads locate text information that may be helpful in answering the questions.

A THEME   11–16

---

1   What is the film's primary concern or focus: plot, character, emotion, or idea? On the basis of your decision, answer one of the questions below.
   a.   If the film's primary concern is plot, summarize the action abstractly in a single sentence or a short paragraph.
   b.   If the film centers around a single unique character, describe the unusual aspects of his or her personality.
   c.   If the film is structured around a mood or emotional effect, what is the mood or feeling it attempts to convey?
   d.   If the film's primary focus is an idea, answer the following questions.
      (1) What is the true subject of the film? What is it really about in abstract terms? Identify the abstract subject in a single word or phrase.
      (2) What comment or statement does the film make about the subject? If possible, formulate a sentence that accurately summarizes the idea dramatized by the film.
2   Although a director may attempt to do several things with a film, one goal usually stands out as more important than the others. Decide which of the following was the director's *primary* aim and give reasons for your choice.
   a.   Providing pure entertainment, that is, temporary escape from the real world.

    b. Developing a pervasive mood or creating a single, specialized emotional effect.

    c. Providing a character sketch of a unique, fascinating personality.

    d. Pointing out a "truth of life" by making the kind of statement that sharpens the viewer's awareness of reality and helps him to accept that "life is like that."

    e. Criticizing mankind and human institutions, and increasing the viewer's awareness of a social problem and the necessity for reforms.

    f. Providing insight into human nature (demonstrating that human beings *in general* are like that).

    g. Creating a moral or philosophical riddle for the viewer to ponder.

    h. Making a moral statement to influence the viewer's values and/or behavior.

3 Which of the above seem important enough to qualify as secondary aims?

4 Is the film's basic appeal to the intellect, to the funnybone, to the moral sense, or to the aesthetic sense? Is it aimed primarily at the groin (the erotic sense), the viscera (blood and guts), the heart, the yellow streak down the back, or simply the eyeballs? Support your choice with specific examples from the film.

5 How well does your statement of the film's theme and purpose stand up after you have thoroughly analyzed all the film elements?

6 To what degree is the film's theme universal? Is the theme relevant to your own experience? How?

7 If you think the film makes a significant statement, why is it significant?

8 Decide whether the film's theme is intellectually or philosophically interesting, or self-evident and boring, and defend your decision.

FICTIONAL AND DRAMATIC ELEMENTS

B *Characteristics of a good story*   **20–28**

How does the film stack up against the five characteristics of a good story?

1 How well is it unified in plot or story line?

2 What makes the story believable? Pick out specific scenes to illustrate what kind of "truth" is stressed by the film: (a) objective "truth" which follows the observable laws of probability and necessity, (b) subjective, irrational, and emotional "inner truth" of human nature, or (c) the "semblance of truth" created by the film-maker?

3 What makes the film interesting? Where are its high points of suspense and action, and where are its dead spots? If you are bored by the film as a whole or by certain parts, what causes you to have this reaction?

4 Is the film a proper blend of simplicity and complexity?
    a. How well is the story suited in length to the limits of the medium?
    b. Is the film a simple "formula" treatment, allowing you to predict the outcome at the halfway point, or does it effectively maintain suspense until the very end? If the ending is shocking or surprising, how does it carry out the tendencies of the earlier parts of the story?
    c. Where in the film are implication and suggestion effectively employed? Where is it simple and direct?
    d. Is the view of life reflected by the story simple or complex? What factors influenced your answer?

5 How honest and sincere is the film in its handling of emotional material? Where are the emotional effects overdone? Where is understatement used?

C *Dramatic structure*   29–32

1 Does the film use the expository (chronological) or the *in medias res* beginning? If it begins with expository material, does it capture your interest quickly enough, or would a beginning "in the midst of the action" be better? At what point in the story could an *in medias res* beginning start?

2 If flashbacks are used, what is their purpose and how effective are they?

D *Symbolism*   32–42

1 What symbols appear in the film and what do they represent?

2 What universal or natural symbols are employed? How effective are they?

3 Which symbols derive their meaning solely from their context in the film? How are they charged with symbolic value? (In other words, how do you know they are symbols, and how do you arrive at their meaning?)

4   How are the special capabilities of film (the visual image, the sound track, and the musical score) employed to charge symbols with their meaning?

5   Which symbols fit into a larger pattern or progression with other symbols in the film?

6   How are the major symbols related to the theme?

7   Is the story structured around its symbolic meanings to the extent that it can be called an allegory?

8   Which of the symbols' meanings are clear and simple? Which symbols are complex and ambiguous? What gives them this quality?

9   Are visual similes employed effectively? Are they primarily extrinsic (imposed artificially into the scene by editing) or intrinsic (a natural part of the setting)?

10 How fresh and original are the film's symbols and similies? If they seem clichéd or time-worn, where have you encountered them before?

E *Characterization*   43–52

1   Identify the central (most important) character or characters. Which characters are static and which ones are developing? Which characters are flat and which ones are round?

2   What methods of characterization are employed, and how effective are they?

3   Which of the characters are realistic, and which ones are exaggerated for effect?

4   Is each character's motivation sound? Which actions grow naturally out of the characters themselves, and where does the filmmaker seem to be manipulating them to fit his purposes?

5   What facets of the central character's personality are revealed by what he chooses or rejects?

6   Which minor characters function to bring out personality traits of the major characters, and what do they help reveal?

7   Pick out bits of dialogue, visual images, or scenes which you consider especially effective in revealing character, and tell why they are effective.

8   Which characters function as stock characters and stereotypes, and how can the presence of each be justified in the film?

F *Conflict*   53–55

1   Identify the major conflict.

2 Is the conflict internal (man against himself), external, or a combination of both? Is it primarily a physical or psychological conflict?

3 Express the major conflict in general or abstract terms (for example, brains versus brawn, man against nature).

4 How is the major conflict related to the theme?

G *Setting* 56–61

1 Which of the four environmental factors (temporal, geographical, social and economic levels, and customs, moral attitudes, and codes of behavior) play significant roles in the film? Could the same story take place in any environment?

2 Which environmental factors are most important, and what effect do these factors have on the plot or the characters?

3 Why did the director choose this particular location for filming this story?

4 How does the film's setting contribute to the overall emotional atmosphere?

5 What kind of important interrelationships exist between setting and the characters, or between setting and plot?

6 Is the setting symbolic in any way? Does it function as a microcosm?

H *Significance of title* 62

1 Why is the title appropriate? What does it mean in terms of the whole film?

2 How many different levels of meaning can you find in the title? How does each level apply to the film as a whole?

3 If the title is ironic, what opposite meanings or contrasts does it suggest?

4 If you recognize the title as being an allusion, why is the work or passage alluded to an appropriate one?

5 If the title calls your attention to a key scene, why is that scene important?

6 How is the title related to the theme?

I *Irony* 63–67

1 What examples of irony can be found in the film?

2 Is irony employed to such a significant degree that the whole film takes on an ironic tone? Is an ironic world view implied?

3   Do any particular examples of irony achieve comic and tragic effects at the same time?

4   Where in the film is suspense or humor achieved through dramatic irony?

5   How do the ironies contribute to the theme?

VISUAL ELEMENTS

J *Cinematic qualities*   68–86

1   To what degree is the film "cinematic"? Cite specific examples from the film to prove that the director succeeds or fails in (a) keeping the image constantly alive and in motion, (b) setting up clear, crisp visual and aural rhythms, (c) creating the illusion of depth, and (d) using the other flexibilities and special properties of the medium.

2   Does the cinematography strive for clear, powerful, and effective communication of the dramatic scenes in a natural way, or does it self-consciously show off the skills and techniques of the cinematographer?

3   Which methods does the director use to draw our attention to the object of greatest interest or significance?

4   Does the director succeed in keeping the screen alive by avoiding large areas of dead screen?

5   What are the primary or most memorable techniques used to create the illusion of a three-dimensional image?

K *Editing*   87–98

1   How does the editing effectively guide your thoughts, associations, and emotional responses from one image to another so that smooth continuity and coherence are achieved?

2   Is the editing smooth, natural, and unobtrusive, or is it tricky and self-conscious? How much does the editor communicate through creative juxtapositions, such as ironic transitions, montages, and the like, and how effective is this communication?

3   What is the overall effect of editorial intercutting and transitions on the pace of the film as a whole?

4   How does the cutting speed (which determines the average duration of each shot) correspond to the emotional tone of the scene involved?

5 What segments of the film seem overlong or boring? Which parts of these segments could be cut without altering the total effect? Where are additional shots necessary to make the film completely coherent?

L *Cinematic viewpoints and visual effects* 99–111

1 Although the director will probably employ all four cinematic viewpoints in making the film, one point of view may predominate to such a degree that it leaves the impression of a single point of view. With this in mind, answer the following questions:
   a. In terms of your reaction to the film as a whole, do you feel that you were primarily an objective, impersonal observer of the action, or did you have the sense of being a participant in the action? What specific scenes can you remember that used the objective point of view? In what scenes did you feel like a participant in the action? How were you made to feel like a participant?
   b. In what scenes were you aware that the director was employing visual techniques to comment on or interpret the action, forcing you to see the action in a special way? What were the techniques used to achieve this, and how effective were they?
2 Although a thorough analysis of each visual element is impossible, make a mental note of those pictorial effects that struck you as especially effective, ineffective, or unique, and consider them in light of the following questions:
   a. What was the director's aim in creating these images, and what camera tools or techniques were employed in the filming of them?
   b. What made these memorable visual images effective, ineffective, or unique?
   c. Justify each of these impressive visual effects aesthetically in terms of its relationship to the whole film.

M *Lighting* 112–115

1 How would you characterize the lighting of the film as a whole: (a) direct, harsh, and hard, (b) medium and balanced, or (c) soft and diffused? Does high-key or low-key lighting predominate?
2 How does the lighting contribute to the overall emotional attitude or tone of the film?

3 In what individual scenes is the lighting especially effective, and what makes it effective?

N *Color, black and white, and screen size* 116–121

1 Was the filmmaker's choice of black and white or color film correct for this story? What factors do you think influenced this decision? Try to imagine the film as it would appear in the other film type. What would the important differences in total effect be?
2 Is the film designed for standard or wide-screen projection? What factors do you think influenced this decision?

O SOUND EFFECTS AND DIALOGUE 122–130

1 Where in the film are off-screen or invisible sounds effectively employed to enlarge the boundaries of the visual frame, or to create mood and atmosphere?
2 What sound effects in particular contribute to a sense of reality and a feeling of "being there"?
3 Where is sound employed to represent subjective states of mind, and how effective is it?
4 If voice-over sound tracks are used for narration or internal monologues (thoughts of a character spoken aloud), can you justify their use, or could the same information have been conveyed through purely dramatic means?
5 Is dialogue used unnecessarily, repeating information already adequately communicated by the visual image? Where?
6 Where in the film is silence employed as a sound effect to intensify suspense, to increase the impact of sounds which follow, or to create other special dramatic effects? How effective are the results?
7 How do the pace of the dialogue and the rhythmic effects of the sound effects influence the pace of the film as a whole?

MUSICAL SCORE

P *General functions* 132–135

1 Where in the film is music used to match exactly the natural rhythms of the moving objects on the screen? At what points in the film

does the music simply try to capture a scene's overall emotional mood?

2   Where does the film employ rhythmic and emotive variations on a single musical theme or motif?

3   Does the musical score remain inconspicuous in the background, or does it occasionally break through to assert itself?

4   If the music does demand your conscious attention, does it still perform a subordinate function in the film as a whole? How?

5   Where in the film is the main purpose of the music to match structural or visual rhythms? Where is it used to create more generalized emotional patterns?

6   How would the total effect of the film differ if the musical score were removed from the sound track?

Q _Specialized functions_   136–143

1   Which of the following functions of film music are used in the film, and where are they used?
    a.   To cover weaknesses and defects in the film.
    b.   To heighten the dramatic effect of dialogue.
    c.   To tell an "inner story" by expressing a state of mind.
    d.   To provide a sense of time or place.
    e.   To foreshadow coming events or build dramatic tension.
    f.   To add levels of meaning to the visual image.
    g.   To aid in characterization.
    h.   To trigger conditioned responses.
    i.   To characterize rapid movement (traveling music).

2   Does the music accompanying the titles serve basically to underscore the rhythmic qualities of the title information, or to establish the general mood of the film? If lyrics are sung at this point, how do these lyrics relate to the film as a whole?

3   Where are sound effects or natural noises employed for a kind of rhythmic or musical effect?

4   If lyrics sung within the film provide a kind of interior monologue, what feeling or attitude do they convey?

5   How effectively does the score perform its various functions?

R ACTING   144–155

1   Which actors did you feel were correctly cast in their parts? Which actors were not cast wisely? Why?

2 How well were the physical characteristics, facial features, and voice qualities of the actors suited to the characters they were attempting to portray?

3 If a performance was unconvincing, was it because the actor was miscast in the role to begin with, or did he simply deliver an incompetent performance?

    a. If faulty casting seems to be the problem, what actor would you choose for the part if you were directing the film?

    b. If the actor proved incompetent in the part, what were the primary reasons for his failure?

4 Based on your knowledge of their past performances, classify the actors in the major roles as "impersonators," "commenters and interpreters" or "personalities."

5 Try to determine whether the following actors and actresses are impersonators, interpreter/commenters, or personalities: George C. Scott, Cary Grant, Laurence Olivier, Steve McQueen, Robert Duvall, John Wayne, Marlon Brando, Sophia Loren, Elizabeth Taylor, Faye Dunaway, Dustin Hoffman, Anne Bancroft, Shirley MacLaine, Clint Eastwood, Gene Hackman, James Stewart, Racquel Welch, Glenda Jackson, Peter O'Toole, Woody Allen, Diane Keaton, Humphrey Bogart, Doris Day, Joan Crawford, Gary Cooper, Sean Connery, Al Pacino, Mia Farrow, etc. Justify your decision in categorizing each actor or actress by describing the degree of similarities or differences in his or her roles in at least three movies. Which of the actors or actresses are most difficult to categorize and why?

6 Consider the following questions with respect to each of the "staring" actors:

    a. Does the actor seem to depend more on the charm of his own personality, or does he attempt to "become" the character he is playing?

    b. Is the actor consistently believable in his portrayal of the character he is playing, or does he occasionally fall out of character?

    c. If the actor seems unnatural in his part, is it because he tends to be overdramatic, or does he seem wooden and mechanical? Is his unnaturalness more apparent in the way he delivers his lines, or in his physical actions?

7 In which specific scenes is the acting especially effective or ineffective? Why?

8 Where are the actors' facial expressions used in reaction shots? What reaction shots are particularly effective?

S DIRECTOR'S STYLE   157–164

1 After viewing several films by a single director, what kinds of general observations can you make about his or her style? Which of the adjectives listed below are descriptive of his or her style?
   1. Intellectual and rational *or* emotional and sensual.
   2. Calm and quiet *or* fast-paced and exciting.
   3. Polished and smooth *or* rough and crude-cut.
   4. Cool and objective *or* warm and subjective.
   5. Ordinary and trite *or* fresh, unique and original.
   6. Tightly structured, direct, and concise *or* loosely structured and rambling.
   7. Truthful and realistic *or* romantic and idealized.
   8. Simple and straightforward *or* complex and indirect.
   9. Grave, serious, tragic, and heavy *or* light, comical, and humorous.
   10. Restrained and understated *or* exaggerated.
   11. Optimistic and hopeful *or* bitter and cynical.
   12. Logical and orderly *or* irrational and chaotic.

2 What common thematic thread is reflected in the director's choice of subject matter? How is this thematic similarity revealed in the nature of the conflicts he or she deals with?

3 In the films you have seen, what consistencies do you find in the director's treatment of space and time?

4 Is a consistent philosophical view of the nature of man and the universe found in all the films studied? If so, attempt to describe the director's world view.

5 How is the director's style revealed by the following visual elements: composition and lighting, "philosophy of camera," the nature of the camera movement, and methods of achieving three-dimensionality?

6 How does the director use special visual techniques (unusual camera angles, fast motion, slow motion, distorting lenses, and so on) to interpret or comment on the action, and how do these techniques reflect his or her overall style?

7 How is the director's style reflected in the different aspects of the editing in the films, such as the rhythm and pacing of editorial cuts, the nature of transitions, montages, and other creative juxtapositions? How does the style of the editing relate to other elements of the director's visual style, such as the "philosophy of camera" or the point of view emphasized?

8   How consistent is the director in using and emphasizing setting? What kind of details of the natural setting does the director emphasize, and how do these details relate to his or her overall style? Is there any similarity in the director's approach to entirely different kinds of settings? How do the sets constructed especially for the film reflect the director's taste?

9   In what ways are the director's use of sound effects, dialogue, and the musical score unique? How are these elements of style related to his or her visual style?

10   What consistencies can be seen in the director's choice of actors and in the performances they give under his or her direction? How does the choice of actors and acting styles fit in with the style in other areas?

SPECIAL PROBLEMS

T *Film adaptation of a novel*   **185–204**

After reading the novel, but before seeing the film, consider the following questions concerning the novel.

1   How well is the novel suited for adaptation to the screen? What natural cinematic possibilities does it have?

2   Judged as a whole, does the novel come closer to stressing Hemingway's sensuous and emotional rendering of experience, or James's intellectual analysis of experience?

3   How essential is the author's verbal style to the spirit or essence of the novel? Could this verbal style be effectively translated into a pictorial style?

4   What is the novel's point of view? What will necessarily be lost by translating the story into film?

5   If the novel is written in the first-person point of view (as told by a participant in the action), how much of the spirit of the novel is expressed through the narrator's unique narrative style—that is, the particular flair or flavor built into his *way of telling* the story rather than the story itself? Could this verbal style be suggested through a minimum of voice-over narration on the sound track, so that the device would not seem unnatural? Is the feeling of a warm, intimate relationship between reader and narrator established by the novel, as though the story is being told by a very close friend? How could this feeling be captured by the film?

6   Is the novel's length suited to a close adaptation, or must it be drastically cut to fit the usual film format? Which choice would seem most logical for the filmmaker in adapting this novel:

    a. Should he try to capture a sense of the novel's wholeness by hitting the high points without trying to fill in all the gaps? What high points do you think must be dramatized?

    b. Should he limit himself to a thorough dramatization of just a part of the novel? What part of the novel could be thoroughly dramatized to make a complete film? What part of the story or what subplots should be left out of the film version?

7   How much of the novel's essence depends on the rendition of mental states: memories, dreams, or philosophical reflections? How effectively can the film version be expected to express or at least suggest these things?

8   How much detail does the author provide on the origins and past history of the characters? How much of this material can be conveyed cinematically?

9   What is the total time period covered by the novel? Can the time period covered be adequately compressed into a normal-length film?

After seeing the film version, reconsider your answers to the questions above, and also answer those following.

10   Is the film version a close or a loose adaptation of the novel? If it is a loose adaptation, is the departure from the novel due to the problems caused by changing from one medium to another, or by the change in creative personnel?

11   Does the film version successfully capture the spirit or essence of the novel? If not, why does it fail?

12   What are the major differences between the novel and the film, and how can you explain the reasons for these differences?

13   Does the film version successfully suggest meanings that lie beneath the surface and remind you of their presence in the novel? In which scenes is this accomplished?

14   Did having read the novel enhance the experience of seeing the film, or did it take away from it? Why?

15   How well do the actors in the film fit your preconceived notions of the characters in the novel? Which actors exactly fit your mental image of the characters? How do the actors who don't seem properly cast vary from your mental image? Can you justify, from the director's point of view, the casting of these actors who don't seem to fit the characters in the novel?

U *Film adaptation of a play*   206–213

1   How does the film version differ from the play in terms of its concept of physical space?   How does this affect the overall spirit or tone of the film version?

2   How cinematic is the film version?   How does it use special camera and editing techniques to keep the visual flow of images in motion and to avoid the static quality of a filmed stage play?

3   What events does the filmmaker "show" happening that are only described in dialogue during the play?   How effective are these added scenes?

4   Are the play's structural divisions (into acts and scenes) still apparent in the film, or does the film successfully blend these divided parts into a unified cinematic whole?

5   What stage conventions employed in the play are not translatable into cinematic equivalents?   What difficulties and changes does this bring about?

6   How does the acting style of the film differ from that of the play? What factors enter into these differences?

7   What basic differences can be observed in the nature of the dialogue in the two versions? Are individual speeches generally longer in the play or in the film?   In which version is the poetic quality of the language most apparent?

8   What other important changes have been made in the film version? Can you justify these in terms of change of medium, change in creative personnel, or differences in moral attitudes and sophistication of the intended audiences?

V *The silent film*   214–217

1   Is the acting style melodramatic, with broad and exaggerated gestures and facial expressions, or is it subtle, refined, and even understated?

2   What is unique about the acting styles of each of the major actors? Which actors depend most on facial expression, and which ones depend more on gestures and bodily movements?

3   How many different emotions are expressed by actors through their walks?   Which actors in the film have unique walks that become a part of their acting style and the total personality they project?

4 How effective is the film in telling its story without words? How much does the film need to rely on subtitles to make the action absolutely clear?

W *The foreign language film*   **218-222**

1 Which method is used to translate the dialogue into English—subtitles or voice dubbing? Was this the best way to solve the language problem for this particular film? Why?

2 If subtitles are used, how well do they seem to capture the essence of what is being said by the actors? Are the subtitles ever difficult to read because of light-colored backgrounds? Is the film's pace slow enough to allow for both reading the subtitles *and* following the visual image?

3 If voice dubbing is used, how closely do the English words spoken on the sound track correspond to the mouth and lip movements of the foreign actors? Do you get used to the fact that the voices are dubbed, or is it a constant irritation? How well-suited are the voice qualities and accents on the sound track to the actors with which they are matched? Does the overall emotional quality of the English translation match the facial expressions and gestures of the foreign actors?

4 How does the foreign director's style differ from American cinematic styles? What effect does this have on your response to the film?

5 How does the film reflect the culture of the country that produced it? How is this culture or lifestyle different from what we know in America? How is it similar? What different aspects of this foreign culture do you find most fascinating, and why?

X *The historically important film*   **222-224**

1 Based on your knowledge of the films produced prior to this film, what innovations in cinematic style or technique did this film introduce? Which of these innovations are still being used in the modern film?

2 Does the film seem crude, time-worn, or full of cliches when compared to the modern film, or is it still fresh and powerful? What specific elements or qualities in the film led to your decision?

3 What is the film's contribution to the overall development of the motion picture? What would the modern film be like if the innovations introduced by this film had never been tried? How have the innovations introduced by this film been polished and refined in the modern film?

Y *The feature film on television*   **224–227**

1   To what degree is the film's continuity destroyed by commercial breaks? Which of these breaks occur at appropriate times in terms of the film's dramatic structure, and which breaks weaken the dramatic tension appreciably?
2   If you saw the film in a theater, can you remember portions that were cut out of the television showing? How important were these segments to the spirit or plot of the film? Can you justify these deletions in terms of the new medium or its mass audience? Were these segments cut out for reasons of time limits or censorship?
3   If the film is a made-for-television film, how successful is it in solving the problems of the theater film on television?

Z *The social problem film*   **227–228**

1   Does the social problem being attacked by the film have a universal and timeless quality, affecting all people in all time periods, or is it restricted to a relatively narrow time and place?
2   Is the film powerful enough in terms of a strong story line, enduring characters, good acting, artistic cinematography, and so on, to outlive the social problem it is attacking? In other words, how much of the film's impact is caused by its relevance to a current problem and its timing in attacking that problem?
3   If the immediate social problems on which the film focuses were permanently corrected tomorrow, what relevance would the film have to the average viewer twenty years from now?

AA *Viewer-centered problems*   **228–234**

1   Do you have any strong prejudices against this particular type of film? If so, how did these prejudices affect your response to the film? Does this film have any special qualities which set it apart from other films of the same genre?
2   How much do your personal and highly subjective responses to the following aspects of the film affect your judgment: actors and actresses in the film, treatment of sexual material, and scenes involv-

ing violence? Can you justify the sex and violence in the film aesthetically, or are these scenes included strictly for box-office appeal?

3   What were your expectations before seeing the film? How did these expectations influence your reaction to the film?

4   Do you have some specialized knowledge about any subject dealt with by the film? If so, how does it affect your reaction to the film as a whole?

5   Was your mood, mental attitude, or physical condition while seeing the movie less than ideal? If so, how was your reaction to the film affected?

6   If the physical environment in which you watched the film was less than ideal, how did this influence your judgment?

ANALYSIS OF THE WHOLE FILM

BB   *Overall analysis and evaluation*   **235–243**

1   What is the director's purpose or primary aim in making the film?

2   What is the true subject of the film, and what kind of statement, if any, does the film make about that subject?

3   How do all the separate elements of the film relate to and contribute to the theme, central purpose, or total effect?

4   What is the film's "level of ambition"?

5   In terms of the director's intentions and the film's level of ambition, how well does the film succeed in what it tries to do? Why does it succeed or fail?

6   What elements or parts make the strongest contribution to the theme and why? What elements or parts fail to function effectively in carrying out the director's intentions? Why do they fail?

7   What were your *personal* reactions to the film? What are your *personal* reasons for liking it or disliking it?

OTHER APPROACHES TO THE FILM FOR
ANALYSIS, EVALUATION, AND DISCUSSION

CC   *The film as a technical achievement*   **244**

1   How well does the film utilize the full potential of the medium?

2   What inventive techniques are employed, and how impressive are the effects they create?

3 Judged as a whole, is the film technically superior or inferior?

4 Technically speaking, what are its strongest points and what are its weakest?

DD *The film as a showcase for the actor* 245

1 How well are the actor's special personality traits or acting skills suited to the character he plays and to the action of the film?

2 Does this role seem tailored to fit his personality and skills, or does he "bend" his personality to fit the role?

3 How powerful is his performance in this film compared to his performance in other starring roles?

4 What similarities or significant differences do you see in the character he plays in this film and the characters he has played in other films?

5 Judging in terms of past performances, how difficult and demanding is this particular role for the actor?

EE *The film as a product of a single creative mind* 245–246

1 In terms of this film and other films by the same director, how would you describe his style?

2 How does each element of this film serve to reflect the director's artistic vision, his style, and his overall philosophy of film or even his philosophy of life itself?

3 What basic similarities does this film have to other films by the same director? How is it significantly different?

4 Where in the film do we get the strongest impressions of the director's personality showing through, imposing his unique creative intelligence on the material?

5 What is the quality of this film compared to the other works in his canon? As compared to his other films, how well does this film reflect the philosophy, personality, and artistic vision of the man who made it?

6 Does this film suggest a growth in some new direction from his other films? If so, describe that new direction.

FF *The film as a moral, philosophical, or social statement* 246–247

1 What is the statement the film makes, and how significant is the lesson or "truth" we learn from it?

2 How effectively do the different film elements function to get the film's message across?

3 How does the film attempt to influence our lives for the better? What changes in our beliefs and actions does it bring about?

4 Is the message stated by the film universal, or is it restricted to our own time and place?

5 How relevant is the theme to our own experience?

GG *The film as an emotional or sensual experience*   247–248

1 How powerful or intense is the film as an emotional or sensual experience?

2 Where in the film are we completely wrapped up and involved in the reality of the film? Where is the film weakest in emotional and sensual intensity?

3 What role does each of the film elements play in creating a hard-hitting emotional and sensual response?

HH *The eclectic approach*   249

1 How technically sound and sophisticated is the film, and how well does it utilize the full potential of the medium?

2 How powerful is the star's performance?

3 How well does the film reflect the philosophy, personality, and artistic vision of the man who made it?

4 How worthwhile or significant is the statement made by the film, and how powerfully is it stated?

5 How effective is the film as an emotional or sensual experience?

II DEVELOPING PERSONAL CRITERIA   254–256
FOR FILM EVALUATION

1 Try to construct a set of five to ten questions that *you* think should be answered in judging the merits of a film, *or* list the five to ten qualities *you* think are essential to a good movie.

2 If you fall short on the questions asked for above, or lack confidence in the validity of your essential qualities, try another approach: List those ten films which you consider to be your personal all-time favorites.

3 Now answer the following questions about your list, and see what your answers reveal about your personal criteria for film evaluation:

a. Consider each film on the list carefully, and decide what three or four things you liked best about the film. Then decide which of these played the most important role in making you like or respect the film.

b. How many of the films on your list share these qualities which most appeal to you? Which films seem to be most similar in the characteristics you like best?

c. Do the qualities you pick out show an emphasis on any single critical approach, or are you eclectic in your tastes? To decide this, answer the following:

(1) How many of the films listed do you respect primarily for their technique?

(2) Do several of the films you chose feature the same actor?

(3) How many of your favorite films are done by the same director?

(4) Which of the films listed make a significant statement of some kind?

(5) Which of the films have a powerful, intense, and very real emotional or sensual effect?

d. What do your answers to questions (1) through (5) above reveal about your personal preferences? How narrow and restricted are your tastes?

e. How does your list of favorite films measure up against your first attempt at establishing personal criteria for evaluation? How can your standards be changed or added to in order to better match your list of film favorites?

INDEX

9868